BAYWATCH

RESCUED
FROM PRIME TIME

BAYWATCH

RESCUED
FROM PRIME TIME

The Official, Behind-the-Scenes Story
of the World's Most Popular TV Show

by GREGORY J. BONANN

with BRAD ALAN LEWIS

NEW MILLENNIUM PRESS

Beverly Hills

The author gratefully acknowledges the following for selected photographs and images: Yasmine Bleeth; Blue Saint Music; Leigh Brecheen; *Broadcasting & Cable* (copyright 1997 by Cahners Publishing Company); Kim Carlsberg; Corbis photographic agency; Harold Dunnigan; *Entertainment Weekly*; *The Hollywood Reporter*; *Inside Sport*; Los Angeles County Lifeguards; *Los Angeles Times* (copyright, 1989, Los Angeles Times; reprinted by permission); *MacLean's*; Playboy material from the Archives of *Playboy* Magazine. Copyright © 1990, 1993, 1994, 1996, and 1998. PLAYBOY, MR. PLAYBOY DESIGN, PLAYMATE, and RABBIT HEAD DESIGN are trademarks of Playboy Enterprises International, Inc. Used with permission. All rights reserved; PSO Limited; Tim Ryan; Roman Salicki; Sky Garden Music; *The Star*; *Swim Magazine*; *TV Guide* (reprinted with permission from the TV Guide Magazine Group, Inc., publisher of *TV Guide* magazine; copyright August 13, 1994, and May 27, 1995, TV Guide, Inc.; TV Guide is a trademark of TV Guide Magazine Group, Inc.); *Variety*; Warner Bros. Music Corporation.

New Millennium Press
a division of NM WorldMedia, Inc.
350 S. Beverly Drive, Suite 315
Beverly Hills, California 90212
www.newmillenniumpress.com

10 9 8 7 6 5 4 3 2 1

Library of Congress Cataloging-in-Publication Data

Bonann, Gregory J.
    Baywatch : rescued from prime time: the official behind-the-scenes
story of the world's most popular tv show / by Gregory J. Bonann
and Brad Alan Lewis.
      p.   cm.
    ISBN 1-893224-09-0
    1. Baywatch (Television program) I. Lewis, Brad Alan.
II. Title.
PN1992.77.B383 B66 1999
791.45'72--dc21   99-018253

                                    CIP

CONTENTS

FOREWORD

When Greg Bonann first showed up at GTG, the television production company in which I was partnered with Gannett, he impressed me immediately with his energy and his enthusiasm, to say nothing of his considerable likability. At the time I had no inkling of his aptitude for fictional storytelling, though others in the company, particularly Stu Erwin, knew of his documentary film experience. And we all knew of his celebrated status as a lifeguard on the beaches just a few miles from our Culver City studio.

Without Greg Bonann, there never would have been a *Baywatch*. It was Greg who married the idea of a show about lifeguarding with all of the disciplines represented by his various colleagues. My own role was one of cheerleading and ultimately convincing NBC that the show belonged on its schedule.

I have been frequently associated with "quality programming," and some people have found the fact that I actively championed *Baywatch* to be inconsistent with that reputation. It is true that I expected the show to be "commercial"—potentially a cash cow for GTG, which was woefully in need of such an animal at the time.

Wherever there are beaches, and we have plenty of them in Southern California, there are heroes called lifeguards. Moreover, they happen to work in a setting that is not only very photogenic, but one that is obviously appealing to viewers, especially those far removed from our beaches and climate.

The further appeal of healthy young people in trunks and bathing suits was not lost on me. I don't think it's a crime that *Baywatch* is a physically attractive show, and that *Baywatch* provides any number of positive lessons and messages in a context where young viewers, in particular, might absorb them. This book makes the point.

I was stunned when NBC failed to pick up the show for a second season. But that wasn't the first time a network has blown a schedule call; I have been party to similar gaffes.

For the producers of *Baywatch*, NBC's decision was devastating, as you will read in the pages ahead. Greg Bonann then led the "we won't let it die" charge, and against daunting odds, the show was reborn—in a form that would prove to be far healthier and far more rewarding for Greg and his colleagues.

It's a good story, with a happy ending, and it's true.

Grant A. Tinker

DEDICATION

To my mom and dad. Over the course of a lifetime they taught me and showed me through their own example that I could accomplish anything.

To my sisters Debbie and Kathe. Although Kathe's name is not as evident in the text as Debbie's, her spirit certainly is. She set a great and lasting example for me to follow—hard work, persistence, and sacrifice are essential when questing after a challenging goal.

To the lifeguards who sat in the tower with me, who kept saying "go for it, go for it." In 1999, I worked nine days as a lifeguard, which was enough to keep my lifeguard status up-to-date. To the day I die, I want to be able to say that I am a lifeguard.

To my mentors, Hal Dunnigan, Jack Hennessy, Stu Erwin Jr., Grant Tinker, and Jay Sandrich. Their guidance and friendship were and are invaluable.

To Peggy, who stood by my side through some exceptionally dark days and is still there for me.

To Doug, Michael, and David, three exceptional men, whom I am fortunate to have as friends and partners. We're a good team.

Most importantly, to Tai. Her dedication to creating a better world, especially for children, keeps me grounded, honest, and inspired. You truly are a remarkable person. I am so lucky to have met you. To know you. To have been able to share the best part of my life with you. Thank you.

—Greg

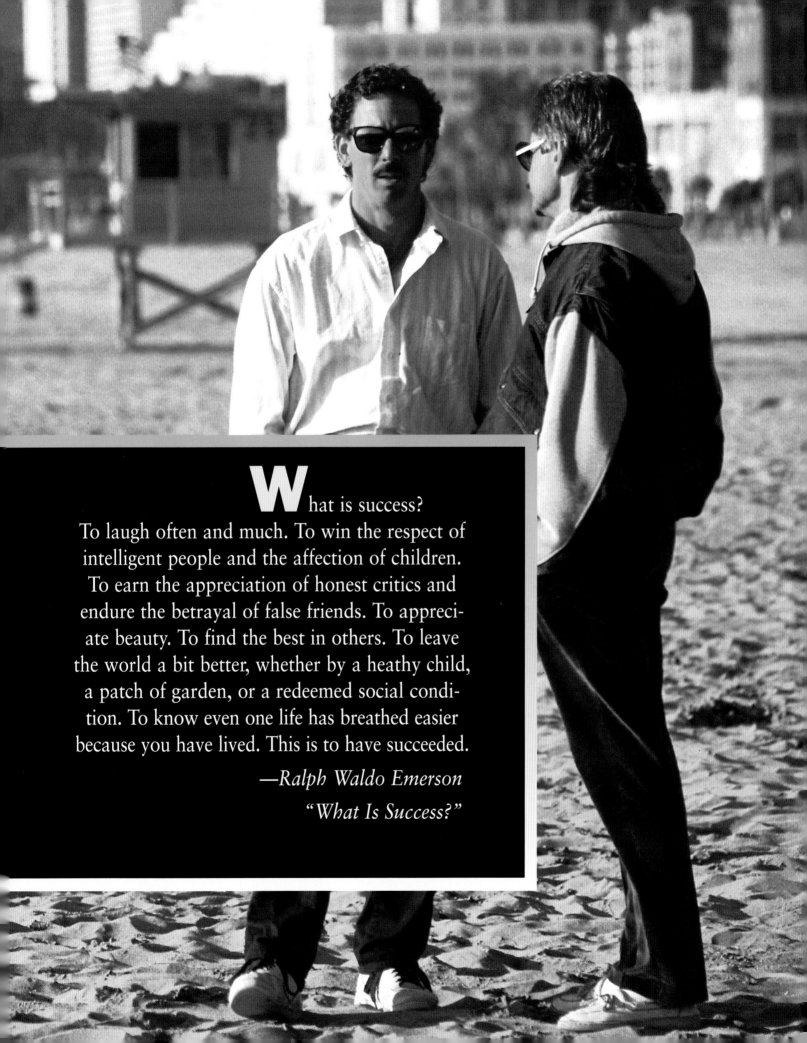

What is success?
To laugh often and much. To win the respect of
intelligent people and the affection of children.
To earn the appreciation of honest critics and
endure the betrayal of false friends. To appreciate beauty. To find the best in others. To leave
the world a bit better, whether by a heathy child,
a patch of garden, or a redeemed social condition. To know even one life has breathed easier
because you have lived. This is to have succeeded.

—*Ralph Waldo Emerson*
"What Is Success?"

CHAPTER 1

Watching the Water

Five days after NBC canceled *Baywatch*, I went back to lifeguarding. I had no choice. My most recent payday had been months before. The quickest way to make some money was to do what I knew best: lifeguard.

Don Rohrer, the chief lifeguard, assigned me to my old tower at Will Rogers Beach, Tower 18. The busy summer season had not yet commenced, and during the day only a dozen or so patrons took up residence in my stretch of sand. As I stared at the water, I had lots of time to think about life after cancellation.

At irregular intervals my thoughts were interrupted by the phone, lifeguard friends calling from their towers to say they were sorry to hear that *Baywatch* was finished. One call was from Hal Dunnigan, my teacher from lifeguard rookie school. He said, "Welcome back to the beach."

In the late afternoon, just before I closed up the tower, one of the lifeguard rescue boats cruised past, 100 yards offshore. I saw the lifeguards on board waving to me. I waved back, and then I felt my whole body slowly sag toward the wooden floor, defeated. That rescue boat, as much as anything, symbolized *Baywatch*. As it went off into the sunset, I cried for the first and last time, mourning the loss of something intensely special, intensely personal to me. Gone forever.

On duty, late afternoon at Tower 18, watching the water—while thinking about the loss of Baywatch *at NBC.*

W hen I was six years old, my family often went to Castle Rock beach, near our home in Pacific Palisades. On one visit I brought an inflatable raft. Just as I was about to go into the water, a lifeguard walked up, knelt beside me, and patiently explained why I couldn't take the raft into the ocean: It might deflate and I'd be out too far; the line encircling the raft might break; the brass nozzle might cause me injury. Then the lifeguard walked back to his tower. My mother said that I never took my eyes off that lifeguard for the rest of the day.

I was not a particularly healthy young boy. Once or twice a month, whenever I had a severe asthma attack, my dad would take me fishing. We'd go to the Malibu pier, rent a fishing pole, and then ride the shuttle boat out to the deep water barge permanently anchored three miles off-shore. While on board for a few hours, I breathed clean, moist air, absent of any pollen or dust. I remember the barge, the ocean air, the sun warming my shoulders, the long, rolling swells, the silvery fish inches below the surface. The barge is now long gone.

A tower during the winter, silently awaiting the summertime crowds.

Because of my severe asthma, my parents felt that we should live near the ocean. Yet despite both my asthma and a severe allergy to grass, I wanted to play baseball. In my life, my father has asked me to do only two things of a relatively monumental nature: the first was that I drop baseball and take up swimming.

My dad didn't know that my school, Palisades High, had one of the best swimming teams in the city. Nor did he know that I had zero chance of even making the team. He just knew that swimming would be good for me.

As a 10th grader, I went to the freshman swim team tryouts. Our high school had only 10th, 11th, and 12th grades. I had never competed in swimming in my life. I was over-weight and out of shape. I wore baggy shorts to the tryout, too embarrassed to wear Speedos like everyone else. On the coach's command, I swam 50 yards, up the length of the pool and back, flailing the whole way. Immediately after touching the wall I hauled myself out of the pool, retreated to the locker room, and promptly threw up. Then I went back to the pool and asked for one more chance.

After tryouts, the coach, Pete Nelson, called me aside. He was the king of high school swimming coaches. His teams had won the city championship for years. Coach Nelson said, "I'm sorry Greg, but we don't have room for you on the freshman team. And you're too big for the junior varsity. The only team you could be on is the varsity, but you're just not good enough. If you want to continue swimming, I'll let you work out with the team. But forget about competing." I immediately agreed. He said, "Okay, you'll swim two events, the distance freestyle and the individual medley (IM). The freestyle will get you into condition and the IM will teach you the strokes."

The next day Coach Nelson put me in a lane with Bob Janis, who was a senior. I remember in the first workout, a 400-yard set, Bob lapped me four times. As the months went by, I measured my progress by how many times I was lapped. Another good swimmer, Randy Bartley, was also in our lane. Invariably I would finish behind Bob and Randy, although by the end of the year I had made some progress—at least I wasn't being lapped anymore. In fact, when we went to the preliminaries of the all-city finals, I finished third, behind Bob and Randy. As it turned out, I'd been training with the two best distance swimmers in the whole city of Los Angeles. By making the city finals, I earned a varsity letter, which was a big deal to me in those days.

That was in 1968. Today, over 30 years later, Bob Janis and I are still swimming against each other, in the same pool, in the same exact lane.

At the end of my freshman year, Bob graduated and became a lifeguard. The next year I finished third once again, behind Randy Bartley and another a swimmer who had switched over from sprints to the distance event, Mark Newman. (Mark's brother, Mike "Newmie" Newman, later became one of my best friends, and later yet an important actor on *Baywatch*.)

During my senior year I swam well enough to compete against anyone in any event. When my school swam against Westchester High, I raced Steve Grainer in the IM; against Venice High, I raced against Steve Sharp in backstroke; against Hollywood High, I swam against Sandy Levee in distance freestyle—altogether the best swimmers from across the city. Sometimes I won; many times I lost.

The training and swim meets served as excellent preparation for the single biggest competition of my life: the lifeguard test.

In April 1970, on the morning of the test, my dad drove me to Venice Beach. I was nervous and scared, and he knew it. He said, "You're only as good as your competition. If these guys are good, they're going to make you even better." Win or lose, qualify or not, I knew he would be proud of me. He had not missed one of my races all through high school, and he was going to be there for this race, the most important of my life.

The only way to become a lifeguard at a Los Angeles County beach is to succeed in this annual spring test: Run into the water, swim straight out 200 yards, round a buoy, swim down the beach for one mile, round another buoy, and then swim back to shore.

The test took place in April, long before the Pacific Ocean had managed to lose its winter chill. Three hundred young men were lined up, poised at the starting line, ready to sprint into the water. As I looked over the competition, I saw practically every rival I had competed against over the last three years—Grainer, Sharp, Levee—all of them shaved down, tapered, and ready to kill. In the back of my mind, I didn't think I could pull it off. I'd beaten Steve Sharp at the city finals in the backstroke, but I didn't know if I could ever do it again. The guy was huge, 6'6", and very strong. I naturally assumed he'd be a great open water swimmer.

My biggest problem, besides the tough competition, was my frighteningly poor vision: 20/650. (What most people can see at 650 feet, I can barely see at 20 feet.) I was and still am legally blind. Lifeguard rules, not surprisingly, do not tolerate bad eyesight. I had recently begun wearing contact lenses for the sole purpose of helping me conceal my vision problem from the lifeguards. I wasn't wearing my contacts for this competition, however, since I hadn't yet learned how to swim while wearing them.

In the days leading up to the race I had taken several practice swims, previewing the course. The buoys were set only a short distance offshore. Obviously the quickest way to traverse the course would be to swim in a straight line between the buoys. But when swimming in the ocean, the natural tendency is to follow the contour of the shoreline, which is often not the shortest distance. With some practice, I learned to stay true to the fastest course despite my lousy eyesight.

Just before the start, the chief lifeguard at the time, Myron Cox, gave a brief speech. "This is going to be one of the toughest things you'll ever do, and one of the most worthwhile. Someday you may hold a person's life in your hands."

My first professional competition was moments away. If I made it through, I stood to make $3.11 an hour as a rookie lifeguard. Otherwise I would be joining my friends at Safeway, bagging groceries for $1.25 an hour, minimum wage.

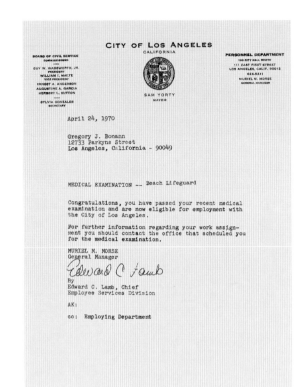

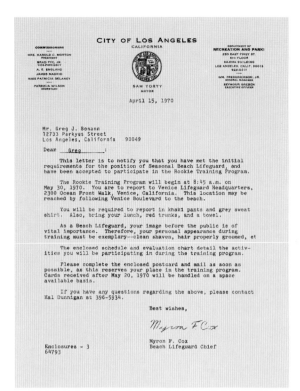

Chief Cox raised his starter's pistol. For a moment he glanced around, allowing one last infusion of adrenaline into my body. I felt the guy next to me raise his elbows in preparation for the mad dash. An instant later Chief Cox fired his starter's pistol and we all sprinted toward the surf. Once in the water, it was unreal. Guys climbed all over me. I was kicked in the face, gouged, scratched. Going around the first buoy, someone wrapped his hand around my ankle and tried to pull me under. I fully knew, going in, that this was not going to be a pool swim, where each lane is neatly cordoned off. Still, I hadn't expected such unbridled physical aggression.

At the first buoy, I went wide, way outside, and then swam as hard as I could in a direct line for the next buoy. My practice swims paid off. While the other swimmers wrestled among themselves, and swam a longer distance, I stayed true to my solo course, charging straight for the buoy.

Finally, after what seemed like an eternity, I rounded the second buoy, sprinted to shore, and ran out of the water. Because of my poor eyesight, I couldn't see anyone. All I could see was the flag-funnel, set up to guide the competitors from the shoreline through the finish area. As I ran up the funnel I could hear my dad cheering me on. Immediately after crossing the line, I surmised that I had either come in far, far behind or way, way ahead. I looked around—I was alone. I'd outpaced everyone. I had won. It was *the* single greatest day of my life.

Out of the original 300 competitors, the top 50 finishers made it to the next phase, a thorough physical exam. A lifeguard official told us, "Show up at 9:00 in the morning and don't plan anything for the rest of the day." He was right. The physical took six hours, with careful attention paid to ears, eyes, nose, blood pressure, and agility. The demands of professional lifeguarding necessitate that guards be top physical specimens. Flawed eyes and ears eliminated many of the 50 candidates. I prayed that the nurse would not ask or notice that I wore contacts. If my poor eyesight had been discovered, I would have been kicked out immediately. Suffice to say, my desire to become a lifeguard was far stronger than any sense of impropriety I might have felt. I survived the physical exam—contacts unnoticed—and advanced, along with 24 other hopefuls, to rookie school.

During the six weeks of rookie school, they taught us everything we needed to know in order to be lifeguards: first aid, correct rescue procedure, how to calm frightened mothers and lost children. I would always come to work with a few toys in my gear bag, something I could use to distract a distressed, anxious child. We had to learn pages of communication codes: Code 3, red lights and siren; 10-7, out of service; 10-4, it's all over. Knot tying, as simple as it sounds, was a major deal. If you were to improperly tie up the rescue boat, it might later cause a rescue to be delayed.

All of the training was conducted like a Marine boot camp, with plenty of "yes sirs" and "no sirs." Excuses were not tolerated. You did it the proper way or you were gone. Fear of the instructor was instilled at every turn, along with a healthy, overall respect for the profession of lifeguarding.

Throughout rookie school, while secretly wearing my contact lenses, I lived in fear of being caught by one of the instructors or by a fellow candidate. Had another rookie found me out, he would have turned me in without a second thought, thereby moving up a notch and improving his chances of getting the job.

Hal Dunnigan, my rookie school teacher, watching us swim around a distant buoy.

Before and after every swim I sat in a toilet stall to remove or replace my contacts. Gradually, over the course of rookie school, I noticed that someone was invariably sitting in the stall next to me. Because he always wore the same shoes, I knew it was always the same guy: Mike Konig. Sure enough, he, too, wore contacts. We kept each other's secret and from this rather duplicitous beginning we eventually became good friends. We stayed friends through the first few years of guarding. Then he moved on.

I could not have made it through rookie school without the help of Bret Clark, one of my teammates from Palisades High. Bret knew all about my vision problems. On beach runs, I would stay directly behind him, stepping into the sand exactly where he had stepped only moments before. Bret always guided me through the ocean swims, staying right next to me so that I wouldn't stray far. Until I finally learned to wear my contacts while swimming, Bret saved my lifeguarding career.

Hal Dunnigan was one of our most important rookie school instructors. Hal was a Navy SEAL. He was always away "at training" during any big international security incident in such places as Vietnam, the Falklands, the Middle East, or Grenada. In the fraternity of SEALS, he was well respected as an expert in underwater demolition. Certainly he is one of the finest men I've ever met. Early in my lifeguarding career, he took me aside and said, "You don't know it, but someday you're going to be important to this group." Later, at his suggestion, I joined a coalition of lifeguards, becoming a member of the leadership committee that steered the guards toward forming a union.

Nowadays, I still look up to Hal the way I did 30 years ago. When I guard with him, I worry that he will run faster, swim faster, and get to a victim first. At 68 years of age, he is still lifeguarding. Off the beach, Hal is equally amazing. His full-time job is educating handicapped and learning disabled children at a Los Angeles inner-city school.

After six weeks of rookie school, 21 rookies graduated, listed in order from 1st to 21st. I ended up being No. 1, the top-ranked graduate.

One of the rewards for having successfully completed rookie school was getting a chance to meet Myron Cox, the chief lifeguard. Myron was one of those people about whom others were always talking. One day you'd hear, "Don't screw up around Cox. He'll tear your head off." The next day you'd hear, "Myron Cox is a real lifeguard's chief. He'll go to the mat for you." Both statements were accurate, especially the latter.

With a few other rookies I went to Myron's office. He was a big man, very strong, very intense, and more than a little intimidating to a 17-year-old kid. After quickly shaking hands he said, "You're lifeguards now. I want to be proud of you. If you don't make me proud, you're gone." He was a tough, old-school, demanding guy who insisted that the job be done well. No quarter given.

I survived the school, coming out on top.

On the wall behind his desk was an enlarged, black-and-white photo. It showed Myron (when he'd been a regular lifeguard) trying in vain to comfort a distraught mother whose little girl had just drowned. As Myron spoke, I found myself staring at that photo. It seemed to contain the essence of lifeguarding: This wasn't simply a summer job, taken to earn a few dollars. Lives hung in the balance. As I looked at the photo, I knew my life would never be the same now that I was a lifeguard.

From my rookie school days I made good, lifelong friends: Steve Grainer, Bret Clark, Bob Seamon, Billy Astudious, Tom Doman. Yet from that group, I am the only guy still guarding. It's too bad, especially since many of the others left for the wrong reasons. When they married, their wives didn't want them at the beach anymore, not with all the young women around. And later, most of the guys got divorced anyway. When I was divorced, the first place I went was to lifeguard headquarters. My lifeguard friends helped me get through it.

I can't imagine not belonging to the fraternity of lifeguards. You cannot buy your way into it. You can't politic your way in. Certainly it is one of the most exclusive clubs in the world.

Years ago, the son of a prominent California congressman got it into his head that he wanted to become a lifeguard. We were given specific instructions to get this congressman's kid through the rookie test by any means necessary. Unfortunately the kid couldn't swim well enough to save his own life. In the initial swim test, he finished near last out of 300 hopefuls. Still, he was slipped into rookie school, where he again finished near last. Despite his lack of ability, the kid was chosen to be a lifeguard. On his first week of work, a woman almost drowned at his beach. Soon afterward the kid quit. Lifeguarding is not a place to compromise any standards whatsoever. The stakes are simply too high.

T he night we graduated from rookie school, a half-dozen new guards went to Playa del Rey to celebrate. We built a huge bonfire on the beach and drank some beer, too much beer, as is the habit of kids this age.

Suddenly one of the senior guards, Mike Whittington, drove up in his patrol truck and said, "We have a possible drowning in Ballona Creek. I want you guys down there right now."

As Mike drove away, we all started laughing. We assumed he was playing a prank on us, the new guys. We stopped laughing as Mike, seeing in his rear view mirror that we weren't moving, spun his truck around and raced back. In a dead-serious tone, he said, "You think I'm kidding? If you're not down there in five minutes, you're all fired."

We immediately began running to Ballona Creek, about half a mile away. As I ran I could feel the alcohol emptying out of my stomach and going straight into my bloodstream. I felt sick, nauseated, by the time we arrived, my head pounding, wanting only to throw up.

Three people were standing on the edge of the creek, staring into the water. A fourth member of their group, on a dare, had jumped off the small bridge that spans Ballona Creek. He never surfaced.

Was he dead? Most likely, yes. He was either on the bottom, near where he had jumped, or swept out to sea by the outgoing tide. If he was nearby, it was our job to find him. The rookie guards formed a line, shoulder-to-shoulder, and slowly waded in, deeper and deeper, into the icy water. I found myself praying that the missing man would come running up, laughing, saying it was all a joke, for his sake, his friends' relief, and so that we could get the heck out of the slimy, polluted waters that make up Ballona Creek.

In unison we dove down, searched, came up, shifted the line to the right, following the tide, and dove again. We couldn't find him. Suddenly I noticed that the tide was moving in, not out as we had first determined. I yelled that we should move the line in the opposite direction. This we did, then we dove again. This time, after going no more than a few feet underwater, my left hand touched a cold, unresponsive leg. I immediately tried to pull the man to the surface but nothing moved. What was going on? I came up, took a deep breath, and dove down. As I felt around in the pitch black, I realized that he was impaled on a length of concrete-reinforcing steel rod, a half-inch in diameter. The steel was rammed straight through his chest.

I came up gasping for air, from the horror, from the cold, from the adrenaline in my blood mixing horribly with the alcohol. When I finally caught my breath I yelled to the other rookies that I'd found the victim, and that I needed help. Five of us surrounded the man, lifted him off the steel rod, and carried him to the rocky edge of the creek. Barely a moment later, his girlfriend approached me. I happened to be wearing white Speedos, as opposed to everyone else's dark colors. The woman, seeing me dressed differently, must have assumed that I was in charge. She asked me, "Is he going to be okay?" I wanted to say, "Okay? He's been underwater for 50 minutes." Clearly, she was in shock. I responded by saying, "He's going to be taken to the hospital."

Lifeguard Myron Cox trying to comfort a distraught mother. This photo brought home to me the seriousness of being a lifeguard.

Could we have had a worse night? I doubt it. We'd been drinking, which happens to nearly everyone at some point in their life, but we shouldn't have been drunk on a public beach, not to mention our being under the legal drinking age. I felt guilty that we had hesitated in carrying out Mike Whittington's original orders. In different circumstances, the time we wasted might have made a difference in the survival of the victim. No doubt some lessons were learned that night, but those lessons came at the cost of one horrible, awful, lousy experience, which none of us will ever forget.

This was my welcome to lifeguarding.

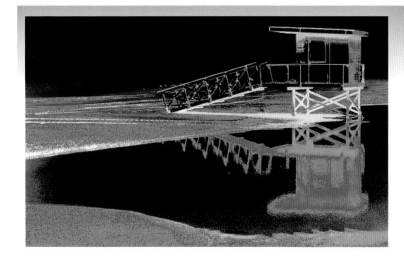

CHAPTER 2

Night Fire

Through the course of rookie school, we were observed by the head lifeguards from different L.A. County beaches. Finally, when it was over, these head guards picked the rookies they wanted to man their towers, somewhat like a professional draft.

Being the top rookie, however, I was allowed my choice of beach. I selected Will Rogers State Beach, where I'd spent many summer days as a kid. I had dreamed of guarding at that beach as long as I could remember. Unfortunately, I didn't know one important fact about lifeguarding at Will Rogers: The man in charge, Lieutenant Bud Clark, had his own strict, carefully defined way of doing things. For starters, Bud Clark hated the fact that I had chosen his beach. Each year he was given new lifeguards, but only those men whom he had personally selected. I had chosen Bud, and he did not like that at all.

Bud Clark's whole existence was lifeguarding. He literally lived at lifeguard headquarters, in a small apartment set above the garages. He was always on duty, always supervising.

I soon found out that Bud was a difficult man and an even more difficult boss. Like the strident Jack Webb character in the film *The D.I.* (Drill Instructor), Bud employed a leadership style that demanded all his guards to live in complete and utter fear of him. He didn't want us working

(Opposite) A picture of the Will Rogers Headquartes during the 1920s. It was a lighthouse before it became the lifeguard headquarters.

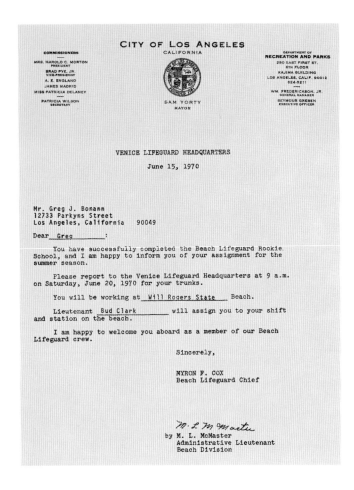

With this letter I became an official member of the lifeguard fraternity.

CITY OF LOS ANGELES
CALIFORNIA

COMMISSIONERS

MRS. HAROLD C. MORTON
PRESIDENT
BRAD PYE, JR.
VICE-PRESIDENT
A. E. ENGLAND
JAMES MADRID
MISS PATRICIA DELANEY
PATRICIA WILSON
SECRETARY

SAM YORTY
MAYOR

DEPARTMENT OF
RECREATION AND PARKS
250 EAST FIRST ST.
6TH FLOOR
KAJIMA BUILDING
LOS ANGELES, CALIF. 90012
624-5211

WM. FREDERICKSON, JR.
GENERAL MANAGER
SEYMOUR GREBEN
EXECUTIVE OFFICER

VENICE LIFEGUARD HEADQUARTERS

June 15, 1970

Mr. Greg J. Bonann
12733 Parkyns Street
Los Angeles, California 90049

Dear Greg   :

      You have successfully completed the Beach Lifeguard Rookie
School, and I am happy to inform you of your assignment for the
summer season.

      Please report to the Venice Lifeguard Headquarters at 9 a.m.
on Saturday, June 20, 1970 for your trunks.

      You will be working at Will Rogers State   Beach.

      Lieutenant Bud Clark   will assign you to your shift
and station on the beach.

      I am happy to welcome you aboard as a member of our Beach
Lifeguard crew.

                              Sincerely,

                              MYRON F. COX
                              Beach Lifeguard Chief

                              by M. L. McMaster
                              Administrative Lieutenant
                              Beach Division

out or competing in the Lifeguard Games, competitions held throughout the summer. In his opinion, the best way to keep the beaches safe was for his guards to watch the water and nothing else.

By regulation, however, lifeguards, while on duty, were required to exercise an hour each day, always within the guard's area of responsibility. Like many new guards, I cherished this required workout, looking forward with great anticipation to running, swimming, paddle boarding, or dory rowing. (A dory is a fixed-seat rowboat used by guards for making ocean rescues.) Bud Clark didn't follow this exercise rule. With Bud, when you were on duty, you were watching the water. If you came in early to work out, he would say, "It's too busy. Start watching the water. Right now!"

During my first year of lifeguarding, I lived in fear of missing a rescue. This fear served as an astoundingly powerful motivation. The first time I worked at a crowded beach, with thousands of heads bobbing in the water, I was partnered with Glen Hughes, who was a five-year lifeguard. To me, a five-year lifeguard seemed like a god. Now I look back and see that even at five years, in many respects, a guard is still a rookie. Glen was a swimmer at UCLA, a great butterflyer. I had gone to UCLA swim meets just to watch him compete.

Glen told me, "Don't count heads. You'll screw up by counting heads. Look for the guy who is caught in a riptide. You can tell because he's facing toward the shore but going out to sea. Go get him even if he's not yet struggling."

If you don't take action, the lifeguards on either side might think you don't see the victim. Then they will be forced to get involved, which is the last thing a guard wants. By causing an adjacent lifeguard to get involved in your territory, you're creating a situation where they could miss a rescue in their own turf. Plus, it is very embarrassing, since it infers to the other guards that you didn't see the situation as it was escalating.

At the beginning of my third season, summer 1972, I told Bud Clark that I was planning to go to the Munich Olympics in late August and would not be able to work the full summer.

After considering this for a moment, Bud said, "In that case, you're out of here." I couldn't believe it. The most important part of my life, guarding at Will Rogers, had abruptly ended. Bud, who had been looking for any excuse to get rid of me, said that he couldn't tolerate a guard at his beach who would not commit to being around for the whole summer.

I was transferred to Playa del Rey, which is much further south, under the take-off zone for Los Angeles International Airport (LAX). It was awful. Certainly I wanted to go to the Olympics, but I hadn't imagined that it would cause me to lose my job at Will Rogers. I nearly cried on my way to Playa del Rey that first day.

Of all the L.A. County beaches, Playa del Rey is the only one where a patron can legally build a fire. We had many happy families coming to Playa del Rey in the late afternoon to have a barbecue, and we had a great number of angry, drunken gangbangers coming down to have a raging riot that would last long into the night.

20 • *Baywatch*: Rescued from Prime Time

The del Rey guards had a shift called "Night Fire." Many times I worked Night Fire, Playa del Rey. We weren't rescuing swimmers, we were breaking up fights, dealing with kids who were overdosing on drugs, treating people who had gotten drunk and fallen into a fire pit, attending people who had been stabbed in knife fights or been hit over the head with a beer bottle. For a kid like me, fresh from Palisades High School, my first few days on Night Fire were a real awakening to the ways of the real world.

I soon learned that any legitimate ocean dangers, riptide and rough surf, are hugely multiplied if a beach patron has been taking drugs, drinking alcohol, or both. One time at Playa del Rey, six barrio kids were on the beach, drinking at 11:00 in the morning. The lifeguard on duty told them drinking wasn't allowed, so they moved behind a sand dune, where the lifeguard couldn't see them. Hidden away, they continued drinking. At about 1:00 P.M. they went swimming. A short while later they came back to their towels, drank some more, and then fell asleep. Around 6:00, they went to their car, but realized that the keys were missing. After much arguing, they noticed that their buddy, who had been holding the car keys, was nowhere to be seen. As it turned out, he had drowned five hours earlier. They were so drunk, they never missed him.

When a lifeguard sees a swimmer struggling, arms flailing, thrashing about in the water, the guard immediately comes to that person's aid. But when a swimmer is drunk, he doesn't struggle. An incoming wave washes over him, and he simply never surfaces. He's gone. The guard on duty has no chance of making the rescue.

The man in charge at Playa del Rey, Eddie Hoffman, was altogether different from Bud Clark. Eddie inspired his guards using positive motivation, rather than through fear and intimidation. Eddie's ability to inspire was even more amazing if you consider that Playa del Rey, and especially the Night Fire shift, was undoubtedly the worst assignment in all of L.A. County, perhaps the worst in the whole state of California. The esprit de corps that existed among the del Rey guards was unbelievably strong; this spirit showed in our camaraderie, our teamwork, the back-up response. If I made a call for back-up at 9:00 P.M. on a Sunday night, it seemed as though the whole lifeguard world would come charging down the beach to my aid.

One section of Playa del Rey was directly under the take-off zone for LAX. The departing jets, about one every two minutes, were so low when they crossed the beach that you could wave to a passenger on-board and see them wave back. Not surprisingly, the noise was deafening. Eddie made sure his guards didn't work under the jets for more than an hour or two at the most.

Eddie loved to have his guards represent Playa del Rey in assorted lifeguard competitions. If you needed a day off to compete in a swim race, he gave it to you. If you won, he would put you in the truck and parade up and down the beach, telling everyone. He would have the trophy on the dashboard, showing you off as one of *his* guys. He was a great boss.

During my five years at Playa del Rey, I ended up making some of the best friends of my life. A few of these men decided to stay on as guards and have made it their career. Others have sought out careers elsewhere. My attorney, John Balent, was a lifeguard, as was my insurance man, Mike Dorsey, and my doctor, Mark Newman. Fellow lifeguard John Johnson became an artist. He designed my Tower 18 logo, which has become the *Baywatch* logo, one of the most famous logos in the world. Some of my guard friends now work in the entertainment business. Tom Moore is script supervisor on *Baywatch*, in charge of continuity; Devon Clark is our production coordinator; and the production consultant on the show is Scott Hubbell, a jack-of-all-trades who can solve seemingly impossible problems.

I recruited Hans Fassnacht, a West German swimmer who won a silver medal at the 1968 Olympics, to swim for Long Beach State. He later became a Los Angeles County lifeguard—even later he joined TYR, where, with TYR founder Steve Furness, he helped supply *Baywatch* with our men's and women's signature swimsuits.

The calendar for a seasonal lifeguard is set up in this manner: The guard works the whole week of spring vacation; then he works every weekend until summer. During the days of summer he works full-time, five days a week, until Labor Day. After Labor Day he again works weekends until Thanksgiving. Altogether a seasonal guard has the equivalent of 18 full weeks of employment.

After Los Angeles city beaches merged with L.A. County in 1975, I was transferred to Santa Monica South. It's always a little strange at first to be thrown into a new situation, but right away I realized that I had a lot in common with the guards at Santa Monica South. Most of them were like me. Their idea of a good time was not going to a smoky bar but bodysurfing or working out. I even caught up with the man who had originally inspired me to become a lifeguard: Paul Debello. Once, when Paul and I were working together, we figured out that he had almost certainly been the guard who had told me not to use my inflatable raft on that long ago trip to the beach with my family. At the time he was about 18 years old; I was six.

The Santa Monica beaches have huge parking lots. In fact the world's largest collection of parking lots is found in and around the Santa Monica beach area. If a beach has plenty of parking, you can be certain that it's going to have plenty of patrons. On a summer day, when the surf is big, and you're guarding at Santa Monica, North or South, you'd better be ready to pull out lots of people.

At Santa Monica South, I usually worked next to a rock jetty that was notorious for having a strong "gutter rip." This rip didn't pull a swimmer out to sea, it drew them laterally, into the rocks. Lifeguards put up flags, yelled at swimmers—anything to keep them away from the jetty.

One hectic afternoon, I made a rescue to the south of my tower, about 70 yards to my left. From where I returned to the shore, my view north was obstructed by the jetty. By the time I returned to my tower, a young swimmer had been swept down from the north and was being pulled into the jetty. I sprinted back into the water and swam to the kid as fast as I could. As I came near him, I could see that he was panicking, his eyes wide with fear, his face drained of all color. His fear was well founded—behind him a huge wave was building, a wave that would certainly drag us into the rock jetty, an experience akin to getting pulled into a giant, spinning blender. I yelled to him, "Grab my hand, grab my hand." He reached out, but as he did, the current pulled him away from me, to the outer edge of the rocks. As I swam toward him, I glanced to my right and saw the immense wave bearing down on us. Just as it was about to crest, I yelled one last time, "Grab my hand." Again the kid reached out. This time I grabbed his hand and pulled him toward me. I managed to swim us a few yards away from the jetty before the wave crashed over us. We tumbled over and around, but luckily we missed the rocks. As soon as we surfaced, I swam us out to sea, so that the gutter rip would lift us around the tip of the jetty and then take us down the beach, where we could return to shore. When we finally made it in, I couldn't believe that we'd escaped without a scratch. If I had arrived even a second later, we both would have been dragged into the jetty, the razor sharp barnacles scraping off our flesh. For weeks afterwards, I woke up in the middle of the night shouting, "Grab my hand."

Lifeguarding is a tough job. It carries an immense responsibility. But a lifeguard's day is not always filled with frantic rescues. When I think of lifeguarding, I often imagine a young man or woman sitting in his or her tower, feet up on the railing, watching the water while talking on the lifeguard phone, a party line that connects to other towers and to headquarters. It's a great setting for telling stories. For some reason, people have always liked to tell me stories, and I liked to hear them. I spent countless hours on the phone talking to other lifeguards. If nothing else you can really practice giving your pitch.

LA CO. LIFEGUARD

COUNTY OF LOS ANGELES LIFEGUARD DEPT. OF BEACHES & HARBORS

LOS ANGELES COUNTY LIFEGUARD

BEACH LIFEGUARD LOS ANGELES CITY

SANTA MONICA LIFE GUARD RECREATION

BEACH LA GUARD

L.A. RECREATION PARK DEPT. LIFEGUARD

SANTA MONICA LIFE GUARD RECREATION & PARKS DEPT.

LIFEGUARD GOLD COAST LIFES LUMEN ET OCEANUM

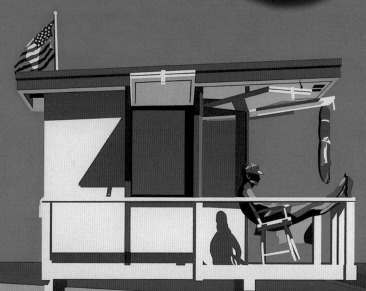

Moon over Malibu on the way to Dodger Stadium.

Here I am with my friends at the game. From left: myself, Pam, Chris, Barbara, and Peter.

One hazard of the profession is somewhat unique. Lifeguards, since they're supposed to be watching the swimmers, carry on all their conversations, whether on the phone or in person, while looking at the water. This habit becomes so ingrained that even away from the beach we often have a difficult time making eye contact when we're having a normal conversation.

After a quiet day in the tower, most young lifeguards have enough pent-up energy to keep them going long into the night. And during the summer it seems as though someone is always having a party. It's at these parties that off-duty lifeguards eagerly switch from beach savior to energetic, oversexed adolescent (regardless of age), with all the accompanying appetites and desires.

Over the years I became celebrated among the lifeguards for staging huge parties, many of which went on to become mythologized in lifeguard lore. Each year I organized a rolling lifeguard party. I'd rent a huge bus, stock it with a few kegs of beer, and we would head to Dodger Stadium to watch a game. Toward the later innings, the announcer would say over the public address system, "We would like to welcome the L.A. County lifeguards." By this time the beer would have taken its toll and the guards would invariably yell something obscene in response.

The announcement served as our cue to depart the stadium and make our way to The Ball, a notorious strip joint on Wilshire Boulevard. One time we accidentally left Captain Rohrer (who later became chief) at Dodger Stadium. He passed out in the ivy, finally waking up at 3:00 in the morning when the sprinklers came on.

The biggest party of the year was always our end of the summer bash—500 raging lifeguards celebrating the end of another season. For many years I organized this event. Once, to make it special, I decided we should have it at a fancy locale. Why not the Sand and Sea Club? I donned a suit and tie (one of maybe a dozen times in my life) and went to the Sand and Sea, a ritzy club that usually wouldn't let a lifeguard in the door, much less rent us their main ballroom for a party.

I told the Sand and Sea representative, a cheerless, stocky woman of about 50, exactly what would happen: "Our gathering will start at 7:00 P.M. Our demeanor will be appropriate. The music will be played at a low level. No alcohol will be permitted. You will be proud of us." On the strength of my presentation, she rented us the ballroom.

In the weeks leading up to the party, an army of lifeguards canvassed the beach, flyers in hand, looking for women to recruit. While the flyer itself was considered high art by the guards, it clearly exceeded the bounds of propriety even for those sexist, male-dominated times. The chief lifeguard, Jerry Cunningham, was so offended by the flyer that he demanded we cease its distribution. Then he wrote a scathing letter, protesting the flyer as a degrading affront to "professional beach lifeguarding." Naturally his furor only served to jack up the interest in the party to an even higher plane. When the big night finally arrived, the band was rocking out, 80-proof punch was flowing like water. As the hours passed and the punch was consumed, the party evolved into a raging steamer. Guys were diving off the clubhouse roof, doing two-and-a-half flips into the pool.

Finally we reached the party's climax, the traditional "hot legs" contest. A dozen women, in various states of undress, took turns dancing to the cheers of the lifeguards. Then I heard a bell go off—the elevator bell. Suddenly, at the far end of the hall, the elevator doors parted and out stepped the woman to whom I had originally spoken about renting the hall. For a moment it seemed as through I was looking through a telescope: I could see her advancing, double-time, her face frozen in a scowl, arms crossed. Cruella De Vil could not have looked meaner. She walked straight toward me, sparks flying off the heals of her shoes.

I was standing on a table, microphone in hand, acting as the emcee for the hot legs contest. Without thinking twice, I said, "Wait a minute, guys. Here she comes. A LATE ENTRY." The guys went wild. Then someone switched off the lights and we all bolted for the exits.

CHAPTER 3

Lights, Camera, Action of a Different Sort

Besides lifeguarding, my great passion has always been the Olympic Games. When I was a young boy I stayed glued to the television when the Olympics were being broadcast. To me, the Olympics were, and still are, one of the greatest celebrations of the human spirit. The Olympic Games always bring out the best in people.

For several years I trained to make the U.S. Olympic modern pentathlon team. Modern pentathlon is a relatively obscure sport, made up of five events: swimming, cross-country running, pistol shooting, equestrian, and fencing. Naturally I excelled at swimming, but I couldn't fence my way out of a phone booth.

In 1972, I qualified for the Olympic trials but I didn't make the team. The next best thing, I figured, was to go to the Olympics and watch in person. Within hours of arriving in Munich, I met another tourist, Jimmy Langkop, who was accompanying his mother, Dorothy Franey Langkop. She had been a champion figure and speed skater, and was now covering the Olympics for a Dallas newspaper. They had extra tickets to various events, which they were nice enough to give me. Through the course of the Games, Dorothy, Jimmy, and I became good friends.

Months later, on a visit to Los Angeles, they introduced me to one of their friends, John "Jack" Hennessy. Jack was an extremely likable, charismatic man. He was also a very competent

(Opposite) Ready to film at the Lake Placid speed skating rink, where Eric Heiden won his five gold medals.

filmmaker. His company, JJH Productions, made industrial, educational, and documentary films.

Jack and I eventually became close friends. Essentially he was my first mentor. For many years Jack and I had lunch together about once a month, during which we talked about all things: life, work, and play. When I failed to get into law school, Jack, a Harvard Business School, Baker's Scholar graduate, advised me to try business school. Because of Jack's advice, I went to UCLA Business School where I earned an MBA.

The value of having a business education is not to be underestimated. At *Baywatch*, I handle everything financial: the budgets, completion bonds, insurance, bank loans, float. I do it all—not because I'm smarter but because I'm not intimidated by that stuff, thanks to a large degree to having studied. Having this business knowledge frees me up to make my own decisions. Entrepreneur's Rule No. 1: Make your own business decisions. A business manager should *not* make your decisions, but take your decisions and make them a reality.

After graduating from UCLA Business School in 1977, I soon found a full-time job working for West-Nally, a worldwide sports marketing firm. This was in addition to my ongoing part-time job as a lifeguard. At West-Nally, I was an account executive for two sports, soccer and gymnastics, and also for the Tall Ships event. My job was to raise money for those entities any way that I could. For soccer, I arranged for Coca-Cola to sponsor a tour of the United States by the Chinese national team.

Training for the U.S. Olympic pentathlon trials, 1972.

As part of their sponsorship, Coke wanted to have a documentary made about the tour. At that time the only filmmaker I knew was my friend Jack Hennessy. I went to Jack and said, "Coca-Cola has advanced me a lot of money toward making a movie about this soccer tour. Will you make it for me?" He gladly agreed to do so.

Later I took a Tall Ships project to Jack. Finally I asked him to make a documentary for the U.S. Gymnastics Federation, sponsored by Armor Dial.

After I brought this third film to Jack, he said, "It's really exciting making films, but it's damn hard to find someone who will give you the money to make them. You seem to be good at finding the money. Why don't you work for me as a sales rep?" I had always wanted to work in the film and television industry, and I had often considered working for Jack. Without thinking twice I resigned from West-Nally and joined JJH Productions.

Filmmaking is a strange business. If you want to buy a new car, most likely you wouldn't consider talking to the guy who works on the assembly line or the manager of the factory or even the chairman of the board. You'd talk to a car salesman, let him give his song and dance. Filmmaking is quite different. The buyer wants to talk to the actual filmmaker. From day one, Jack said, "In order to be a good sales rep, you have to become a producer–director. Otherwise you will never have any credibility with our clients." I could not have been happier at the prospect. Over the next few years Jack taught me everything I needed to know about the craft of making films.

Soon after arriving at JJH, I sought to combine my love of the Olympic Games with my new career as a filmmaker. I went to the Montgomery Ward corporation and asked their special projects representative, "Would you be interested in sponsoring a film about the U.S. athletes as they compete in the 1980 Winter Olympic Games being held in Lake Placid?" He said, "Wow, can we do that?"

I said, "Sure."

I then took the Montgomery Ward commitment to the United States Olympic Committee (USOC) and asked their rep, "Would you like to have a film made that would celebrate the accomplishments of all U.S. athletes as they compete in Lake Placid?" My proposed film would differ from the International Olympic Committee film, which could be counted on to feature only athletes who finished first.

He said, "Yes, that would be great. But I don't think we can afford it."

I said, "Don't worry about the costs. I've taken care of it."

I had an ally at the USOC: its head at the time, Colonel F. Don Miller. He liked the fact that I was an athlete and that I had tried out for the Olympic team. Through Don, I was able to get the necessary credentials to film at Lake Placid. I then hired four of the premier documentary cameramen in the business, including Joe Longo, a great sports photographer as well as a renowned battalion cameraman from World War II.

Before leaving for Lake Placid, I talked to Bob Paul, a well-respected USOC expert who was often consulted on all-things-Olympic. With dozens of events taking place in Lake Placid, and with our finite resources, I needed some insight into which events I should consider capturing on film. Regarding the ice hockey competition, Bob Paul said, "Shoot lots of footage of the U.S. team at the very beginning of the Games. I doubt if you'll have an opportunity later."

We arrived at Lake Placid and went straight to the ice hockey competition.

In the first game, United States vs. Sweden—with only seven seconds to play—the U.S. team tied the score. Over the next two weeks the U.S. team kept winning, defeating four consecutive opponents. Naturally we kept filming. By the time the final match was played, we were nearly out of film stock. (So much for expert advice.)

In the now legendary final match, U.S. vs. U.S.S.R., I gave each of the cameramen three rolls of film. I told them, "Use it judiciously, but don't miss a goal."

With the cameramen positioned around the stadium, I took my place behind the U.S. bench where I could hear U.S. Coach Herb Brooks yelling instructions to his players. All through the match, as the lead went back and forth, I kept in contact with my cameramen over a walkie-talkie. Suddenly, with 10 minutes to go, Mike Eruzione broke away and scored what turned out to be the winning goal. As the stadium erupted into cheers, I yelled over the walkie-talkie, "Did you get it?" The first cameraman said, "No, I didn't get the goal, but I caught the breakaway." I asked the second cameraman, Bill Hefner, up in the crow's nest, "Did you get it?" He said, "Yeah, but it's a wide shot. I don't think you can even see the puck." I asked the third cameraman, Ray Ambraizunas, "Did you get it?" Ray said, "Yeah, but a guy stood up right in front of me just as Mike made the goal." By this time I was in a panic. Three of the four cameramen had missed the most important footage of the Olympic Games. I had only one more chance. I said, "Joe, are you there? This is Greg. Did you get it? Did you get it?"

"Greg?" he said, "I'm ready any time you are."

The whole thing was set up, an amusing little trick played on their 28-year-old direc-

(Above) With our homemade armbands firmly in place, cameraman Ray Ambraizunas takes direction. (Below) Our crew take over the podium at Lake Placid. From left: myself, Jack Hennessey, Joe Longo, Ray, and Bill Hefner.

tor, who felt about 100 years old by the time they let me in on the joke. They had all captured the shot.

The completed film, *Fire and Ice*, won many, many awards, including the Cine Golden Eagle for best documentary, and it helped establish my reputation. Whenever I walked into a meeting, the people would say, "You're the guy who made *Fire and Ice*? Sit right down." It opened up many doors.

started at JJH in 1978. Over the years, I spent a lot of time with Jack Hennessy. One project, a six-hour PBS documentary about Saudi Arabia, required that we travel countless times between Los Angeles and Saudi Arabia, a 26-hour flight each way. You get to know someone pretty well sitting next to them on a plane or in an airport for 26 hours.

In many ways, I was the son he never had. And like many people in his situation, he was happiest when sharing the life wisdom he had acquired over the years.

Eventually Jack, who wasn't a particularly healthy guy, wanted to retire. He had two daughters, but neither was interested in running JJH Productions. I was. Jack and I agreed that he would give me the opportunity to buy 5 percent of the company, each year, for five years. Then I would be awarded 5 percent for the following five years. After 10 years I would own 50 percent of the company and Jack would retire.

Sarajevo Olympic Film Team. From left: Arnie Serlin, Joe Longo, Mark Ulano, Frank Conway (in front) Gay Hennessey, Ray Ambraizunas, me (in beard), Bill Hefner. Gay wears one of our home-made "official" arm bands.

That seemed fair. I would be buying goodwill and film equipment, although the equipment turned out to be worth very little since the technology used in filmmaking, much like computer equipment, quickly goes out of date. For instance, when we made the Saudi Arabia–PBS documentary (narrated by Orson Welles, his last project before he died), we bought a state-of-the-art Kem Flatbed editing machine. Within weeks of taking delivery, the editor we hired said, "I can work on this machine, but I'll be here 16 weeks. If you get the newer model, I'll be out of here in eight weeks." Our supposedly state-of-the-art editing machine was already obsolete.

Sadly, Jack Hennessy died in 1983. His passing was a huge loss to me. Jack was a great guy, a good friend, and an irreplaceable mentor. I learned a tremendous amount about filmmaking and about life from him. Over the years I've wished many times that I could once again ask his advice. I miss his counsel and our friendship.

My first film without Jack was a documentary about the '84 Olympic Winter Games held in Sarajevo. To keep JJH going, and to keep me going as a filmmaker, this film *had* to be a success.

Filming in a foreign country greatly increased the degree of difficulty. Proper Olympic credentials, which we had been given without any undue hassle for Lake Placid, were now unavailable. Rather than get shut out of events, I made up our own credentials that said OFFICIAL OLYMPIC FILM CREW. As it turned out, these credentials worked just as well as the real ones.

The best thing about making this film was undoubtedly my association with Frank Conway. Frank served as my A.D., assistant director. We each took a different side of the process. I put my energies into the creative side: Where should we position the cameras? Who is going to win the men's downhill? Frank worried about how to move the cameras in and out of the country without being taxed, logistics, housing, visas, exchanging money. Plus, he kept a close ear to the frozen ground, finding out things that constantly saved my ass.

The Sarajevo Olympics marked the first time assorted information was placed on-line: schedules, athlete bios, results. Being somewhat computer literate, I was constantly tapping into the nearest computer terminal to access information. After the Mahre brothers, Steve and Phil, finished first and second in the slalom, I read on the computer that the awards ceremony would take place later that evening at the ice rink, before the finals of the ladies figure skating. This made sense. It's always more exciting to hold these ceremonies in front of 12,000 fans, with all the accompanying noise and excitement. At the appointed time, we were ready to go, one of our cameras trained on the parents of the Mahre brothers, who sat expectantly in the crowd waiting for the proud moment when their twin boys would be awarded the gold and silver medals.

Orson Welles in his final production. That's me on the right.

Suddenly Frank tapped me on the shoulder and said, "They're not awarding the slalom medals here. They're awarding them downtown."

I said, "No way. That must be wrong. I read it on the computer. And why else would the Mahres' parents be sitting in the stands?"

He said, "They're wrong too. It's downtown." We hopped in a cab and raced away. Frank was right. In a windswept, deserted square in downtown Sarajevo, three small boxes had been set up. Compared to the ice skating rink, it seemed as though the only people in attendance were the Mahre brothers, the third place French skier, and the town mayor who was awarding the medals. Thanks to Frank, we got the shot.

The key to good filmmaking is in having good people on your team. I was damn lucky to have Frank Conway, Joe Longo, Bill Hefner, Ray Ambraizunas, Arnie Serlin, editor David Hagar, and Steve Rivele, who wrote the film's narration. (Years later, Steve wrote the Oscar-nominated screenplay for Oliver Stone's *Nixon*.)

The men's downhill is always a premier event. In '84 the United States had a good downhill skier, Bill Johnson. He had boldly predicted he would win the gold medal, something no American male had ever done in this event. When the day of the downhill arrived, we lugged hundreds of pounds of film equipment up the side of Mt. Bjelasnica. Not long after we settled into place, the race was postponed due to heavy wind and snow. The whole scenario was repeated the next day, and then a third day. Each time we hauled the gear uphill only to have the race postponed.

As I was cursing the downhill, Mt. Bjelasnica, and the Olympics in general, my cameraman Arnie told me that one of the best stories was taking place all around me. I just hadn't seen it: the weather. He was right. The bad weather was working wonders to build up the tension for this event. On his advice we filmed flags being torn to shreds, huge drifts of snow. It made for some great footage. Despite the delays, Bill Johnson eventually went on to win the downhill. We filmed that too.

With Jack now gone, I was running the whole show at JJH. We had quite a few films in production, including another Olympic film, this time about the '84 Los Angeles Summer Olympics.

The task of filming the L.A. Games was hugely complicated by the mammoth security effort being mounted by the L.A. Olympic Organizing Committee.

However, being a Southern California native, a UCLA grad, and an established maker of Olympic films, I had strong expectations of getting legitimate media credentials. Unfortunately, my friend at the USOC, Col. F. Don Miller, was having a serious, ongoing pissing match with Peter Ueberroth, the head of the L.A. Olympic Organizing Committee. Ueberroth was angry over a bad deal he had made with the U.S. Olympic Committee. As his revenge, Ueberroth was denying F. Don Miller everything he wanted, including my credentials, although at the time I was still hopeful of receiving them.

On the morning of opening ceremonies, my dad called and said, "I'm at church praying for you. I'm not leaving until you get a call from the U.S. Olympic Committee." I said, "Dad, I appreciate your support, but I'd hate to have you sitting in church all day." No matter what I said, I couldn't dissuade him from seeking divine intervention on our behalf.

As I replaced the phone on the hook—my hand still holding the receiver—it rang again. Baaron Pittenger, the U.S. Olympic Committee's new head man, was calling. He said, "I have an idea. Get down to the Biltmore Hotel as quickly as you can."

I'd dealt with the U.S. Olympic Committee for years—in my opinion Baaron was perhaps the best executive director the USOC ever had. He was a classy, elegant man who seemed to embody the ideals for which the Olympics stood. Most importantly, he always considered the best interests of the U.S. athletes and of the Olympics at the forefront of his decisions.

At the Biltmore, the U.S. Olympic Committee's temporary headquarters during the Games, Baaron said, "I have some bad news. You're not going to get your credentials. But I have some good news. I can give you all the tickets you need. Shoot your film from the seats."

The Southland Corporation, which owns 7–11 stores, had already given me the money to make the film. I had hired the crew. I had rented the equipment. Besides the money, my reputation was on the line. I had to do something, so I said, "Great, we'll go for it."

First, I called my crew and said, "Meet me at the Coliseum for the Opening Ceremonies." Then I sat with Baaron and we worked through my 10-page shot list: tickets for opening and closing ceremonies, gymnastics finals for men and women, track and field finals, volleyball finals, on and on. As I drove to the Coliseum I thought up a nickname for the film: *A View from the Seats.*

With tickets in hand, my crew and I adopted a guerrilla filmmaking strategy. For example, we would arrive at each venue long before the event started. Then we would carefully study the arena and decide which seats would give us the best angle for filming. Gradually the arena would fill up around us. When the rightful owner of the seat arrived, I'd offer them another seat, one that would give them equally good viewing but was not as suitable for filming. I'd also give them a couple of U.S. Olympic pins, which Baaron had given us by the dozen.

I pulled out every trick to get the footage I needed. I hustled the crew through the underground passageway at Pauley Pavilion, which took us right onto the hardwood floor, just in time to capture women's gymnastics. I had OFFICIAL FILM CREW armbands made up, including one printed in German. I told my guys, "When in doubt, pretend you speak only German." From having been to practically every Olympics since the 1968 Mexico Games, I knew that the security guards would most likely be grossly underpaid, under-trained, flustered, tired, discouraged, and generally disorganized. With a few kind words and a dozen pins, we were able to move our equipment through the security barriers without undue hassle. Although this was great for us, it was a little unnerving. These supposedly super-secure Olympics were not secure after all—a clever terrorist could have sneaked in and caused all sorts of problems.

Again, cameraman Arnie Serlin came through for us. When Mary Decker tripped over Zola Budd's feet in the women's 1,500 meters, only Arnie kept his camera trained on Mary Decker as she writhed on the track. The other cameramen jumped from Mary to the other runners. That was a mistake: Mary Decker was *the* story.

Event by event, using mono-pods to hold the cameras steady instead of big, bulky tripods, we filmed our way through the Games. At the gymnastics finals, as the U.S. men were winning the team gold, all five cameramen were in prime filming locations, and all five were collectively going for it. Over the walkie-talkie I could hear them hooting as they captured the most perfect shots possible. I knew then, if I ever made it to the big time of entertainment, these were the guys I wanted with me.

Not once, over the two-week span of the Games, did we get shut out of an event. Also, at every venue I had seen all the other cameramen corralled into a cordoned off pit, which was often placed in a less-than-optimal filming area. They could only get the same, exact, often inferior shot. Our film had a much greater variety of camera work.

By the end of the Games, I had become a great believer in the saying, "Power is 10 percent given, 90 percent assumed." In this instance, power was expressed as permission-to-enter. We assumed all 90 percent and more.

Besides developing my producing and directing skills, I learned the importance of motivating the crew. They didn't want to shoot without credentials. They didn't want people milling around as they worked. But I convinced them that this was the opportunity of a lifetime, which it was. Through our hard labor we formed a true team, as valid as any in the athletic arenas we covered. More than anything, more than the film itself, I came to love our team. Most of the guys who worked with me at the '84 Games are still with me today.

We needed tickets in order to shoot from the seats.

Before he died, Jack Hennessy had legal papers drawn up that would have finalized our deal-in-principle, wherein I would become the co-owner of JJH. Unfortunately when Jack passed away in 1983, he had not yet signed the documents.

By nature, I'm a very nonconfrontational person, or at least I was back then. I didn't want to discuss the ownership issue with Ruth, Jack's widow, until the time was right. I waited a year, during which time I continued running the day-to-day events of the company, overseeing every aspect of selling and making films. Midway through the second year, I called Ruth and said, "I'd like to talk about my future with JJH." She said. "Great, but can it wait a little longer?"

Just before Jack died, their daughter, Gay Hennessy, got a divorce, moved from San Francisco, and joined the company. Gay wanted to learn the business, so I started her as a trainee–editor.

When Ruth and I finally sat down to talk about my future, she said, "This is a family company. You're not family. I'm not going to offer you any ownership." I said, "Fine, I want double the money," which meant going from 5 percent commission to 10 percent. She reluctantly agreed to pay me the increased commission, although I could tell she and Gay thought I was extorting money from the company. This arrangement continued for three years. I made the films and sent the profits to Ruth, which was quite a bit of money.

One day in late summer 1987, with a great slate of films set up for 1988, out of the blue Gay walked into my office and said, "My mother and I feel you're making too much money." I said, "Well, do you want me to take a pay cut?" She said, "No, we want you to leave." I said, "I'm not going to leave." She said, "Okay, you're fired."

I drove home in shock. No warning, nothing. I discussed it with my friends and parents, and they all said, "Hey, maybe it's better this way." At the same time I was going through a divorce. It was a low period, to say the least. I lost my job, I lost my wife, and in the process I also lost my house—all at the same time.

Some months later, the lawsuit I had brought against JJH finally came to arbitration. I felt that JJH owed me back commissions for the last few films I'd brought into the business, about $7,500, which was a lot of money to me at the time.

I could hardly get an attorney to look at the case. Then JJH countersued me. They claimed that I had stolen business away from them, which was not true. But JJH's countersuit worked tremendously in my favor. Suddenly I had no trouble finding an attorney to take my case, and for one simple reason: If we won, JJH would have to pay my attorney's fees.

Sure enough, through arbitration, JJH had to acknowledge that they owed me the back commissions. They paid me $7,500. Then JJH paid my attorney almost $50,000. Six months later, in a sad, disappointing end to Jack Hennessy's creation, JJH went out of business.

CHAPTER 4

Entertainment 101

Exactly 10 years before being fired from JJH, one of the most important events of my life took place. On a summer afternoon in 1977, while guarding at Will Rogers State Beach, I made a rescue. It was not a particularly dramatic rescue but it was special in one singular aspect.

From the Will Rogers headquarters rooftop deck, I saw two kids, about six or seven years old, who seemed to be caught in a riptide. I picked up my rescue can, ran toward the water, swam out to the kids, and pulled them in. Their father, who had been on his towel, saw me running into the water. When I came out he was standing knee deep, anxious about the well being of his young son and daughter.

They were fine, just a little shaky and cold. After getting them dried off and settled on a towel, their father came up to lifeguard headquarters to assist me in filling out the rescue card. He told me the names of his kids, Tommy and Jacey Erwin, and his own name, Stu Erwin.

I said, "You're not *Trouble with Father* are you?" Stu Erwin, the star of the sitcom *Trouble with Father*, was a very famous name to me.

"No," Stu said, "that's my father."

As it turned out, Stu and his family lived on Oakmont Drive in Brentwood, just up the street

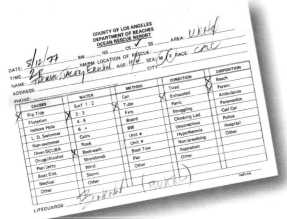

The card filled out after my rescue of Stu Erwin's son and daughter, Thomas and Jacey.

from where I grew up. When I asked Stu what he did for a living, he said, "I'm in charge of development at MTM."

I said, "MTM? Grant Tinker's production company?"

In parting Stu said, "Let me know if I can ever do anything for you."

A few years earlier I had begun imagining a movie or a television series about lifeguarding. Why didn't I envision a book about lifeguarding? I was not a reader while growing up. I was a fan of television and movies so naturally I leaned toward those media forms. Also, lifeguarding is a visual occupation. I felt the visual component of lifeguarding would translate well to the medium of television. Gradually I put my ideas on paper, detailing the characters, outlining a few possible episodes. The series I had in mind would capture the excitement of the rescues we made. By meeting Stu Erwin Jr., I now had that all important "friend in the business" to whom I could pitch my idea.

In November 1977, I drove into the parking lot at CBS Television City on Radford Avenue in Studio City, where MTM had its headquarters. Stu showed me around and even introduced me to Grant Tinker.

Grant was, and in my opinion still is, the single most important individual in the history of entertainment television. Under Grant's guidance, more than a dozen landmark shows were created at MTM, starting with popular comedies: *The Mary Tyler Moore Show* (1970–77) and *Rhoda* (1974–78). Later MTM evolved toward more dramatic shows, such as *Lou Grant* (1977–82).

Back in his office, I described my *Baywatch* idea to Stu. He said, "I like it. Why don't you come back in one week and properly pitch me the show." He went on to tell me exactly what questions a pitch should answer: What is the series about? Who are the characters? What time of night would it air, and on what day of the week? For which network is it best suited? Is it an anthology like *Outer Limits* or a regular series like *Magnum P.I.*? Is it an ensemble show like *M*A*S*H* or a star vehicle like *Rockford Files*? What was my idea for the pilot and the first 10 episodes? Lastly, how much would it cost?

Leaving Television City I went straight to Larry Edmunds Cinema Bookshop and bought every book that I could find on pricing out a television show.

A week later I came back to Stu's office and pitched him *Baywatch*, although at the time I called it *A.C.E.S.*, which stood for Aquatic Corps for Emergency Service. Stu listened patiently and finally said, "It's a good idea but I'm concerned that it's too much like *Emergency*" (a show that had gone off the air only two months earlier, after a five-year run). Further, Grant and Stu had recently tried to develop a light, action adventure series with Brian Clemens, the creator of *The Avengers*. The series hadn't worked out. If an experienced producer like Brian Clemens couldn't meet the challenge, how could a neophyte like me pull it off? Stu politely showed me the door.

Baywatch/A.C.E.S. had not made the MTM cut. But still I had received an invaluable lesson in how to properly pitch a television show. Even better, Stu and I began a lasting friendship that continues to this day. Back then, at least once a month, we would get together for lunch, always at The Tail of the Cock restaurant, an old industry hangout, and discuss life, liberty, and the pursuit of filmmaking success.

My *Baywatch* dream languished for a time. It was revived in 1981, after I had been working at JJH for three years. Early on Jack Hennessy taught me which clients were moneymakers and which were not. Texaco, yes. McDonalds, yes. A one-line pitch could sell a $250,000 film. U.S. military, no. Quite often, a 60-page proposal would gain nothing and cost thousands of dollars to prepare.

36 • *Baywatch*: Rescued from Prime Time

One of the Most-Recognized Logos in the World

The evolution of one of the most famous logos in the world: My lifeguard buddy John Johnson created the logo over a course of weeks, sometimes while also working as a guard in his tower (quiet afternoons only).

I like this shot. We do need to eliminate the structural clutter.

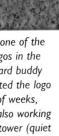

But even our moneymaking films required an amazing amount of work to complete. In early 1981 Jack and I began talking about steering JJH into a new arena, where the profits might equal the amount of work we were investing. The most likely option became fictionalized television series. Jack and I agreed that I would devote a certain amount of my work week to pitching a new project.

The first show I pitched? The one I knew best: *Baywatch*. Immediately I started collecting my requisite 1,500 rejections, something every producer endures early in his or her career. I was told countless times that *Baywatch* was already being done. Where? By whom? Show me? They would say *Chips* or *Magnum P.I.* or *Rescue 911*. To me, these shows contained only the slightest similarity to the elements of *Baywatch*.

I was told an equal number of times that the *Baywatch* concept was dull, that nothing exciting ever happened at the beach. I said, "Wait a minute. Last month you said it was already being done. Now you're saying it's dull. Which is it? Make up your mind."

My own experiences as a lifeguard convinced me that the concept was unique and that it was exciting. Hollywood, Television City, is only a few miles from the Pacific Ocean but you would never know it by talking to the people who work in the entertainment industry. Except for a handful who live in The Colony, Malibu's ultraexclusive beachside enclave, most Hollywood citizens never go near the beach. Everything they know about beach life was learned from watching *Jaws*.

In my naïveté I didn't realize that the industry loves to "niche" people. That is, they lock a person into a tight little pigeonhole: He's an editor, therefore he can't direct. He's a director, therefore he can't produce. She's a producer, therefore she can't write. I was coming from JJH Productions, where we made documentaries, industrial films, and educational films. No one took me seriously. I would have been better off coming from nowhere, in the manner of Quentin Tarantino, rather than trying to get into entertainment through JJH.

Nonetheless I went all over town with *Baywatch*, pitching it at every possible outlet: network television, cable, motion picture studios. Over time I refined my pitch, and like anything it improved with practice. Gradually I began taking meetings with more important people. When I

Contrary to the beliefs of many studio execs, exciting stuff did happen at the beach, such as this small plane crash. From left: Bob Chambers, Bill Powers, Bruce Sailors, Ralph Lee, Don Spitler, and Don Rohrer (in uniform).

had a meeting lined up, I tried to learn as much as possible about the person: What did they like? What had they just canceled? Naturally I had assiduously avoided pitching anything close to what this executive had recently axed.

I also read every industry-related biography and autobiography that I could find, taking careful notes as I went. Eventually I owned hundreds of books, by and about people such as Frank Capra, Roger Corman, Sydney Lumet, Michelle Phillips, Linda Obst, Michael Eisner. The classics. What did I learn from all these biographies? For one thing, I learned that every successful producer or director achieves his or her success through an altogether unique manner. Basically, no "formula for success" exists. Every successful person does it his or her own way.

Although I had imagined *Baywatch* as a weekly television series, over time I pitched it in every possible shape, form, and permutation, changing the show to match where I was pitching and what I thought the market was buying. I tried a one-hour drama series, a documentary, a major motion picture, animation, miniseries, children's show, reality show.

I pitched *Baywatch* to Kim LeMasters, who at the time was the head of CBS Television. After my morning swim workout, I drove straightway to the International House of Pancakes restaurant near the CBS studio. I wanted to get the drive out of the way good and early, just in case a tanker truck flipped over on the Santa Monica Freeway and closed it down. Then I sat at the restaurant for an hour and a half, going over my pitch notes. Over time I had written out my complete pitch, starting with "Hello, my name is Greg Bonann," all the way to "Thanks for your time." This way, if the executive was interrupted for any reason, which nearly always happened, I could resume my pitch at the right place.

At the appointed time, I drove to the studio, waited in the outer office until being ushered in by his secretary, gave my pitch to Kim LeMasters, and left. Afterward, I found a quiet place nearby where I could write up my notes about the meeting, specifically what problems he had with the show. Kim didn't like the blending of drama and comedy. Two years later, when I pitched him a second time, I referred to my notes from the first meeting and made sure that I didn't suggest the same aspects.

My first, best, and preferred version of *Baywatch* was as a one-hour, action-drama series. A drama must be about *something*. Jay Sandrich, the legendary director and a man who, like Jack Hennessy, became a mentor of mine, told me time after time, "Be precise when telling people what *Baywatch* is about." Sitcoms, on the other hand, are usually character-driven: Jerry, George, Elaine, and Kramer chatting over a bowl of soup. Each character was crucial to the show and could not have been replaced. Drama is a story-driven medium. *Law and Order* lives by the story, not the actors. That series wins Emmy after Emmy even though over the years every cast member has been replaced except Stephen Hill.

Baywatch is about the life and times of lifeguards, on and off duty. It's about heroes. These young attractive, spirited people save lives during the day and then go home at night to their real world problems and pleasures.

During my years at JJH, I spent part of each week pitching *Baywatch*, getting nowhere, getting told time and again that nothing exciting ever happened at the beach. Then on weekends, back at my lifeguard tower, I'd hear about a small plane that crashed on the beach, or about a rescue that had happened the day before—where a guy's leg was trapped under a rock, and the tide was coming in, and he was about to drown, and the only way to free the guy was for five lifeguards to hoist up the rock. That's exciting stuff. On occasion, I was the lifeguard who made the rescue, so I knew firsthand what was going on. Unlike most producers, who get beaten down with time as their projects are rejected again and again, I would be reenergized over the weekend. Then I would go back to work the next week and do battle all over again.

n 1981, NBC was the lowest-rated of the three networks. In an attempt to revitalize their entertainment programming, Grant Tinker left MTM and took over as chairman of NBC. When Grant arrived at NBC, Brandon Tartikoff was in charge of entertainment programming. Following a long-standing Hollywood tradition, most executives, upon coming into a new position, would have cleaned house—firing anyone who might have contributed to the lowly ratings. But Grant left Brandon in place—a brilliant move because it put incredible pressure on Brandon to produce the goods.

Gradually, over the next five years, NBC rose from last place to first. Brandon and Grant led this dramatic turnaround by presenting such shows as *The Cosby Show*, *Cheers*, *Hill Street Blues*, and *St. Elsewhere*. The victory of NBC over CBS and ABC firmly established the reputation of both Brandon and Grant as television programming and management geniuses.

Grant left NBC in 1986 and formed a new production company, GTG. It should be noted that Grant did not leave in order to make more money, as is often the case. The producers of successful television shows are paid enormous sums of money because they generate astronomical profits for the networks who buy their shows. Grant Tinker left NBC because the original challenge, bringing the network to the top, had been met and conquered. Basically Grant was now seeking out new challenges. GTG was funded by Gannett, a huge conglomerate which owned, among other things, a syndicate of newspapers, including *USA Today*. Gannett's only caveat to the new relationship was that Grant Tinker produce a daily television newsmagazine called *USA Today*, comparable to today's *20/20* and *Dateline*. Gannett would use this new show as another medium through which to distribute news and information.

Using Gannett's money, Grant bought the old Laird Studios in Culver City and thoroughly remodeled it. The GTG studio eventually featured five levels of underground parking topped by a garden, 12 sound stages, and state-of-the-art editing equipment. Nothing was overlooked. Even the ornate facade that faced Culver Boulevard, patterned after the mansion in *Gone with the Wind*, was totally remodeled.

GTG immediately became a very desirable place to work. Grant Tinker had a reputation for allowing his people to maintain their creative freedom. Gannett was liberally funding the whole operation. The best people in Hollywood—directors, producers, actors, and writers—wanted to join Grant's team.

My first ever meeting with Grant necessitated a lengthy stop at the guard shack, where I received my first ever Visitor's Pass.

In early 1987, my sister Deborah began working as a receptionist at a television production company, ITC, owned by Sir Lew Grade. Like several production companies, ITC rented office space on the GTG lot. Whenever I had lunch with Stu Erwin Jr., who was again working with Grant, I always stopped by ITC to say hello to Deb.

During one of these visits, I met an ITC writer, Doug Schwartz. Doug seemed like a nice guy, very personable. He was quite interested in the Olympic documentaries I had been making. Some months later, my sister announced that she and Doug were engaged to be married.

Doug worked with a writing partner, his first cousin Michael Berk. Starting in their late teens, Doug and Michael had worked together as writers of television movies and series, with many shows to their credit. At the time, Doug and Michael's biggest credits were two television movies called *The Incredible Journey of Dr. Meg Laurel* and *The Ordeal of Dr. Mudd*. Like most writers, Doug and Michael were always searching for new opportunities. Likewise, I was looking for writers who might be interested in my ideas.

When Doug and Michael's overall deal at ITC expired, they asked me, "Can you introduce us to Stu Erwin at GTG? We know he's a friend of yours." I said, "Sure, I would be glad to." I set up a meeting and introduced them. Eventually Doug and Michael were hired to develop new shows at GTG.

Finally, in terms of *Baywatch*, all the key elements were coming together. I knew Grant Tinker, who ran his own studio. I knew his trusted associate, Stu Erwin Jr. A member of my own family and his first cousin were now working as writers at GTG.

Only a few problems remained. At this point, late summer 1987, I had pitched *Baywatch* to Doug and Michael dozens of times. I showed them my *Baywatch* script, the outline, the treatment. Each time they had said, "What else do you have?"

Over and over they said it just wasn't their sort of show. Finally, with the help of my sister Debbie, I was able to make some headway. One of the most exciting lifeguard events of the year

AVISO
AGUA
CONTAMINADA
EVITE CONTACTO
CONDADO DE LOS ANGELES
DEPARTAMENTO DE SALUBRIDAD

Masked dory racers prepare for battle.

was about to take place, the annual Lifeguard Games. This summer ritual, part competition, part voodoo-rite, is held over the course of two nights, with bonfires, helicopters, rescue boats, and a cast of thousands. Debbie had been around lifeguarding for 20 years, and she was intimately familiar with the Games. She told Doug, "Please, just go down and check it out. You'll like it." Finally Doug agreed.

The competition began with the Coast Guard's $7 million, French-built Dauphin jet-helicopter flying in low and then hovering overhead. Three lifeguards suddenly leaped out of the helicopter and into the water, where they proceeded to execute a mock rescue. Then the search-lights positioned on the Manhattan Beach Pier flashed on all at once. The featured event, a Taplan Race, was about to commence.

A Taplan Race, named after Supreme Court Judge and lifeguard Irwin Taplan, consists of a relay race featuring four events: running, swimming, paddling, and my own specialty, dory row-ing. Each Los Angeles County lifeguard division fields a team of its best athletes to compete in the Taplan. For instance, the Will Rogers team had four swimmers, four soft-sand runners, four paddlers, and four two-man dory teams.

For an hour and a half, Doug watched the swimmers, runners, paddlers, and dorymen race each other. Sitting in the grandstands next to Doug were more lifeguards and their family and friends, all cheering for their comrades. The whole night was an unrestrained riot of action, noise, narrow victories, disputed losses—the perfect introduction to lifeguarding.

The Lifeguard Games

As part of the Taplan Race, lifeguard divers jumped from low-hovering helicopters. (Top)
I jump from the dory while Kenner Snyder steadies the boat.

Knowing that Doug liked to write character-driven scripts, I introduced him to some of the more colorful, eccentric characters like Kenner Snyder, my sprint dory partner.

Doug loved it and insisted that Michael head to the beach and see it in person. The following Sunday, the three of us drove down the coast. Michael sat next to me, tape recorder in hand, asking question after question. For starters, he wanted to know the basics of lifeguarding. He asked me, "What is this 'can' thing?"

The can is the ubiquitous red, hard-plastic, flotation device, three feet long, which is attached to a length of line and a shoulder strap. Lifeguards use the can to haul people out of the water. A guard never wants to have direct physical contact with a drowning person. In a panicked state of mind, the victim will often pull the guard under if given a chance. The best alternative is to hook the victim to the can and then pull them through the water using the line and shoulder strap.

Michael asked, "Why are the guards always swinging their cans?" It's simple but important: Lifeguard towers are set about 300 yards apart. On a crowded day, a guard walking toward the ocean will swing his can above the heads of the patrons to inform the guards on either side of him of his whereabouts.

Therein lies the beauty of collaboration, which became the strength of our eventual partnership. The beach had been an intimate part of my life for over 20 years. I knew it *too* well. Doug and Michael, both fresh and new to the scene, came to it with a naïve, curious perspective. (Later I organized a "lifeguard-story" brainstorming session at my house—at the time across the street from Malibu's beachside Gladstone's Restaurant. Besides Doug and Michael, in attendance were the Newman brothers, Phil Topar, Will Maguire, Hal Dunnigan, and Kenner Snyder. Here we hashed out a whole season's worth of story lines.)

Doug quickly realized that lifeguarding was unique. Lifeguards were exciting. Doug became a believer: *Baywatch* was an exceptionally good subject for a television series. All three of us left the beach that Sunday knowing that we had something special. But could we make it happen?

(Above) Kenner Snyder and I made 16 straight L.A. County Taplan teams as rowing partners. (Below) The can: the basic tool of every lifeguard. It also became one of the symbols of the show.

Doug and Michael were earning a salary at GTG. I was not. To generate an income I created my own production company, Tower 18, named after my favorite tower on my favorite beach. I continued making documentaries. My first assignment came from a familiar source, Baaron Pittenger, head of the U.S. Olympic Committee. Just after I was fired by JJH, Baaron called me and asked, "Do you want to make a film about the 1988 Olympic Winter Games in Calgary?" I said, "Wow, do I." He said, "Great, it's yours."

After the challenge of making two Olympic films without credentials, I promised my crew that we would never again do a film without having our own official, laminated, authentic credentials. But as the '88 Games approached, the usual hassles

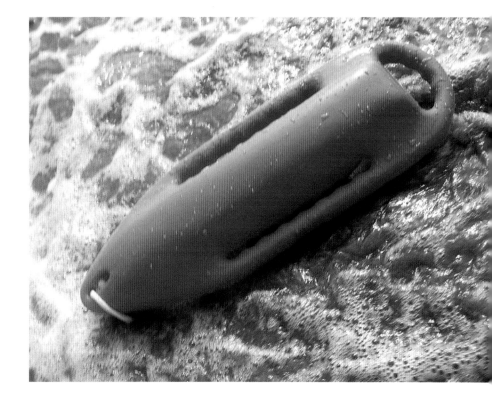

reappeared. The possibility of our getting credentials became more and more unlikely. In hopes of sorting out the problems with the Canadian Olympic officials, I flew to Calgary a week early. No luck. It was a classic case of déjà vu. I had rented the equipment; the crew was already heading to Calgary. A half-dozen people were depending on me, not to mention the fact that a ton of money had already been spent. Somehow we had to make the film.

When the crew gathered at our Calgary headquarters, The Sunbow Hotel—Joe Longo, Gordon Forbes, Gary Capo, Stuart Asbjornson, Ray Ambraizunas, Frank Conway, Terry Erwin, Steve Kovner and David Hagar—I gave them the bad news: sorry guys, no credentials. It was going to be another view from the seats. Joe Longo immediately started laughing. He assumed I was making a joke. It took a while before I was able to convince Joe that I wasn't kidding. Still, they all agreed to stay on and give it their best shot.

On this film we tried something new. Usually the editor waits until all the footage has been shot before piecing it together. But for an Olympic documentary, if you haven't captured the shots you need before the closing ceremony, you're flat out of luck. To make the best possible film, we had our editor, David Hagar, come to Calgary and set up his editing machine in an adjacent hotel room. Each day he studied the footage we had shot the day before. He would then tell us where we needed more coverage, what shots didn't work, what looked good. Having David Hagar edit on-site worked exceptionally well.

For an Olympic wanna-be like me, making these Olympic documentaries was the next best thing to being on the team. Altogether I made six Olympic films. Over the years I have seen the Games evolve; some changes I find distasteful. God knows we don't need multimillionaire Charles Barkley punching out a basketball player from Angola. But in the big picture, the beauty of the Olympics lives on. It is a glorious celebration of the human spirit, one that I still find incredibly inspiring.

On the flight home from Calgary, our film crew rode on the same United Airlines jumbo jet as most of the U.S. Olympic team. As soon as we were airborne, the pilot said over the loudspeaker: Welcome to United's cocktail flight. For those of you who might not know, the Olympic hockey team, the Olympic alpine team, the Olympic speed skating team, and the Olympic filmmaking team are on board. Congratulations on a great job in Calgary. No one bothered sitting down the whole flight.

Nothing like a big Hollywood premiere to symbolize the completion of a project. The cover art for this invitation became the logo for my production company, Tower 18.

City of Gold, my last Olympic film, came in on budget and on schedule. With its completion, I earned a little money. And with that money, I was able to do something that I had been wanting to do for a long, long time.

By this time, March 1988, I'd been pitching *Baywatch* in one form or another for 10 years—an entire decade. Gradually I had come to realize that my presentation lacked one key element: a way to describe the visual beauty of the beach. No matter how eloquent I tried to be, I simply could not convey the essence of this unique, wonderful beach world.

While my crew was still on a high from having done such good work at the '88 Games, I called them together. Sitting around my kitchen table, I told them, "Something big is coming up in a few days. I need your help, but I can't pay you. However, if it goes well, it may eventually mean a lot of work for all of us. Will you shoot it for free?" Gary Capo, my cameraman, said yes. Gordon Forbes agreed to be assistant cameraman. David Hagar agreed to edit.

By good fortune, the lifeguard tryouts were being held that very next weekend, 17 years after I had participated in the same test. I called the senior lifeguard in charge of the tryouts and asked if we could shoot it. I was well-known at lifeguard headquarters by that time, not only as a lifeguard but as a documentary and Olympic filmmaker. The senior lifeguard in charge said, "Fine, great. Come on down."

Shooting the Baywatch *presentation. From left: Gordon Forbes, David Hagar, Gary Capo (kneeling), and me.*

With the help of Scott Hubble, a lifeguard/master organizer, we acquired the necessary permits on short notice. We bought a mountain of 16-mm film stock. The weather was spectacular. The crowds were huge. Our film crew attacked the challenge with abandon.

Tryout day is always special: The lifeguards in charge are extremely officious. The trucks are buffed and waxed. The boats look great. It's a showcase day.

Much the same way as when I had taken the test, the coordinating lifeguard—Terry Hearst in this case—gave a speech just before the competition began. Using a wireless mike we captured his words on tape: "This is the toughest job in the world. Some of you are not going to make it. Don't go down with the ship. We don't need any people drowning out there." He made the test sound very dangerous, and for those who weren't prepared, it certainly could be. As the director, I knew that his words would convey a tremendous sense of drama when reproduced on film.

We opened the film on Terry and then flashed away to the young men and women who were preparing to compete. Terry's speech continued in voice-over: "When we pull you out, you're out. We are going to take 50 candidates to rookie school. From rookie school we may hire only the top five."

I called upon all my Olympic directing experience—quick set-ups, no second takes. Film stock is relatively cheap, so we shot plenty of footage. After the tryouts, I used the rest of the afternoon to film several lifeguards, including Mike Newman, high-stepping into the water and making mock rescues.

David Hagar and I then pieced the footage together. On his suggestion, we tried marrying the footage to the song *The Boys of Summer*, by Don Henley. David's suggestion was just right. The song brought the presentation to life. When we were finished, I felt that we had managed to capture the exquisite, irresistible beauty of *Baywatch*. The presentation proved to be an invaluable selling tool in the weeks ahead.

As an immense Santa Monica crowd watches, we film the lifeguard tryouts. (Top) Terry Hearst addresses lifeguard hopefuls. Gary Capo is behind the camera, with Gordon Forbes to his left. (Above) Filming Mike Newman tossing the can. He is the senior actor on Baywatch, predating even Hasselhoff.

Timing is everything. At the time, Grant, because of his track record at MTM and NBC, had an unprecedented deal: CBS had promised to buy 10 new shows from Grant over a five-year period, no matter what he might propose.

The significance of the 10-show deal cannot be overestimated. Any series that Grant supported would be made. Period. No messing around, no pilot, no "maybe we will buy six episodes." With this deal in mind, a commitment by Grant meant that years of hassles could be leaped over in a single bound. It's no surprise that every creative person in town wanted to work for Grant. In all the years since then, only Steven Bochco and Aaron Spelling have had anything to compare with this remarkable deal.

In early spring 1988, CBS found itself in need of a show to fill its fall, Friday night, 10:00 time slot. And just as we completed the *Baywatch* presentation, several new shows that GTG had been developing (including one that I conceived called *Laugh Trackers*) were discontinued. After seeing the new presentation, Stu said, "The time is right for *Baywatch*." Stu told us to start developing *Baywatch* for CBS. We promised to do our best.

After a month of development, Stu called us into his office. Grant was already sitting on the couch. Jay Sandrich sat next to him. With Doug, Michael, and me looking on, anxious as schoolboys, Stu said, "Okay, this season *Baywatch* is going to be one of our CBS shows, and it's going to be a hit!"

Champagne. Everything was great. *Baywatch* was going to be *on the air*. This particular CBS version of *Baywatch* did not match my original vision, but I didn't care, not after 10 years of pitching *Baywatch* and getting nowhere. We walked out of Stu's office hardly bothering to touch the ground. The feeling was almost as good as winning the rookie lifeguard tryouts.

CBS had all manner of caveats: No nicknames. No CPR. No mouth-to-mouth resuscitation. They were intent on making *Baywatch* into a very serious, very dramatic show.

I had always thought that *Baywatch* should be an action-adventure show set on a fantasy beach. In real life, L.A. County beaches have some degree of urban problems. How could it be otherwise when the beaches are adjacent to 13 million people? We have a few fights, some drugs, no shortage of homeless people. But overall, our beaches are not like a hospital emergency room or a police station. The beach is where people go to have fun. Under the circumstances, however, I kept my opinions mostly to myself.

Using the guidelines set down by CBS, we developed a script for a two-hour television movie. Then we met with CBS, handed them the script, and waited. And waited and waited. We waited for weeks but never heard back.

Finally, on Friday, July 1, 1988, Stu told us that CBS had passed. I was stunned. I said to Stu, "What do you mean CBS passed? Grant has a 10-show deal. Guaranteed. He can do any show he wants. I read it in *The Hollywood Reporter*. I read it in *Variety*. Grant told me himself."

"Well," Stu said, "that's the way it is." While Stu kept his cool when breaking the news to me, I later discovered that he had taken the CBS rejection to heart. Not only was the network rejecting a show he'd nurtured from the beginning, but CBS was not fulfilling their 10-show agreement with GTG.

Eventually we found out that the lower-tier executives at CBS resented the fact that Bill Paley, the chairman of the network, had given Grant this unprecedented deal. Yes, Grant had a 10-show deal, but the lower-tier executives at CBS found ways to derail it. If Grant had insisted, CBS would have bought *Baywatch*. Then they would have promptly thrown it away, putting it up against NBC's *Cosby*, where our ratings would certainly have suffered and the show would soon have perished. In the process Grant and GTG would have lost millions.

That was a miserable, sad day.

CHAPTER 5

In the Back Door

Grant Tinker, however, was not saddened by the turn of events at CBS. He was pissed off. Absolutely furious.

At the time, a strike was underway at the WGA (Writers Guild of America). Guild writers like Doug and Michael could not go to work. But I was not a Guild writer, and so I was not governed by the union's rules. (Of course, I was a writer by trade—I had written scripts for many films at JJH. Subsequently I joined the WGA.)

Grant called me into his office and told me that he wanted to offer *Baywatch* to Brandon Tartikoff at NBC. My task was to write and produce a new presentation, and then direct it.

According to Grant, Brandon favored shows that captured the professionalism of the craft, whether it be police detectives, paramedics, or pilots. He wanted to see lifeguards as highly trained, competent guardians of the ocean. He wanted to see badges, uniforms, patches. He wanted to see the L.A. County seal on the lifeguard trucks—things that would serve to denote *Baywatch* as the one and only official lifeguard show.

After I finished writing it, I prepared a shot list for each of our three units. Then Doug, Michael, and I teamed up to shoot the presentation. With a shot list in hand, a cameraman by our side, and lots of 35-mm film, we set to work. (We switched from 16-mm to 35-mm in order

(Opposite) The romantic leads for "Baywatch: Panic at Malibu Pier" were Parker Stevenson and Mädchen Amick. They tested very high when matched together before sample audiences.

to capture a slightly improved image.) Thanks to the Coast Guard, who lent us the use of their helicopter, I spent most of the day in the air, shooting the beach, the patrons, the rescue boats. Doug's shot list took him from Will Rogers State Beach to the Palisades Cliffs. Michael shot from Venice to Marina del Rey. By the end of the day we had shot pretty much everything under the sun.

Grant was scheduled to play tennis with Brandon Tartikoff at 3:00 in the afternoon the next Saturday. This became our deadline.

We picked up the film from the lab on Monday. David Hagar and I edited the footage together in three days. I showed it to Grant. He suggested changes, which we made. I showed it to him again on Friday afternoon. Some parts of the presentation still made him uncomfortable, so we agreed to make more changes.

Grant was new to rock videos. That's basically what we'd created, an extended rock video—without dialogue or voice-over—but with the visual images complementing the lyrics of the song. Certainly it was quite different from anything Grant had ever done before.

On Saturday morning, David Hagar and I went to the editing studio, On Time, On Line, in the Fairfax district, to make the final changes. When I pulled on the double doors leading into the building, I was met with firm resistance. Locked! Closed for the weekend. Damn it, we had to finish the presentation and get it to Grant in five hours. I said to David, "Hell, this is our future." Without further discussion, on the count of three we both jammed one foot against the middle of the double doors. Like magic the doors sprung open and we were inside.

Finally, after David and I modified the presentation until it was just the way we wanted, we closed the doors behind us and I raced over to Grant's house. As I walked to the front door, he came out, wearing tennis clothes, racket in hand. I handed him the tape and that was it. We had done all we could do.

A week later I was on a rafting vacation with Doug and Debbie along the Sacramento River. Toward the end of our stay, Michael reached us at the American River Inn. He told us that he had just heard from Stu Erwin. Brandon Tartikoff had liked the presentation and he'd agreed to buy a two-hour *Baywatch* pilot for NBC. The only caveat was that NBC would have script approval.

Baywatch became the first series ever to be sold on the strength of a concise video presentation, without prepackaged creative elements such as a lead cast member, director, writer, or producer. Not long afterwards, this sort of presentation became widespread. Why waste all the money doing it the other way?

Big celebration. More champagne. We immediately came back to Los Angeles and began writing the script.

In traditional network television, a series concept evolves into an actual living, breathing weekly series through one or two different means, often based around the pilot. One-hour pilots are the most common. The network commissions the producer to create a one-hour super-episode, which will introduce the audience to series elements, A to Z. After taking a look, the network will decide if this one-hour pilot merits being made into a series. The less promising one-hour pilots are put on a shelf, permanently, never to be seen by the viewing public.

The network sometimes commissions a mammoth two-hour Movie of the Week. This movie is shown—the ratings tabulated. If the rating numbers are good, or if someone in power at the network decides the concept has merit, the producer is given an order for a certain number of episodes, usually a 13-episode order. When a Movie of the Week is used for audience-testing purposes, with an eye toward it being made into a series, the movie is called a "back door pilot."

For a producer, a back door pilot is always preferred to the one-hour variety. The back door has roughly twice the chance of success, since it's guaranteed to be shown to two audiences, the network execs and the viewing audience.

If this pilot whets *someone's* appetite for more, a 13-episode order will be given by the network. If those 13 episodes generate decent ratings, they'll order another 9 episodes. At the end of the year, the network will evaluate the show—its ratings and its costs—and decide whether to renew it or not for a second season.

The number of episodes per season has changed dramatically over the years. For example, in the 1950s, a full season of *Gunsmoke* meant 40 new episodes. Over the years, the number was reduced—a full season of *Sea Hunt* consisted of 32 new episodes. Eventually the number came down to 26—half the year—so that each episode would be rerun once to fill a whole 52-week year. Today the number of new episodes needed to fill a season is a mere 22. They are rerun once, with the remaining eight weeks filled with assorted specials, from "The American Accordion Music Awards" to "The Making of Cindy Crawford's Fitness Video Special."

The concept, from the producer's perspective, is to make as few episodes as possible—to keep the costs down—and still get a full season's order.

Over the next two months, our initial euphoria gradually dissipated as the *Baywatch* script became a problem. In simplest terms, NBC wanted murders; NBC wanted the lifeguards to wear guns like policemen. Doug, Michael, and I tried to accommodate the wishes of NBC and at the same time keep the aspects of the show we wanted—the lifeguard's world, which in reality has nothing to do with murders, committed or solved. Before long, a sense of alienation developed between NBC and Michael Berk, Doug Schwartz, and myself.

The cover of our first Baywatch script.

Being our designated point man, I typically received the phone call from GTG's designated point man, Stu Erwin. Stu wanted to get both sides together without jeopardizing the integrity of the project. Over and over he asked me, "What is wrong with your guys? Why can't they make the network happy?"

For the most part, Grant was detached. At GTG, Stu was in charge of developing new shows. Grant, in his tried-and-true managerial style, left Stu alone. Also, Grant had other projects going at the same time, including at least four series in production: *Dick Van Dyke, Raising Miranda, TV 101, Why on Earth,* plus *USA Today,* the daily newsmagazine. Grant was concerned with keeping those shows on the air and keeping the company afloat. Stu's job was to get new shows up and running, which he'd done successfully many times with *Hill Street Blues, St. Elsewhere,* and *Remington Steele.*

Finally NBC, specifically Brandon Tartikoff, Warren Littlefield, and Perry Simon, approved our script, "Baywatch, Panic at Malibu Pier."

Brandon Tartikoff was well-known in the industry as the man who led NBC. But he didn't work alone. With him were Warren Littlefield, head of programming (and now head of the network, Brandon's old job), and Perry Simon, in charge of drama development.

While I had little contact with either Brandon or Warren, I had daily contact with Perry Simon. We got along very well—I greatly enjoyed his boundless energy and his enthusiasm for the show. Development guys, I knew, did not cancel shows. They want them to be successful. Perry gradually came to understand and to appreciate what we were trying to do with *Baywatch.* In the big picture, were lucky to have Perry as our main ally at NBC.

The script had what Brandon Tartikoff wanted: *Fatal Attraction* Goes to the Beach. In the main story line, Laurie Harris, a character played by Mädchen Amick (a beautiful actress who

A great cast for the Baywatch pilot/Movie of the Week. From left: Parker Stevenson, from Hardy boy *to* Baywatch *lifeguard; Mädchen Amick as an obsessive woman stalker; Richard Jaeckel, who captured the essence of an actual lifeguard captain. (Opposite) former* Knight Rider *David Hasselhoff.*

went on to star in *Twin Peaks*) is dramatically rescued by lifeguard Craig Pomeroy, played by Parker Stevenson. After fantasizing about the Stevenson character and then stalking him, she finally tries to kill him. Brandon considered this *Fatal Attraction* story line to be highly promoteable, and therefore a necessary element of the pilot.

Within the secondary story line, an older lifeguard, Ben Edwards, played by Richard Jaeckel, dies while trying to save people on a fishing boat that has exploded. The Ben Edwards character was based on Hal Dunnigan, the legendary lifeguard who was my teacher during rookie school. This story line, and some of the other minor ones, salvaged at least some of the real lifeguarding aspects that Doug, Michael, and I wanted the show to contain.

Also, we managed to keep the title. NBC had wanted to change it to something other than *Baywatch*. Their reasoning was that viewers would be confused—is the show taking place in a bay? Finally I convinced them that the title, which my mother had suggested at the dinner table one night, came from a nickname given to the rescue boats that patrolled the huge Santa Monica Bay. This bay stretches 50 miles, from Point Vicente in the south to Point Dume in the north, and is hardly baylike, since it is wide open to the Pacific Ocean. Like all good titles, *Baywatch* is easy to remember, easy to say, and unusual enough to capture the interest of viewers.

Preproduction marched ahead at a steady pace, except for one significant area: finding an actor to play the lead character, Mitch Buchannon. A dozen actors a day—essentially every leading man in Hollywood who was searching for work at the time—came before us. We looked at Tom Wopat from *The Dukes of Hazard* and William Katt from *Greatest American Hero*. We saw Adrian Paul (before *Highlander*), Lorenzo Lamas (before *Renegade*), and Jack Scalia (before *Pointman*), a great actor but New York through and through.

NBC wasn't going to do the show unless we came up with somebody they liked. We, the producers, wanted to make sure the actor was someone *we* liked. The physical challenge alone

eliminated about 95 percent of the available actors. Our lead man would have to be ready to swim through the surf, run along the beach (in fast and slow motion), pull people off burning oil platforms and out of sinking sailboats—in general he'd have to be up for the whole *Baywatch* challenge, whatever that might entail. In my opinion, he didn't necessarily have to be the premier Shakespearean actor of our day or the most classically good-looking man in town—just the right actor for the part, that's all.

NBC suggested we use David Hasselhoff.

At first we weren't quite sure if Hasselhoff was the one we had all envisioned. As would any producer, we first took a look as his Q factor. The measure of an actor's relative stardom is such a key part of the entertainment industry that the Nielson company devised a test called the "Q factor" (short for TV Quotient) to calculate an actor's relative star rating. The Q factor for David Hasselhoff was tremendously high. No doubt about it—he could definitely attract viewers, and on a nationwide, network scale.

At the time, however, Hasselhoff was thoroughly niched because of *Knight Rider*. But we definitely needed a David Hasselhoff-type, an actor with a lot of sincerity and a strong physical presence—a true leading man who could share the limelight with other actors (some of whom might not be as experienced or talented). But I just couldn't picture him outside of that souped-up, jet-black Knight Rider car.

Finally Hasselhoff came in and discussed the part with us. I was immediately struck by his physical presence: he's a big, strong, fit man. To me Hasselhoff looked as though he could be a true lifeguard. We wouldn't have to fake the physical side of his character in the least. To give him a sense of *Baywatch*, we showed him the *Boys of Summer* presentation. He loved it. In general, he liked the whole *Baywatch* concept. He turned out to be a great guy *and* he was perfect for the role.

Parker Stevenson, formerly of the *Hardy Boys* television series, was already on board. Then Erika Eleniak joined the cast. Years earlier Erika had been in *E.T.*, playing the little girl who kisses the creature. Unbeknownst to us, in the weeks before we signed Erika she had become a *Playboy* magazine Playmate. Her photo spread was scheduled to appear in the July '89 issue. When the NBC executives found out, they immediately wanted to drop Erika from *Baywatch*, thinking her bared breasts might offend some of their more conservative affiliates. Fortunately we were able to prevail upon the network not to discriminate against her, and she stayed in the cast. After all, she had been hired for her acting abilities and not because of *Playboy*.

We introduced the whole *Baywatch* franchise in the pilot: cast, setting, and characters. Every character on the show was, and still is, based on a real person. Through the years, I had gradually filled a notebook with photos and biographies of interesting, real-life lifeguards. When the time came to cast the show, I brought out the notebook and, one by one, we found actors who somehow captured the unique qualities that these real guards brought to the beach.

My good friend and top lifeguard, Phil Topar, was the model for the character named Mitch Buchannon—played by David Hasselhoff. Phil Topar's son, Beau, was the model for the character named Hobie

(*Opposite and above*) Erika Eleniak: Playboy *Playmate, red-suited actor.* (*Below*) Richard Jaeckel and me. Richard played Ben Edwards, modeled after lifeguard Hal Dunnigan.

Mitch Buchannon

. . . played by David Hasslehoff was based on real-life lifeguard. . .

Phil Topar

Eddie Kramer

. . . played by Billy Warlock was based on real-life lifeguard. . .

Mitch Flyer

Jill Watson

. . . played by Shawn Wetherly was based on real-life lifeguard. . .

Diane Grainer

Shauni McClain

. . . played by Erika Eleniak was based on real-life lifeguard. . .

Natalie Locus

Buchannon—played by Brandon Call. Natalie Locus, a veteran lifeguard, was the model for a character named Shauni McClain—played by Erika Eleniak. Chuck Locko, Richard Mark, and Will Maguire (all three lifeguards, attorneys, and good friends) were models for Craig Pomeroy, played by Parker Stevenson.

One of the best casting jobs was to find actor Billy Warlock to portray the real lifeguard, Mitch Flyer. I'd known Mitch for years, first as a young swimmer at Palisades High, then as a Los Angeles County lifeguard. Mitch was an ultra-confident, incredibly capable lifeguard—in many ways Billy Warlock was able to capture that brash, young, cocky attitude. It worked out well.

The whole casting process was a long, drawn out affair, with every actor (except Hasselhoff and Stevenson) reading for their part a total of five times. First, the casting people had a precasting reading. Then the actor read for us, the producers. If that reading went well, we had them read again, just to be sure. Next we took them to Stu and Grant for a fourth reading. If they approved, we had the actor read one last time for the network.

Diane Grainer and Natalie Locus, posing together.

We auditioned Pam Bowen to play a character based on Diane Grainer, a champion, stud-ass swimmer/lifeguard. I was excited about Pam Bowen from the first reading. Doug, Michael, and I all loved her. She had exactly the right chemistry for the part, and eventually we hired her.

Some weeks later, when we shot Pam's first scene, we had a rude awakening. When the director shouted "action," Pam ran to the water's edge—and stopped. Only then did we realize she had a debilitating fear of the water. All through casting she had told us that she could swim—and swim well. Wrong. That was the last time we ever cast an actor without first conducting a thorough swim test. Now we are famous for the rigorous swim test we give to all our prospective actors before they're offered a contract.

Overnight we replaced Pam with Shawn Weatherly, a former Miss South Carolina, Miss USA, and Miss Universe, who had recently done a series called *Oceanquest*. The only reason we didn't cast Shawn earlier was NBC's reluctance about having both a *Playboy* Playmate *and* a Miss Universe in one series. That, clearly, was the wrong reason. A large percentage of the audience was quite excited to see actors like Shawn Weatherly and Erika Eleniak together. NBC just didn't get it. Nor did NBC understand, despite my best efforts to inform them, that the real lifeguards the characters were based on, Natalie Locus and Diane Grainer, were actually as beautiful, glamorous, and sexy as fashion models, the only difference being they also saved lives.

The reasons NBC resisted having a Playmate and a Miss Universe are somewhat interesting. At the most basic level, it starts with the casting directors—they're the voice of the network. The casting director—after years of having observed, studied, and catalogued talent through the watching of innumerable plays and actor's showcases—is suddenly confronted with a producer like myself who says, "Hey, look at this *Playboy* Playmate. She would be perfect for the role." My suggestion totally invalidates everything the casting director knows about the world of actors and acting. Naturally they defiantly resist the corruption of their profession.

In the big picture, no one knows what elements make for a hit show—essentially it's all smoke and mirrors. I've always felt that as far as NBC was concerned, why should they care? All they need are eyeballs fixed on their network. Why those eyeballs chose NBC is not especially relevant, unless that information can be used to bring in more eyeballs. That being the case, I've always believed that a network could be reduced to just a few clever accountants. They would tally up a show's profitability. If a show made money for the network, it stayed. If it didn't, it was canceled.

Shawn Weatherly was superb: good actress, very serious. When I called her up and asked if she wanted the role, she said, "Yes! Absolutely." I offered her $7,500 an episode (a figure we determined by studying the relative market), and she took it. Then I turned the deal over to the GTG people. She called me the next day, ecstatic beyond words. She was now getting $17,500 an episode. We had agreed to $7,500 but her agent had asked for and received $17,500. I was happy for her. That's where the money goes: She would have been stoked to get $7,500, and GTG paid her $17,500. Multiply that out—times 22 episodes. It adds up.

When I made the deal on "Panic at Malibu Pier" with GTG, I also had to negotiate my salary and title as if we were going to series—despite not knowing if we were going to be picked up. From GTG's point of view, they didn't want a guy holding them up for a lot of money in the event the show went to series.

My attorney called and said, "A sticking point has come up in the deal. It's about your title." I said, "I thought we had agreed on my title: Producer." He said, "Yeah, okay, you can be producer. But another guy wants the "produced by" title. I said, "Who?" He said, "A guy named Bob Hargrove."

Producer. Produced by. What's the difference? Any given movie might have a half-dozen or more producers. For a variety of reasons, the producer title has evolved to mean very little. "Produced by," on the other hand, means this whole cinematographic contraption was assembled by the one person whose name comes next: Produced by Bob Hargrove. Bob Hargrove was the unit production manager, in charge of line production: day-by-day hiring, makeup, hair, wardrobe. He was the guy who would eventually let the *Baywatch* pilot go $2 million over budget.

Once it was explained to me, I became quite distressed at the turn of events. I asked everyone I knew, "Am I getting screwed?" My attorney, especially, got me all worked up. He said I should object. I got caught up in it for a few days until Grant called me in and gave me a piece of advice, the best of my career. Grant said, "It is amazing what you can accomplish when you don't care who gets the credit."

It's true. It is amazing. Grant lived by his words. One of the keys to his attracting the best talent was in letting others get the credit for a show's success. Hollywood is a small community. Word soon gets out regarding who actually does what. When you apply for another job, the people will know what role you performed on the show. And if they don't know, they can call up and ask.

Jack Clements, in white hooded sweatshirt, keeps a close eye on me as I direct. From left: Jack Clements, Gary Capo, and me.

The pilot, "Baywatch, Panic at Malibu Pier," started shooting on Wednesday, January 4, 1989. First off, we filmed a scene where Parker Stevenson drives a lifeguard truck under the pier and gets stuck. By the end of the sequence, the water is up to the doors and finally the truck is destroyed. This incident was based on a true story. It actually happened to lifeguard Richard Mark.

To film this sequence properly, we needed to schedule the shoot at exactly the right time, when the incoming tide was nearly high. As a lifeguard and lifelong surfer, tides, to me, were second nature. I knew that the timing had to be perfect. On the day of the shoot, I was in full wet suit—the whole crew was in full wet suit. We were ready to go. Then the director, Richard Compton, showed up—jeans, T-shirt, cigarette, sunglasses. He tried to direct the sequence from the dry sand, 75 yards from the nearest actor. That was a problem.

The choice of director, originally, had not been an easy one. Three kinds of directors inhabit Hollywood: A, B, and C directors. We had wanted an A director, someone with an accomplished track record who had sold pilots in the past, such as Thomas Carter or Jeff Bleckner. However, none of the A team wanted to do *Baywatch*. At the same time, the B team disappeared into other projects. We ended up selecting from the C team. We found Richard Compton, who had done a few episodes of *Miami Vice*. Richard, unfortunately, wasn't prepared to jump into a monstrously difficult shoot. He would go home at night to his regular life—behaving as though the making of

this pilot was just another directing job. He would have had to live and breathe *Baywatch* in order to pull it off.

Three days later, while still shooting at the pier, one of our assistants tapped me on the shoulder and pointed toward Jack Clements, the head of production for GTG, who was motioning for me to join him. I jogged over to see what he wanted.

He said, "It's pretty obvious we made a mistake with this director. We want you to follow him around, look at the dailies, pick up after him—fill any holes you can find."

I said, "But I'm not in the DGA (Directors Guild of America)."

He said. "We've bought you in," which meant that GTG had paid the DGA's $9,000 initiation fee. Despite the somewhat rocky circumstances, this was a great day. For years I had dreamed of being in the Directors Guild. Finally it had become a reality.

The DGA, per member, is the richest labor union in the world. For the most part, you can't shoot a movie or television episode in this town unless you employ a DGA director. If, for some reason, the writer needs to be replaced, another writer is brought in straightaway. If the director needs to be replaced, the whole production is shut down for two weeks while the new director becomes familiar with the production. (It takes 10 years of active directing to become tenured in the DGA. When I came into the DGA I was working on *Baywatch*. Nine years later I am still on *Baywatch*. I may be the only guy in the history of the Guild who becomes tenured while working on only one show.)

I spent the next few hours at GTG headquarters, filling out forms. At the end of the process I saw that I needed three sponsors, people who were already members of the DGA. The first two were easy: Jay Sandrich and Jack Clements. For the third sponsor, Jay suggested that I go back to the beach and seek out Richard Compton. Jay was right. It was better that Richard find out the situation from me, rather than secondhand. Back at the beach I explained to Richard that I wanted to work with him, not against him—and overall we both had the best interests of the show at heart. Richard became my third sponsor into the DGA.

It's interesting to note that directing a pilot can be a very lucrative event in the course of a director's career: nine years later Richard is *still* being paid a bonus of $1,000 per episode for having directed the *Baywatch* pilot.

I watched Richard closely for the rest of the filming, taking notes on what I thought we would need to reshoot. After he finished, I continued to shoot second-unit work. Plus, Doug, Michael, and I spent two more weeks filling the first-unit holes he left behind. This included spending countless hours in GTG's two editing rooms. One room was the domain of editor David Hagar and the other was reserved for editor Steve Kemper. When we had a scene assembled, we would screen it for Stu and Jack Clements, who would suggest further changes that needed to be made.

was handling the directing during one of the first beach scenes we filmed. Before we got started with the day's work, I called together the stars.

(Above) On "Baywatch: Panic at Malibu Pier," a shot of Richard Compton directing Mädchen Amick; and myself directing in full wetsuit. (Opposite) A cast shot for the first year on NBC. Kneeling: Hasselhoff; first row, from left: me, Michael Berk, Shawn Weatherly, Doug Schwartz; second row: Gina Hecht, Erika Eleniak, Parker Stevenson, Mädchen Amick, Billy Warlock; top row: Monte Markham, Richard Jaeckel.

I told them, "Don't expect a stunt double to take your place when we get to the water shots. This show is all about lifeguards rescuing people. You are the lifeguards. The key thing to keep in mind is that your face is the only part of your body sticking out of the water when you're swimming. We've got to be able to see your face."

It's important to note the difference between stunt work and action work. Rolling a car is a stunt. Swimming across a pool is action. Hasselhoff had come from *Knight Rider*, where Jack Gill, the well-known stunt man, had driven the KIT car whenever the scene required some tricky stunt work.

Quite often actors will say they do their own stunts. They can't do their own stunts—they're not insured to do stunts. Almost inevitably the actor means he does his own action scenes—for example, an action star like Steven Seagal mock-kicking someone in the head.

By the *Baywatch* definition, swimming in the ocean and making a rescue is not a stunt—it's action. I said to the actors, "You must swim up and get this victim. If you don't, I will never see your face and the audience will never know that you're the hero." David Hasselhoff and Shawn Weatherly jumped right in without hesitation. The other actors followed their lead.

Overall, GTG threw lots of money at the pilot, but how much?

At JJH, I made my living by carefully scrutinizing "hot costs," the term used to denote the amount of money spent on the day's effort. If we worked two hours overtime, for example, hot costs would significantly increase. Hot costs are then applied against the total budget, giving a cost-to-completion amount.

I knew of only one way to keep tight control over a film's budget and that was to keep a close eye on the hot costs. The premise is simple: A director will go $1,000 over budget before he goes $50,000 over. Hot costs allowed me to see a problem immediately and do something about it.

Bob Hargrove didn't do hot costs. When I asked him why, he said, "There's 250 people working here. The accountant can't keep up." Common sense told me that we should hire another accountant for $1,000 a week to make sure we get our hot costs every night.

We ended up going $2 million over on an original budget of $4 million. Where'd the extra $2 million go? Bob took the whole production company to Hawaii—everyone went, from the stars down to the lowliest cable puller. The costs of housing, feeding, and transporting this army ran into the tens of thousands of dollars. Except for a few essential people, a producer would be better off hiring local people. They can perform the work just as well and the extra costs are eliminated.

Through it all, I watched and listened and took extensive notes on what *not* to do should the opportunity ever arise.

The pilot aired on Sunday, April 23, 1989. NBC did a magnificent job promoting it, including a full-page ad in *TV Guide*. The promos were great, the time slot was excellent. Unfortunately the reviews that came out on the day of the premiere stunk. One reviewer said, "If you have seen one beach party you've seen them all." Yet we hadn't included a beach party in the show, for the very reason that we wanted to avoid any obvious beach clichés. Later I found out that this reviewer had never even seen the pilot.

The reviewers may not have liked it, but the audience did. *Baywatch* earned a 17.1 rating and a 34 share, the highest-rated movie for that week. (Imagine a universe comprised of 100 television sets. The rating number is the percentage of the total 100 sets that are tuned to the show—in this example 17 sets. The share number is derived by taking the number of sets that are in use—50 sets out of 100—and then calculating the percentage that are tuned to the show, 34 percent.)

As time went on, *Baywatch* became the highest-rated movie for the month. Only one question remained: Would *Baywatch* be picked up for a series?

CHAPTER 6

The Medal

T hrough the next four weeks we kept wondering what would happen. Then on Monday morning, May 15, 1989, Grant called me into his office. With Stu looking on, Grant said, "Greg, we are picked up for 12. If *Baywatch* does well, they'll order another 9." Fantastic. Thank you Grant, Stu, Brandon, NBC, my mom and dad, and anyone else who might have helped make this a reality.

In order to deliver the first episode by September, we had to start shooting on August 1. That gave us half of May, June, and July to write scripts and prepare for production.

Besides Doug, Michael, and Terry Erwin (one of Stu Erwin Jr.'s sons), the writing staff consisted of five new writers (foisted on us by NBC), none of whom knew the beach, or the *Baywatch* concept, or the slightest thing about lifeguards, except that they sat next to the pool in an elevated chair with a whistle around their neck, chatting up young women.

The first week, I said to the writing staff, "Let's go on a tour." We started at 8:00 A.M. Just getting the writers out of bed at that hour was an accomplishment. We all rode together in a van, a sleepy crew that included Michael Berk, Ernie Wallengren, Jill Donner, Bill Schwartz, and the writing team of Goldberg & Rafkin whom we called The Twins.

The first stop was Zuma. I showed them the Zuma lifeguard headquarters and introduced

(Opposite) The Medal of Valor

them around. Next we moved south to Malibu, where they learned about that particular beach. The third stop was Will Rogers, where I had begun my guarding career 18 years earlier. Each of these beaches had some unique characteristic, a good surfing spot or a wide sandy beach or even funky roller bladers zipping past the boardwalk.

Lastly we went to Venice, which is division headquarters. We climbed up the stairs to the top floor, where the offices were located. Here we met the chief, Howard Lee, and the captains, Don Rohrer and Bob Buchannon, from whom we borrowed the name for Hasselhoff's character.

As the writers and I were heading out the building, a young boy came flying in, yelling, "Help, help." He ran up to me and asked, "Are you a lifeguard?" I was wearing jeans, a dress shirt, high-top tennis shoes. I definitely did not look like a lifeguard. But I was the first guy this boy saw. And I was, in fact, a lifeguard. So I said, "Yes, I'm a lifeguard."

He said, "My brother is drowning."

I said, "Show me."

As I sprinted out the door with the little boy, Michael ran upstairs to tell the on-duty lifeguards about the unfolding emergency.

Once outside, the boy pointed down the beach. Just offshore I saw the biggest riptide I had ever seen. It was a textbook rip, shaped like the mushroom cloud from an atom bomb. I said to myself, "Oh shit."

For a moment I considered the lifeguard's rule that says 90 percent of the time when this happens, the missing kid turns up on the swing set or at the rest room or in the food line. But you cannot assume it, so I went full speed ahead.

I scrambled out of my high tops, pants, shirt. Now I was wearing only pink underwear. I ran into the water thinking, backup is going to be here any second. But no backup arrived.

I dove through a couple of big waves, swam out, and did my first surface dive. I could hardly see anything. I had to squint just to keep my contacts in. Suddenly I felt that the boy was close— it was the same feeling you get when you are in a dark room, about to walk into something. I knew then that he was not in the food line, not on the swing set. My eyes are so bad that over the years I have developed an acute level of sensory awareness. I sensed he was close, close, close. Underwater. Dying. But where? I came up, swam out a little further, and I dove again. Nothing.

I turned around and looked for backup. All I saw were the writers lined up on the beach, frantically taking notes: "Greg, in pink underwear, dives down."

I swam out further, with the rip, the cold, muddy brown water swirling around me. I shifted to the right and dove down once more. This time, I went straight to him. He was two feet off the bottom, floating in a fetal position. When I touched him at first, he felt like a baby dolphin, smooth and silky. I knew, even as I brought him up, that he wasn't breathing. But for how long? Three, four minutes at least.

While furiously treading water, I tried to give him mouth-to-mouth resuscitation. But I couldn't get a mouth-to-mouth seal, which would allow me to force my air into his lungs. I knew I had to get aggressive. Finally I banged my mouth against his and blew as hard as I could, forcing air into his lungs. That did it. He spit up some water and began to breathe.

I looked again toward the beach. Still no backup. I started screaming, "Help, help." The writers were getting the idea, but they were not going anywhere. I could just imagine these little dots on the beach writing down, "Greg yells 'help help.'"

Slowly I began swimming the boy to shore. We were making good progress until I hit the drop zone, where the waves break. A big set of waves loomed behind us. The second wave of the set lifted us up, higher and higher. Just as we were going over the falls, I wrapped my arms around the boy and prayed that I wouldn't lose him. The force of the wave drove us deep underwater and tumbled us over and around, almost pulling us apart. But I managed to keep hold of him. When we finally came up, I saw that he had stopped breathing again. Once more I applied mouth-to-mouth resuscitation, aggressively. I had to get him to shore or he was going to die.

Still no backup. I thought, what the hell is going on? I'm right next to division headquarters. Finally, the waves stopped for a few seconds. During the lull, with the boy in my arms, I swam as hard as I could toward shore. At last I felt the sandy bottom with my feet. I found my footing and waded into shallow water.

When I tried to pick him up to carry him toward the dry sand, my legs suddenly went out from underneath me. I had not realized how exhausted I'd become through the whole ordeal. Right then, over my shoulder came lifeguard Jeff White. We carried the kid onto dry sand and laid him down. Then Mickey Gallagher arrived with other lifeguards. They managed to stabilize the boy and get him breathing regularly.

Later we found out that the boy's blood-gas level was moments away from causing permanent brain damage. But, miraculously, the rescue and the resuscitation all worked out okay. Two days later he was back in school. For that rescue—the rescue of my life—the City of Los Angeles awarded me the Medal of Valor.

After reading about the rescue in the *Los Angeles Times* the next day, Grant called and told me, "You make us all proud." Suddenly I was a celebrity on the GTG lot. The timing was remarkable. The rescue dramatically showed exactly what *Baywatch* was intended to convey.

I was extremely proud to be a lifeguard, and yet ironically one of the basic rules of lifeguarding had been violated: no backup had come to my assistance during the rescue. To this day nobody has ever addressed the point that this rescue went on for 20 minutes in front of lifeguard division headquarters without any assistance from the on-duty guards.

The day after, I visited the young man, Alan Jenkins, in the hospital to check on his progress, something that lifeguards often do after making a rescue. I met his parents, and eventually I visited them in their home. The family lived in a very dangerous part of South Central Los Angeles. Some months later I managed to get Alan into the lifeguard W.A.T.E.R. program—Water Awareness, Training, Education, and Recruitment.

In the 23 hours of *Baywatch* that were broadcast on NBC (two-hour pilot and 21 episodes), that kind of story, or even that story in particular, was never told. The network was simply not interested—it was not the sort of story they wanted. Something was wrong with that. It was exactly the kind of story Doug, Michael, and I wanted to tell.

Photos of me being awarded the Medal of Valor, plus a photo of me with Alan Jenkins, the young man I rescued. When Grant read the Los Angeles Times article about the rescue, he called me straightaway.

Los Angeles Times

4 inches; 125 words   THURSDAY, JUNE 8, 1989, CALENDAR, PART 6, PAGE 2   000067105
COPYRIGHT 1989 / THE TIMES MIRROR COMPANY   FAX page #1

MORNING REPORT
TV & VIDEO

From the life imitating art file: Gregory J. Bonann, co-creator and producer of the upcoming NBC fall series "Baywatch," made a daring, real-life ocean rescue 100 yards off Venice Beach Tuesday morning saving a teenage boy who had become caught in a riptide. Bonann, a sports television documentary producer and a 20-year veteran lifeguard for Los Angeles County, was giving a tour of the Los Angeles County Beaches and Harbors facilities and its Baywatch rescue unit to the writing staff of the television series when he was approached by a frantic teen-ager who explained that his friend had been swept out to sea. Bonann swam out, found the youth who had been submerged for several minutes and administered mouth-to-mouth resuscitation while treading water. Once on shore the boy received oxygen from the lifeguard unit and was taken to UCLA Medical Center where he is currently recovering.

—Claudia Puig

Successful, opinionated artists are not always the easiest people to be around. When these opinionated artists manage to upset the powers-that-be, something has to change. Inevitably the changes are dictated by the entity that holds the power—in our case, NBC.

Michael Berk is a writer. He is also an artist, a strong, opinionated, determined man, with years of experience creating television shows. The NBC executives who had worked with Michael on the *Baywatch* pilot had found him too difficult. When the series was picked up, they went to Stu and Grant and said they were going to bring in their own head writer, Ernie Wallengren. Both Doug and Michael could remain as executive producers, but with a reduced role in writing episodes.

Over the next three weeks, the relationship between NBC's Ernie Wallengren and Michael

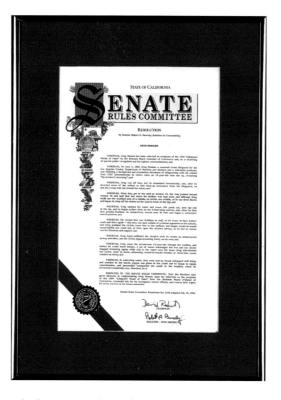 

The California State Senate and Assembly presented me with these resolutions following the rescue of Alan Jenkins.

Berk deteriorated, such that GTG brought in another man, Bob Silberling, to executive produce the show. With the arrival of Bob, Michael became so frustrated that he left *Baywatch* completely and sought out other writing projects.

Not long afterwards, Doug Schwartz also began to have problems, until eventually he saw his dream of becoming the *Baywatch* show runner disappear. "Show runner" is the title given to the person who actually engineers the show, essentially the captain of the ship. In our case, the show runners would eventually be Ernie Wallengren and Bob Silberling.

This phase of *Baywatch* was by far the lowest point. My partners, Doug and Michael, had worked long and hard with me to get *Baywatch* on the air. Now they were essentially gone. I had to deal with my parents, who wanted the best for their son *and* their son-in-law. I also had to deal with my sister, who wanted the best for her brother *and* for her husband. They were understandably upset by this turn of events. On top of that, I was working 18 hours a day just to keep the show from sinking. Without a doubt, this was the most hectic, unpleasant time of my life, especially because this is what I had been working to achieve for so many years.

n June, as preproduction was getting under way, I received a memo from Grant saying, "Greg, I would like David Hasselhoff, Shawn Weatherly, Parker Stevenson, and you to represent *Baywatch* at the big press gathering next week."

I assumed that I was being invited because of the Medal of Valor. I wrote back to Grant saying, "Thanks, this is great. I'll look forward to it." A day later Grant called me and said, "Greg, can you come to my office? I want to elaborate on the memo I sent you." I went right over.

Grant said, "This press meeting is *not* going to be a friendly little get together. Tough questions will be asked. I can guarantee that a reporter will ask you, 'Why is Grant Tinker doing a tits-and-ass show?' If you are not ready for those kind of questions, you'll be raked over the coals."

Since I was the creator as well as being a lifeguard, Grant figured that I was the best guy to respond, "*Baywatch* is going to tell the lifeguard's story. In reality, lifeguarding is not a tits-and-ass job. I should know. I've been doing it for nearly 20 years. Here's the real story…"

Grant gave me about 10 questions that he predicted I would be asked. I went home, wrote out my answers, and rehearsed what I was going to say over and over.

Every year, an army of reporters from around the country gets together to see what the network will be sending out the following season. During our year, this meeting took place at the Century Plaza Hotel in Century City, in the main ballroom. Each of NBC's prime-time shows was given exactly one hour to inform, and hopefully excite, the reporters about the upcoming season. On Friday afternoon, sandwiched between *Odd Balls* and *Mancusco*, *Baywatch* was given its time on stage. I stood at the lectern. To my left sat Hasselhoff. To my right were Parker Stevenson and Shawn Weatherly.

We started by showing a few clips from the pilot—that took all of five minutes. Then the 55-minute question-and-answer session got under way. The very first question cut right to the chase: "Why in God's name have you made a retread like Hasselhoff the star of *Baywatch*?"

Writer, director, artist, and executive producer Michael Berk with me.

I took a deep breath and started rattling off a few of the network's failures during the Friday, 8:00 P.M. time slot: *Sonny Spoon*, *Rags to Riches*. Then I informed them that the last time NBC had won Friday night at 8:00 was in 1985, with David Hasselhoff's *Knight Rider*. "He is hardly a retread," I told them, "he's a proven star."

Sure enough, as Grant had predicted, I was asked in so many words: "Why is Grant Tinker doing a tits-and-ass show?"

"Yes, we have Shawn Weatherly, a Miss Universe, and Erika Eleniak, a *Playboy* Playmate. They are both beautiful women. We also have Hasselhoff, Stevenson, Billy Warlock, a whole bunch of buff guys. And, yes, everyone is running around in a red bathing suit. However, this show is about lifeguards rescuing people. You cannot perform a rescue wearing street clothes. I've been lifeguarding since 1970, I should know. In order to demonstrate the reality of our profession, we must show fit, healthy men and women wearing the appropriate outfits: bathing suits."

Most of Grant's questions were indeed asked. Certainly, had it not been for Grant's advice, I would have been sliced and diced at that meeting. With his help I was able to respond and segue my ass off.

Overall it went well. The press is always looking for a hot new show to write about or some huge, embarrassing mistake made on stage by one of the presenters. Fortunately, *Baywatch* was able to satisfy the first need while avoiding the second. Afterward, someone wrote that I came off sounding more like a producer than a lifeguard, which I think was meant as a compliment—or at least I interpreted it as such.

In Deep

The cast was set, the contracts were signed. Finally, on August 1, 1989, principal filming began on the first series episode, "In Deep."

In this episode, two drunken jet skiers run over and kill a woman windsurfer. David Hasselhoff's character, Mitch Buchannon, tracks down the killers and brings them to justice. That's not, in any way, lifeguarding. That's police work. Nor was it plausible. Drunken jet skiers, to my knowledge, have never killed a windsurfer. The first thing a lifeguard would do in that sort of situation is turn it over to the cops. Then he would go back to watching the water.

If you were to tear the title page off the script for "In Deep," it could have been any of a dozen different TV series. To me, it seemed criminal to turn *Baywatch* into yet another crime show. Why squander the unique elements of *Baywatch*? The answer was simple: NBC was comfortable with the elements that comprise cop-and-robbers shows. They'd had success with them before. That's what they wanted, so that's what they made.

Back when we'd been making the pilot, we'd encountered some major problems, mostly because the wrong director had been hired. Yet for the first series episode, rather than learn from our mistakes, we marched down that same road a second time, again hiring the wrong person to direct. The show had not changed significantly since the pilot—*Baywatch* was still an action

(Opposite) Phil Topar and I racing in the grueling Catalina to Marina del Rey Race, 36 open ocean miles. We won with a time of six hours, six minutes.

show with lots of water work—and as before this necessitated a director who was qualified to meet the challenge. We hired Peter Hunt, who had directed several episodes of *The Wizard*, a show created by Doug and Michael several years earlier. Peter was a fine director, well-qualified to work with actors. But his qualifications for directing water work? Peter's *hobby* was scuba diving. He had never actually directed any water work.

Peter eventually took 10 days to direct an 8-day shoot. Almost without exception, when a director isn't doing well on a show, it is expressed by the shoot running long. Usually he's running long because he didn't take the time to prepare or he didn't foresee certain things that he could have anticipated. If an actor shows up with the wrong wardrobe, it is usually not the wardrobe person's fault. Ultimately it's the director's fault. Sending the actor back to wardrobe creates a 20-minute delay. Add up enough 20-minute delays, and the shoot will go two days over, at a cost of $100,000 per day to GTG.

For this episode, I directed the second unit. (We had to fudge the usual DGA definition of what comprises second-unit work, so that I could direct all the scenes that included water work. These scenes would usually have been directed by the first-unit director. We decided it was easier to change the definition than to teach Peter Hunt how to direct water work.) In one scene my longtime lifeguard friend Mike "Newmie" Newman, serving as stunt double for Hasselhoff, was supposed to jump off the lifeguard boat and onto the back of the bad guy, who was trying to make his escape on a jet ski. If you were to substitute a couple of horses for the boats, the scene could have been right out of a John Wayne western. It was awful.

I was directing this scene from the lifeguard rescue boat. Next to me stood the cameraman. A few feet away, Newmie was preparing to jump. The rescue boat was being driven by Shelly Butler, a longtime friend and champion guard. Keep in mind, we were using the actual L.A. County rescue boat, and Shelly was "on the clock," so to speak—the L.A. County clock.

After hours of preparation, the big stunt was only moments away from taking place. All three cameras were rolling, including one in a helicopter overhead. Newmie, poised on the gunnel, was just about to leap. Then Shelly received an emergency call over the radio. A moment later he turned to me and said, "Sorry Greg, gotta go." Without another word, Shelly cranked over the wheel and went speeding off toward an ocean rescue a few miles away. Of course we didn't have time to off-load the cameraman, the actors, the assistants, and myself. We were gone two hours.

irst comes the script, then the pilot, then the first 13 episodes (in which the pilot is counted as an episode). Finally, if you are lucky, you get to make the back nine episodes. We'd completed the first 13 episodes of *Baywatch*, but I wasn't sure if NBC would want the back nine. Our ratings were good, but not as spectacular as everyone would have liked.

Finally Grant called me into his office to tell me NBC's decision. It turned out to be a quintessential good news, bad news sort of meeting. "The good news," Grant said, "is we're going to get a back order. The bad news is NBC will only give us the order if we bring another actor on board. They've already selected him: John Allen Nelson. He'll be in your office in two minutes."

NBC wanted John Allen Nelson, a former soap actor, to supplement the hunk-factor, which was another way of saying that in their opinion David Hasselhoff, Billy Warlock, and Parker Stevenson were not setting hearts on fire. Naturally, I had to tell our resident hunks that another guy would soon be sharing their turf. Suffice to say, they were not thrilled at the news.

The network loves to play hard ball, and with their decades of experience they can do it quite gracefully. They will say, "We'll give you an order for nine more episodes but only on the condition that you introduce another character. And, we have already selected him for you. If you don't want to bring him on board, no problem. The show will be canceled. It is totally up to you."

To salvage something from this mess, Grant requested that NBC reimburse GTG for John Allen's salary, $17,500 an episode. NBC agreed, but later they failed to fulfill their end of the bargain, never reimbursing GTG. That's the network way. They hold the cards, the checkbook, the keys to the distribution kingdom. What possible recourse did GTG have in seeking reimbursement for John Allen's salary? Essentially none.

It gets worse. Since our ratings were decent and the show had excellent production value, Stu requested an increase in the license fee being paid to GTG by NBC, an increase of $100,000 an episode. NBC agreed to a $20,000 increase, but, as with John Allen Nelson's salary, NBC later reneged on their commitment to pay the increased license fee.

John Allen Nelson, as it turned out, was a great guy. He surprised everyone, especially me, by finding a place for himself within the cast and working diligently to make the best of a difficult situation. We became good friends, and eventually he wrote an episode of the syndicated *Baywatch* and acted in three more.

I learned an important lesson from John. When he first came in, he found a way to establish a good personal relationship with the cast and crew. Only after that was accomplished did he take on the task of establishing a professional relationship. Personal first, professional later—it's a good working rule to live by.

When we did get back to work, we filmed this sequence. Newmie, doubling for Hasselhoff, dives off the rescue boat, barely snagging the bad guy by the ankle.

All our priceless filmmaking equipment lies dormant during lunch.

Many actors first catch the acting bug in high school, performing in a play. I caught the directing bug after making documentaries at JJH.

Like the old cliché says, "Yeah, but what I really want to do is direct." Tune into *Entertainment Tonight* on any given night and I guarantee you'll hear an actor saying that exact line. The reason is simple: Directing is the best job on the set, plain and simple. The director defines the wardrobe; he casts the show; he decides upon locations. He can completely change the story depending on how he stages and directs a scene. Place the camera high and the actor will look cowardly; place it low and the actor looks heroic. The director points to his left, flames leap out. He points to his right, an actor yells "help, help." While a movie or a television episode may have several writers, it's the director who defines the show.

At JJH, we made documentaries and industrial films. I made a film for the military showing how *not* to be abducted by terrorists. We used actors in these films. In fact, some of the actors that I directed in those industrial films, I subsequently hired for *Baywatch*. But Hollywood, with its tendency to put people into niches, wouldn't consider the directing of those industrial films to be real, Hollywood-style directing.

In Hollywood, people create rules to keep themselves in and to keep others out, especially within the world of directing. Over the years I have been on both sides of the equation, and I know what it's like. The toughest thing about directing is getting the opportunity to direct. A lot of capable people, who would certainly be great directors, cannot get a break.

NBC didn't want me to direct. Grant and Stu, however, made the argument on my behalf: "As head of the second unit, Greg, to a large extent, directed the pilot and a large percentage of the episodes so far this season. Let's give him a shot." In Hollywood, you need someone with the power to say yes and then use it on your behalf.

Variety did a poll of the three most significant directors in the history of television. No. 3 was Alfred Hitchcock, No. 2 was Rod Serling, and No. 1 was Jay Sandrich. Jay directed the pilots for *The Dick Van Dyke Show, Lou Grant, The Mary Tyler Moore Show, Newhart, Rhoda,* and *The Cosby Show.* As far as I was concerned he knew everything about directing actors.

My directing mentor is Jay Sandrich—a man I greatly admire. Jay taught me that the director is responsible for a bad script, not the writer. If the script is bad, then the director must meet with the writer and fix it before he shoots. Ultimately, it is the director's name on the screen. He taught me the importance of each department.

Jay taught me to constantly ask the question: Does the script make sense when spoken? In sitcoms, the actors have several "table readings" in the days leading up to the shoot. (In a table reading the actors sit around a table and recite the script, like a slow motion, low-stress rehearsal.) The writers are present at these table readings, and afterward they make any necessary changes in the script. This evolution is repeated each day, until the episode is shot, usually on Friday evening.

That is not the case in one-hour episodic television. Once the season is under way, our actors rarely have time beforehand to read through the script together. Also, even if they had the time, the script is often not ready to be read until the actual shooting begins. Whenever possible, I like to include at least some rehearsal time before the cameras roll. Early on, actors often told me that they didn't need to rehearse. Thanks to Jay, I acquired a pat response: I know you don't need it, but I have 200 people standing here who haven't seen a thing. For their sake and mine, let's rehearse. The sound guy must know if he needs a wireless mike. The lighting guy must see the blocking so that he can position his lights. The grip needs to know if he is required to put down track for the camera and where.

I finally got my first unit directorial debut in Episode 18. Part of the episode involved filming the death of Shawn Weatherly's character. It was a big episode, lots of water work, complete with a mock great white shark attack.

Shawn Weatherly, despite making $17,500 an episode, was not pleased with the character she was playing, Jill Riley. Our writers at the time had not figured out how to use a woman lifeguard, so they never gave her anything substantial to do. By episode 15, Shawn had endured enough. She came into my office and said, "I've read the upcoming scripts. It's all bullshit. My character has nothing to do. I want out of here."

I really hated to see her go. Of all our woman actors, Shawn was my favorite. She never hesitated to jump into the mix. She out-worked, out-hustled, and out-swam all our male actors. She always came in prepared and ready to go.

Shawn Weatherly, not looking too pleased about the way things were going.

For actors, directors, and DPs (directors of photography), preparation is the key. Actors look foolish if they don't know their lines. Directors look inept if they haven't anticipated every aspect of the shoot. Even after a decade of directing, I still stay up late into the night when I'm about to direct an episode, trying to discover anything I might have overlooked. Prepare, prepare, prepare.

Once, while we were scouting locations near the Santa Monica Pier, we came upon a production company that was making a big-time feature film. The size of the operation was immense, with dozens of production trucks lined up in the parking lot. It was bigger than Cirque du Soleil. The director was Richard Donner, making one of his *Lethal Weapon* movies. When I walked across the beach, I noticed the whole film crew was sitting around, doing nothing. After introducing myself to Richard, I asked him, "What are you guys waiting for?" He said, "When we scouted this location, you could drive a truck under the pier. But now the tide is too high."

The clock was running, $1,000 a minute, while they waited for the tide to go down. Yet for 25 cents someone could have bought a copy of the *Los Angeles Times* and looked at the schedule of tides for the day. They would have read that high tide was at 9:00 A.M. They weren't adequately prepared.

As every TV watcher knows, each year the new season starts around mid-September. For a weekly series, such as *Law and Order*, the producer, Dick Wolf, must start shooting new episodes the preceding August in order to have new episodes ready by September. NBC, Dick Wolf's network, must "pick up" or renew *Law and Order* sometime in May to give Wolf enough time to lay the ground work for shooting.

The network, from their point of view, will evaluate the show's ratings for the whole season, September to May. If the ratings are good, as with *ER*, and everyone's happy, the show is renewed. Poor ratings, as with *Ink*, almost certainly translate into cancellation. Shows with fair ratings are the most maddening. Many popular shows, such as *Cheers*, or even *Seinfeld*, suffered through marginal ratings in the first few seasons before becoming runaway sensations.

On Monday, May 7, 1990, exactly one year after being picked up, Grant Tinker called me into his office. When I walked in, Stu was standing in a corner staring out the window. I took my usual chair and we exchanged the usual pleasantries. Then Grant came right to the point: "I thought you should be the first to know: *Baywatch* has been canceled."

I took a deep breath and tried like hell not to curse out loud. Over the weeks I had been carefully watching the ratings as our episodes aired. They had been medium-to-fair. I had also been watching the competition, shows that aired in the same time slot on different networks. We were beating the CBS show *Snoops* with Tim and Daphne Reid, but losing to the ABC shows, *Full House* and *Family Ties*. I had also been sensing the less-than-joyous vibes around Grant, Stu, and Jay. Naturally they would have the early word from NBC. I knew the chances for renewal were slim, but that didn't make the news any easier to take.

Of course I said the usual things, "Can't we do something to save the show?" But it was over. Finished. As far as Grant Tinker, GTG, Brandon Tartikoff, and NBC were concerned, *Baywatch* was history.

Why was it over? It's more complicated than simply low ratings. The license fee is key. NBC had paid GTG a hefty chunk of money, called the license fee, for the right to broadcast *Baywatch* in the United States. In our case, NBC paid a license fee of $865,000 per episode. Added to this amount was the foreign license fee, which was a modest $75,000 per episode.

NBC then sold advertising, about 15 minutes worth for an hour show, to recoup its license fee. Here's the key to TV: The amount of money a network can charge its advertisers is carefully determined by the show's ratings. Advertisers will pay a million dollars to have a 30 second commercial on a smash hit like *Seinfeld*. But for every *Seinfeld*, 70 other shows are struggling to survive. *Baywatch* aired for 22 episodes, averaging a 9.6 rating on Friday night, a number NBC had not achieved since *Knight Rider* five years prior. But NBC had wanted ratings in the 11.0 range, so that they could charge their advertisers more money.

Baywatch's chances for renewal were diminished even further thanks to Brandon Tartikoff, head of NBC. He had spent nearly $50 million developing new one-hour shows for the following 1990–91 season. To justify spending all that money, he had to get them on the air. With a limited number of time slots available, it was good-bye, *Baywatch*.

It's interesting to note that even if NBC had agreed to renew *Baywatch* at the same license fee, GTG would themselves have pulled the plug. *Baywatch* cost nearly $1.3 million per episode to produce. Between NBC and foreign rights, GTG was paid $940,000. Who covers the $360,000 difference? Grant's company, GTG. That's $360,000 per episode, *times 22*, which adds up $7,920,000. At the end of the season, GTG was $8 million in the hole, and that assumes we stayed on budget, something we rarely did.

This practice is called "deficit financing." How can a company possibly stay solvent if it is practicing deficit financing, losing $8 million a season on one show? Good question. In a normal industry, a business with those numbers would soon go bankrupt. But television is not a normal industry. A unique pot of gold awaits any company that can produce a popular show that can eventually be sold into reruns. Almost always a series must go four to five years, or roughly 100 episodes, to generate enough episodes so that it can be sold into reruns. The profit potential is astronomical. *M*A*S*H* is *still* generating millions in rerun revenue for its producers, despite having completed its run a decade ago.

GTG, however, decided it could not afford to lose another $8 million in hopes that *Baywatch* might eventually be sold into reruns. The only way that GTG could continue making *Baywatch* was for NBC to pay GTG a higher license fee, an amount that would come closer to covering the actual costs of the show. This was out of the question since NBC wouldn't even renew us at the old license fee.

Grant had major problems that went far beyond *Baywatch*. Gannett was pulling out of the TV business. GTG's other shows had also been canceled, including the television newsmagazine *USA Today*. In this genre, Grant was a few years ahead of his time. Now these newsmagazines are immensely popular, consistently finishing among the top 10–rated shows.

At the end of our discussion, I walked down the corridor to my office, which was at the end of the hall. As I walked along I noticed that every door was open and every office was empty. Vacant. No one around. Everyone had vanished.

I walked back to Grant's office and said, "Can I follow up this conversation? Where is everybody?" He said, "Come in and sit down."

He proceeded to give me a brief lecture on the facts of TV life: Most series end after one season. Writers know that. They have families to support. They keep a close eye on the ratings. When the white flag is being unfurled, they're updating their résumés. The bottom line: The other producers and writers had already found work on other series.

Grant's parting words stuck with me: "What does it matter, really? I've always told you that *Baywatch* was your show. Since it's your show, you're left holding the bag."

Baywatch was finished. Grant felt bad, especially because of the way the cancellation had been handled. After all that Grant had done for Brandon Tartikoff, and after all the years Grant had spent at NBC, Brandon didn't even bother calling Grant to let him know that the show was canceled. *Baywatch* was the next-to-last show Grant had on the air. His final show, produced the following season for CBS through Orion, was called *WIOU.*

Besides feeling bad about being canceled, I felt bad that I was no longer in business with Grant. Certainly I considered it an honor to have been a member of his team. And as part of his team, I had worked with top-notch people, true all-stars of the entertainment business: Stu Erwin Jr., Jay Sandrich, Jack Clements, Bob Silberling.

Finally, with everything packed in my car, I left. No need to say good-bye to anyone. The offices were empty. Hasselhoff already had another acting job lined up. Except for my job as a recurrent lifeguard, I was out of work.

My father, Dr. Lou Bonann, has given me a lifetime of quiet, steady support and encouragement. What more could a son ask for?

The first call I made was to the chief lifeguard, Don Rohrer, telling him that I was now available to work full-time. He said he didn't need anyone full-time, but weekends were a different story. Five days later I was back at Will Rogers beach. Returning to the beach during this relatively quiet season gave me time to think and to figure out what the hell I was going to do next.

On Father's Day, Sunday, June 17, 1990, a few weeks after we had been canceled, I spent the late afternoon with my Aunt Jenny and Uncle Neal—who had always been very supportive of all my endeavors—and my mom and dad. My father has always been a great sounding board for me. He is refreshingly naïve. He's a wonderful doctor but he knows nothing about television.

After seeing me so unhappy, he asked, "Why don't you go to Grant and ask for your show back? Just go and ask him."

For the rest of the evening I explained to him why I couldn't do that. For starters, it would cost too much money. I could never afford to pay back the $400,000 per episode deficit that I assumed would have to be covered. Besides, *Baywatch* was used goods. Even if I could reclaim the rights, how could I ever get it distributed again, much less raise the money to get new episodes made—at $1 million per episode? Forget it.

At the end of the day, I gave him a Father's Day gift. As I was getting ready to leave, he made a request of me—the second of my life of any lasting significance (the first being that I try out for the high school swim team). "There is one more gift I want from you," he said. "I want you to talk to Grant and ask for your show back." My mother seconded my father's request.

Reluctantly I agreed, mostly to get them off my back.

As I drove down Pacific Coast Highway, I contemplated how a new *Baywatch* might be different from the old. In my head I knew what I wanted: lifeguards making rescues, helping people, being heroes. I had been frustrated at NBC because they didn't want lifeguards to be heroes.

My paddling and dory partner, Phil Topar, represented what I wanted the essence of Baywatch *to be.*

They wanted murders. They wanted detectives. They wanted shootings. They wanted the stuff with which they were most familiar: An escaped convict comes to the beach and the *Baywatch* lifeguards must find him; drunk guys on jet skis run over a windsurfer and Mitch must catch them. Show after show was cops and robbers.

Make no mistake—cops are heroes. They battle against bad guys. Firemen are heroes, fighting fires, saving lives. But NBC could not comprehend a show about a different kind of hero, the lifeguard. Lifeguards sit in their towers, looking at 10,000 people in the water, trying to spot the lone swimmer who is in trouble. If the lifeguard misses, that person is dead.

I knew the personal stories. I knew guys like Phil Topar, my old rowing partner. For a time Phil and I rowed a dory together every morning. He possessed the most important characteristic of a rowing partner: He was always on time for workout. For a new challenge, we had temporarily put aside the dory at the time and switched into a different sort of craft—the two-man surf ski—so that we could compete in the Catalina Channel–Crossing Race, a six-hour, 36-mile marathon. Our usual workout involved paddling out the Marina del Rey harbor, straight out to sea five miles, then around a marker buoy and back.

At the time Phil was trying to decide if he wanted to leave the tower and become a lieutenant. For a career guard, this is a major decision. He loved the tower. He loved to work out. He loved making rescues. He didn't know if he wanted to be in an office, wearing a uniform and hard shoes, and watching other guys make rescues. Being a lieutenant is a whole different world compared to manning a tower.

At the time Phil was also going through a brutal divorce. His wife was suing him for custody of their little boy. I was sitting in the bow of our dory when he told me this was happening. After a moment I could see his whole back shaking as he began to cry. A great man, a great guard, a great friend—a hero we all looked up to—brought to tears. To me, he had an important, personal story. He was a character on whom you could hang a series. Phil Topar was what *Baywatch* should be about.

aydreaming while driving home is one thing. Actually refloating a canceled network series is quite another. How could I do it? First, I knew I needed enthusiastic, experienced, professional assistance. Only two people I knew had the characteristics that would be needed to pull off such a mammoth challenge: Doug Schwartz and Michael Berk.

As soon as I arrived home, I called Doug and Michael. They had found an overall deal at Reeves Entertainment and were trying to develop new shows. They agreed to leave Reeves and start anew—if we could get it going again.

My motivation toward this end was simple: I believed in the show. Their motivation was a little more complicated. Yes, they believed in the show, but they also felt they had been treated unfairly by NBC. You don't need a graduate degree in psychology to know that the desire to inflict a little revenge goes a long, long way in motivating people.

In the broadest strokes, I considered the three big challenges that we needed to meet. First, we needed to reclaim the rights. Second, we needed a ton of money to produce new episodes. Third, we needed a way to distribute the episodes and market the show.

The next day I called Grant and asked for an appointment. As always, he said, "You don't need an appointment. Come right over." An hour later, sitting in his office, I said to him, "I don't know exactly what I'm doing or what I'm asking, but I want *Baywatch* back."

Almost as if he knew what I was going to ask, he immediately responded: "I can't just give you my part of the show for nothing." My heart started sinking toward the floor as I imagined trying to raise 22 times $400,000.00. Then Grant said, "You'll have to pay me $10."

Of course—the first day of business school you learn that something of value cannot be given away. It must be bought, even if only for one measly dollar.

Next he said, "You still have to buy back Gannett's portion of the show. I suggest you meet with Sid Tessler. If that goes well you should call Paul Talbot."

I wrote down their names and numbers. As I was leaving, Grant said, "Good luck, Greg." Grant was sincere. He hadn't wanted guns and knives to dominate the show, as it had at NBC. Now he wanted me to succeed, to present the show as I had originally conceived. Of course, he undoubtedly knew how much work I was getting into. I still appreciate the fact that he was considerate enough not to tell me.

With a water bottle and headphones, I stayed adequately hydrated and entertained during the Catalina Channel-Crossing Race. Here I am in mid-race. We ended up placing first overall.

hen I returned home, my answering machine was flashing. I had two messages, one from Sid Tessler and the other from Paul Talbot. Grant had already spoken to them, and they understood that I wanted to do something with *Baywatch*.

First I met with Sid Tessler, who worked with the accounting firm of Brown Kraft & Co., located in Brentwood. I knew his name from the GTG/NBC year but I had never spoken to him before.

After I explained the situation to him, Sid agreed to assist me in two ways: first, in regaining the rights to *Baywatch* from Gannett. (NBC, after airing the episodes of *Baywatch* twice, was no

*Baywatch Barbie carried to
the extreme.*

longer attached to the show in any way.) As the day wore on, Sid made a dozen phone calls. Finally he gave me some good news: In order to reclaim ownership of *Baywatch*, which would allow me to make new episodes, I wouldn't have to pay off the deficit from the old ones. That saved me a deal-killing $8 million. All Gannett wanted was that I promise to pay them $5,000 per episode for any future episodes that might be produced.

The Gannett executives emphatically made one point: They were not going to spend any more money on *Baywatch*, or in their own words, "Don't ask us for another fucking dime." I promised I wouldn't.

During the negotiations, a few Gannett executives made it clear that they thought I was wasting everyone's time and money by trying to refloat *Baywatch*. Their predictions of my demise made me look forward with great anticipation to the day when I could write the first check for $5,000 to Gannett, then the 10th check, then the 50th check, then the 100th check, each check a way of saying, "I guess you guys were dead wrong."

Sid Tessler's second role was to serve as the show's accountant. Every company needs an honest guy with a lot of integrity to do the books. When the business involves two inherently antagonistic partners, such as NBC and GTG, this guy must be independent of the principals. (Whenever huge sums of money are tossed around, all parties involved are inherently antagonistic.) During the first year of *Baywatch*, Sid had kept the books, to the satisfaction of GTG and NBC. One of the good fortunes I had in refloating *Baywatch* was when Sid agreed to continue as the show's independent accountant.

Over the course of a few weeks, Sid gave me a crash course in episodic television accounting, from letters of credit to cash flow to delivery requirements. Fortunately, Sid was also well-versed in international finance, since so much of the new *Baywatch* would come to rely on foreign money.

On Sid's advice I spent a great deal of time calculating how much each new episode of *Baywatch* would cost. At NBC, the price of each *Baywatch* episode was ultimately $1.3 million.

But I had seen money wasted on a vast scale. Using the old GTG/NBC budget as my pattern, and a clever computer program called Movie Magic Budgeting, I carefully plotted how much the new shows would cost, minus what I considered the obvious and egregious waste—massive overhead, huge writing staff, tremendous salaries above and below the line. My best estimate was $800,000 an episode times 22 episodes: $18 million.

We made good headway toward finding distribution *and* money, thanks to one man, Paul Talbot, the president of Fremantle Corporation. Fremantle, based in New York, distributes American television shows throughout the rest of the world. During the NBC season, Fremantle had sold *Baywatch* to several countries, most of them in continental Europe.

Over the next week, Paul Talbot offered to pay us a tremendous sum of money, $400,000 an episode, for the international rights to the new *Baywatch*. Until then, no show had ever received $400,000 an episode for international rights.

Why the huge increase from the previous year, when Talbot had paid GTG only $75,000? The reason is simple: *Baywatch* had caught fire in Europe. David Hasselhoff was now a huge star in Germany. In fact, contingent on Talbot paying us $400,000 was that Hasselhoff appear in 17 out of 22 episodes.

Paul Talbot licensed *Baywatch* to various distribution companies all over the world. Two of the most important distributors were Beta Taurus and ITV. Talbot, knowing the importance of these two companies in terms of *Baywatch*'s success, had me deal directly with them.

Germany's Beta Taurus (part of the Kirsch Group) was run by three of the most financially savvy men I have ever met: Leo Kirsch, Klaus Hallig, and Fritz Deakman. I frequently spoke to Klaus Hallig, conferring on many aspects of the show. All three men eventually became big supporters of *Baywatch*.

Paul Talbot wanted more episodes of *Baywatch*, the sooner the better. In passing, Talbot said, "If I'm going to give you all this money, I want merchandising and licensing for continental Europe."

I knew my television history. I knew that only a few shows had ever made money in merchandising and licensing. I said, "Take it. No problem. Don't even ask twice. You can have it." (Only continental Europe merchandising was available to him, not U.S. merchandising.)

Now, years later, I can only marvel at Paul Talbot's prescient abilities. *Baywatch* went on to make an astounding amount of money in merchandising and licensing, both domestically and internationally. The *Baywatch*® Barbie® doll sold by the truckload. *Baywatch* would eventually have over 200 licensees. Each licensee created and sold hundreds of products, from air fresheners to cut glass and crystal. Paul Talbot did very well for himself and his family over the years.

Merchandising and licensing became huge revenue sources, with products including Baywatch sunglasses, swimsuits, hats, sandals—even Baywatch Barbie (the Doll of the Year) and Ken.

I immediately called David Hasselhoff. We needed him, badly. Without Hasselhoff, no new *Baywatch*. Over lunch, David Hasselhoff and I, along with his manager, Jan McCormick, set up the deal. Jan is one of the most exceptional people I have met through *Baywatch*. Not only does she look out for her client's interest, but she *also* cares about the show. This makes her unique. Most managers and agents care nothing for the show in question. David was interested in becoming more than a lead actor on a weekly series.

This is a common theme for many experienced actors. They know that acting can only take them so far—they want to explore the producing side of television life. Producing is a whole different challenge: mundane at times and tedious; also wonderfully rewarding when it all comes together. Plus as an actor/producer he would have some control over the many decisions that would affect his career—control over stories, co-stars, guest stars. We arrived at a solution: David would become a full partner in *Baywatch*, our fourth executive producer along with Michael Berk, Doug Schwartz, and myself. Ultimately, this proved to be an exceptionally profitable move by Hasselhoff and it was good for the show. By being vested in its success, Hasselhoff, over the years, proved to be an indefatigable promoter of the show.

The British television market is huge and very competitive. Because of the market's importance, Paul Talbot decided that our British station, ITV, should deal directly with me—same as Beta Taurus.

At the time, England had only a few stations: BBC1, BBC2, and ITV. Unlike American television, Britain has strict rules preventing excessive sex and violence before 9:00 in the evening. But at the stroke of 9:00 P.M., which is called the watershed, everything changes. After the watershed, almost anything can be shown on British television, including programs that are far more graphic than those on our own networks.

During the NBC year, ITV broadcast *Baywatch* after the watershed, paying only $25,000 an episode, which is practically nothing considering the show cost $1.3 million to make. For that one season, the show achieved decent ratings in England.

For the new *Baywatch*, ITV offered to pay us $75,000 an episode as a license fee and another $75,000 as an equity fee, from which they could derive a profit if the show did well. Their $150,000 total was included in Paul Talbot's $400,000 total for Europe.

But ITV would pay that huge amount if, and only if, we made a show that would work *before* the watershed. That was the key.

Warren Breech, our main contact at ITV said, "Here is our stipulation: We don't want you to put women or children into violent situations."

It's a great system once you learn it. No knives. No guns. No rape. No violence against women or children—specifically, no physical harm being done to them by another person. We could show a woman in danger of drowning—otherwise we wouldn't have much of a show. But we couldn't show a woman being physically attacked by a guy. British audiences don't want those elements, not before the watershed.

For $150,000, I could afford to listen. It was that simple. Anyone who is not willing to accommodate the interests of the investor is not going to succeed in this business.

Early on in syndication, we made an episode called "The One That Got Away," in which a fisherman stalked a woman lifeguard. Ultimately, he trapped her under a pier and it looked as if he was going to rape her. ITV hated it.

I flew to London with a copy of the show and met with the ITV people. We sat in their editing booth and started cutting away at the offensive scenes, which put pressure on them as well. They were forced to demonstrate exactly how they wanted the episode to look. Not only did it solve the problem, it helped establish a good working relationship. I was the first American producer to fly in and try to solve a problem rather than simply shoving it back in their face. I came home and described the situation to everyone here, explaining to our staff how we could adjust the scripts to everyone's satisfaction.

We agreed to meet their requests, and ITV agreed to put us on at 5:45 on Sunday night. To the Brits, 5:45 is a very round number. Some of their shows start at 6:17 or 8:39. The British networks either don't show commercials or, if they have commercials, they block them together, showing them for 20 minutes nonstop before or after a program.

In the UK, Sunday night at 5:45 is *the* time to air. Anything that aired in that time slot would earn good numbers. It gets dark early in England. Rugby stops. They eat dinner ridiculously early. Everything leads into it. Sunday nights at 5:45 was the best time of the week, and ITV was the best channel.

Herein lies the secret to *Baywatch*'s runaway, worldwide, ongoing success: By adhering to ITV's rules, we made a show that appealed to a broad range of viewers. It could play in any time slot, on any day, anywhere in the world.

For station programmers, *Baywatch* was a dream come true. Imagine *NYPD Blue* at 8:30 Saturday morning. No thanks. Imagine *Baywatch* at 8:30 on Sunday morning, or any morning— or at 9:00 P.M., any night. It works! Suddenly we could sell the new *Baywatch* to China, Spain, Brazil, Russia, Japan, Iceland, South Africa, South America—eventually 145 countries around the world.

In the big picture, the audience is broken into three groups: kids, middle-aged adults, and older adults. In any of these 145 countries, all three generations—daughter, mother, and grandmother—could watch an episode together and not be embarrassed at any point. You could count on it.

Little did we know that a global audience was hungry for *Baywatch*. Once we found out, we made it our job to satisfy that hunger.

Vanessa Angel starred in "The One That Got Away," an episode that caused us problems with ITV.

hanks to Paul Talbot, we had our international distribution under control. Plus we were halfway toward acquiring the $18 million we needed to make the series. Gaining domestic distribution and finding the remaining $9 million proved to be a lot more challenging.

At first we explored the possibility of getting the new *Baywatch* on an established network. It is worth noting that the established networks—ABC, NBC, and CBS—are actually nothing more than distributors of their product of choice: half-hour and one-hour weekly series, local and network news, sports, and an occasional movie, either bought on the open market or produced in-house. The networks are to television what Barnes & Noble is to books: the traditional way for the product to reach the market. Because the networks are so big and pervasive, they can command some control over the content of the shows they distribute.

Occasionally a show will be canceled by one network and then picked up by another. For example, a few years ago *JAG* went from NBC to CBS.

The new *Baywatch*, however, had no such luck. We were turned down by ABC and CBS.

Next we explored getting *Baywatch* on a budding network, which at the time consisted only of Fox. They were not interested.

We then tried placing *Baywatch* on Lifetime Television, USA, TNT, even the Playboy Channel. Although they all agreed in principle to air *Baywatch*, eventually we concluded that their viewership was simply too small to support a relatively expensive production.

The best place for *Baywatch*, we decided, would be on the independent stations around the country. Los Angeles is a good example. In Los Angeles at the time, Channel 13, owned by United/Chris Craft, promoted itself as "The *Very* Independent Channel 13." Chris Craft wanted first-run, quality programming to compete against the established networks.

In order to sell *Baywatch* to an independent station such as Chris Craft, we teamed up with a small distribution company called LBS, run by twin brothers, Paul and Henry Siegel. Paul and Henry were so identical that I could never tell them apart, at least until Henry shaved off his mustache. Henry Siegel studied the prospective rating numbers and the demographics for the show, and then determined that the new *Baywatch* was going to be a slam-dunk success. For a fee and a share of the profits, LBS agreed to distribute the show around the United States *and* to assist us in finding the necessary funding that we needed to commence production.

Thanks to LBS, we were introduced to United/Chris Craft. Not only did Chris Craft own Channel 13, they owned stations in six other major markets: New York, Chicago, Portland, Phoenix, San Francisco, and Minneapolis. This made Chris Craft the largest distributor of independent programming in the country. The man in charge at Chris Craft, Evan Thompson, turned out to be exactly the sort of executive with whom I prefer to deal. He didn't pretend to be a programming expert, always intruding on the creative side of the business. Evan Thompson made his decisions based on the rating numbers: If a show rated well and the cost was reasonable, he wanted it.

After a few brief meetings, Chris Craft became partners in *Baywatch*. In exchange for 6 percent ownership of the show, Chris Craft agreed to give *Baywatch* good time slots on all of their stations *and* to promote the show. This promotion was absolutely essential, as important as getting the show on the air in the first place. When considering all the pieces that went into remaking *Baywatch*, the smartest single thing we did was to join forces with Chris Craft.

hanks to Chris Craft, we now had a healthy start on domestic distribution. Now we directed our energy toward finding the missing financing: $9 million.

Where does one find $9 million for a speculative project that doesn't promise any sort of return? Perhaps LBS. When we first partnered with LBS, they told us they had access to loans, which was one reason we were excited to work with them. Wrong. Unfortunately we soon learned that LBS, despite the fact that Henry Siegel was a certified genius, had a terrible credit rating among the banks. In truth, LBS was quite close to going bankrupt. While I was counting on LBS to be our financial and distribution partner, they were counting on *Baywatch* to be their savior.

We considered going straight to a bank ourselves. Plenty of banks in Southern California lend money on speculative projects. But banks need collateral. If we wanted to put our houses on the line, our parents' houses, our cars—basically everything we owned—we might have acquired a loan. But if *Baywatch* failed (a likely event in the opinion of many experts), we would lose it all, something none of us could afford to do.

We had two more options: a sponsor or a guarantor.

First, I looked into getting a long-term sponsor, such as Coca-Cola or Procter & Gamble. In the early days of television, a solitary company sponsored a whole TV show, such as *Texaco Star Theater*, but the *Hallmark Hall of Fame* is one of the few remaining examples of this. Why are those melodramatic daytime dramas called soap operas? Originally each show was sponsored by a solitary soap company. We came close with Coca-Cola, but ultimately they decided the venture was too risky.

The second option was a guarantor, someone with a solid credit rating to whom a bank would lend $9 million.

Henry Siegel said *Baywatch* was going to get a slam dunk 5.0 rating. With a 5.0 rating, advertisers would pay plenty of money to have their commercial appear on *Baywatch*. We could recoup the costs of production and have a modest profit left over. At a 4.0 rating we would break even. But suppose the show flopped? Who would guarantee to the bank that their loan would be repaid? A guarantor. (The situation is analogous to a parent co-signing a car loan for a son or daughter. If, for some reason, the kid can't repay the loan, the parent steps in and takes over the payments.) Our guarantor would guarantee the bank's loan if the advertising income didn't match what we needed. And if the ratings were a 6.0, the guarantor stood to take a lion's share of the surplus, literally millions of dollars, their reward for having assumed the risk.

A 5.0 rating is relatively small compared to the 17.1 rating *Baywatch* had at NBC. But our costs at NBC were much higher. When the final profits are calculated, an inexpensive show with a 5.0 rating can generate more income than a show with higher numbers but which costs much more to produce.

Then, through one of my very best friends, Chris Carlson (not to be confused with Chris Craft), I met a wealthy, private individual, Sid Irmis. Chris Carlson and I had been friends for years—Chris knew the show I had in mind from having listened to me yak about it for seemingly forever. He knew exactly what the show could be. Further, Chris knew that wealthy Sid Irmis wanted his son, Matthew, to be in the TV business. With Sid we came very, very close to closing a deal.

At the same time, LBS introduced me to Syd Vinnedge, who worked for Scotti Brothers Records. Scotti Brothers had a small television division whose only credit at the time was *American's Top 10*, with Casey Kasem. Eventually that show went from TV to radio (expanding to the Top 40), where it thrived for many years.

When I first met Syd Vinnedge, I asked him, "By any chance is your son a lifeguard?" Yes, sure enough, his son, Syd Vinnedge Jr., was a lifeguard. I had met him years earlier. (Grant Tinker often asked me, "Do you know anybody who *isn't* a lifeguard?") Syd Sr. seemed like a perfect match for our needs. He had heard about the thrill of lifeguarding for 10 years at the dinner table from his son Syd Jr. Also, Syd Sr. knew *Baywatch* from its season on NBC. Actually, Syd knew *Baywatch* from even earlier. He reminded me that I had pitched him *Baywatch* 10 years earlier, as a musical variety special, something I had totally forgotten. Back then he responded to my pitch by giving me one of my requisite 1,500 rejections—thank God!

Syd Vinnedge Sr. took our proposal to his associates at Scotti Brothers Records, in particular to the head man, Tony Scotti. A week later I got a call from Syd, saying succinctly, "No thanks." With the exception of one man, Myron Roth, they were not interested in *Baywatch*.

Luckily for us, Syd is not the sort of man who can be easily discouraged. Week after week he kept going back to Tony Scotti, presenting some new piece of evidence that further demonstrated that *Baywatch* could be a winner. All that was needed to make it happen was for Scotti Brothers Records to get on board.

Tony Scotti was a tough sell. Yes, he wanted to run with the Big Dogs of Television, but was reluctant to risk his own money. Syd stuck with it. He set up meetings; he brought in the stars. A number of times he invited me to talk to Tony and his No. 1 man, Myron Roth. Myron had run MCA music for years—now he was making the transition to television via *Baywatch*. Myron and I talked nearly every day. Luckily we got along very well on a personal and professional level. Myron's son David is even an aspiring junior lifeguard.

Finally Syd Vinnedge and Myron Roth convinced Tony Scotti and associates to make a bid to serve as the guarantor for *Baywatch*.

For a brief time I had wealthy Sid Irmis bidding for *Baywatch* against Scotti Brothers' Syd Vinnedge. They both wanted the project, which gave us some leverage to cut a better deal. Finally Sid Irmis pulled out of the bidding. For a week I did my best to conceal this fact from the Scotti Brothers, at least until the deal was finalized. I even went so far as to forget to tell my own partners that Sid Irmis had dropped out of the bidding.

Finally Scotti Brothers—since renamed All American Television—signed on as our guarantor. In the grand plan to resurrect *Baywatch*, Syd Vinnedge was a prime mover, and an ongoing champion. Without Syd, we would never have succeeded.

Altogether Berk, Schwartz, Bonann, and Hasselhoff retained 50 percent ownership of the show, which is quite good in this industry. In return for signing on as our guarantors, All American received 25 percent ownership of the show. The remaining 25 percent went to LBS (for finding domestic distribution), Chris Craft (for actual domestic distribution), Fremantle (for worldwide distribution), and ITV (for Great Britain distribution).

In addition to the 25 percent, All American acquired the *Baywatch* copyright and trademarks. Should anything go grossly wrong with the new *Baywatch* in a financial sense, neither

Berk, Schwartz, Bonann, nor Hasselhoff would be liable. However, because we no longer held the copyright, we could not utilize the *Baywatch* name without All American's approval. But by the same token, All American could not use the name without our approval.

n the old days, the term "syndicated" referred to a show that had been sent to rerun heaven on a non-network station, *M*A*S*H* or *Magnum P.I.* or *Murder, She Wrote*. Nowadays, reruns of shows that are broadcast off network have become known as "strip syndication."

Chris Carlson visiting me in the lifeguard tower. The good old days of guarding: battery-powered television, Planters peanuts, and a Slurpee.

The new *Baywatch* was something altogether different and necessitated a new term. Rather than reruns, we were offering a never-before-seen, independently produced, action-adventure show destined for a non-network station. The term we used to define the new *Baywatch* was "first-run syndication."

With the creation of the new *Baywatch*, purchasers of programming for independent stations suddenly had a choice. They could buy a first-run syndicated show with really great looking women and buff guys, for $400,000 per episode, or they could buy an often-seen rerun of *The Cosby Show* for $800,000. It is important to note, however, that *Cosby* was a proven commodity, with relatively predictable ratings, while *Baywatch* was new and untested.

The country is broken into 212 separate markets, ranging from huge, important markets like New York (with 6 percent of the country's total viewing audience), to relatively insignificant markets, such as Wyoming. Within each market is a myriad of stations. Some of the stations are owned by the networks: ABC, NBC, CBS, Fox (and to some extent WB and UPN). Some are independently owned but still linked to an established network. These are called affiliates. Finally, as mentioned earlier, some of the independently owned stations serve up strictly independent programming, stations such as Chris Craft.

The network affiliates are under contract to air the programming offered to them by their network. The independent stations, however, can buy any programming they believe their audience will watch. With Chris Craft we gained entry into seven key markets out of 212. To sell the rest of the country, we took the show to NATPE in January 1991.

NATPE, the convention of the National Association of Television Programming Executives, is held every January in one of the popular convention cities such as Las Vegas or San Francisco. In '91 it was held in New Orleans.

At that time, NATPE was *the* main marketplace. If you had a series to sell, you took it to NATPE, set up a booth, screened it, and if a buyer from an independent station liked it, he would place an order.

LBS and All American concocted a plan to sell *Baywatch* at NATPE. As would be expected, they planned to bring our two main stars, David Hasselhoff and Erika Eleniak—let them meet the various buyers from around the country. But the plan, specifically LBS's contribution, did not include having one of the show's producers—Berk, Schwartz, or myself—in attendance.

The reason? If any credit or kudos was going to be generated through *Baywatch*, LBS wanted it. Or better yet, LBS needed it. *Baywatch* was their best and last hope for financial solvency. If the show's producers were absent, LBS could present the show to the marketplace themselves—

and make people think that *Baywatch* was an LBS-produced show. Also we (Berk, Schwartz, Bonann) were loud, dominant, self-important guys. Doug Schwartz, in particular, possesses a brilliant salesman's persona. Whenever he's in a room, the focus soon gravitates away from everyone else and toward him. That was the last thing LBS wanted at NATPE. LBS wanted to be top dog!

At the last minute, I was able to convince LBS and All American that I should attend. I'm glad I did. Through the course of the convention, Hasselhoff and I were locked to the booth, although "booth" is hardly the right word. All American and LBS had created their own mini-mall within the conference hall. A prospective buyer from Spokane could watch a video of *Baywatch*, meet Hasselhoff, have their picture taken with Erika, and talk to me about the upcoming season. As I had hoped, the buyers were anxious to talk to one of the show's producers about story lines for the upcoming season. Would we have action and adventure? What guest stars would we be having? My time at NATPE was well spent, not to mention that I was able to keep a close, proprietary handle on the LBS situation. I did not want people coming away from the booth thinking LBS was solely responsible for something we had created.

Through the course of NATPE, I observed that some of the production companies were merely pretending that they were for real. I saw ads in the NATPE program saying, "Sure thing," "Commitment to air," and "87 percent of the country cleared." They would say that their show was absolutely, positively happening. That is all bullshit. They were hoping a buyer would say, "My God, if everybody else has this show, I must have it too." What's amazing is that this tactic often works. If you can create enough heat, the fire will soon follow.

For feature films, the NATPE equivalent is the Cannes Film Festival. In 1995, a movie producer flew in Pamela Anderson, stuffed her into a tight leather outfit, and asked everyone to buy *Barb Wire*, the movie. If no one had bought *Barb Wire*, the producer would have exited through the side door, saying, "Just kidding." However, the international presale of *Barb Wire* was sufficient to finance the making of the movie.

At the '91 NATPE, *Baywatch* came in through the front door, guns blazing. LBS's Henry and Paul Siegel were famous in the business, not only for being complete rascals, but also for occasionally getting the job done. The guarantor, All American, had their point man, Syd Vinnedge, in the booth. The star, David Hasselhoff, was nearby standing alongside Erika Eleniak. We even had a representative from our bank, Chemical Bank. Clearly it was not a smoke screen. How serious were we? I was wearing a suit and tie.

The actual advertisement from the 1991 NATPE program.

Our advertisement in the NATPE program summed it up neatly:

> All American Communications, LBS Distribution, and Fremantle Corporation, along with executive producers Doug Schwartz, Michael Berk, Greg Bonann, and David Hasselhoff, proudly announce the commencement of principal photography of 22 episodes of *Baywatch* for first-run syndication. Commencement of principal photography begins July 7, 1991.

The demand for *Baywatch* grew as NATPE progressed. What percentage of the country would we eventually clear? To "clear" a show means to air the show. Some distributors will manipulate this cleared number to their advantage, stating that their show has cleared in 90 percent of the *markets*. However, their show is not airing in the *top 10 markets*. In reality, their show is being aired in front of only 60 percent of the viewing audience. The key number is not markets cleared, but the percentage of the country cleared.

In our first season of syndication, *Baywatch* cleared in 89 percent of the country.

CHAPTER 8

The Make-up of the Deal

N ow that we had distribution and financing under control, we could march ahead with production. As part of that process, Doug, Michael, and I finalized our partnership agreement. We would share the Executive Producer credit and split the profits—if any—equally. The credits would read, Executive Producers: Michael Berk & Doug Schwartz and Gregory J. Bonann and David Hasselhoff. (The "&" denotes a previously established partnership.)

Each of us, Doug, Michael, and I, had our specialties. I loved action, music, and visuals. Doug loved to create characters and story lines. Michael loved to write scripts. Doug and I wanted to direct. By wearing several hats, each member of the Berk, Schwartz, Hasselhoff, and Bonann team stood to make some decent money, when and if *Baywatch* got off the ground.

What we did not love was budgets, business affairs, advertising and promotion, making deals with actors—all the things that a network and a studio traditionally do for you. Doug, Michael, and I agreed to share the less glamorous work in order to participate in the aspects of the show that were more to our liking.

In accordance with the producer's code, I went everywhere, did everything, on my own nickel. A producer specs his time and expenses in hopes that it will eventually pay off. If it does pay

(Opposite) Mädchen Amick getting made up for her next scene.

off, the producer is in a good position to expect a decent piece of the profit pie. Otherwise, he is just a salaried employee. How does a hopeful producer survive for 14 months without a payday? Extremely frugal living.

I burned up gallons of gasoline during this pre-preproduction phase, looking for a new home for *Baywatch*. My first stop was Warner Bros. Studios, which rented space to production companies. I learned right away that GTG wasn't the only studio that charged huge, outlandish fees to producers looking to rent some office space. After visiting a few more studios, all of whom charged huge sums, I decided we would be better off creating our own studio. We could have our whole production team, the editing equipment, the writers, in one place—and save a fortune in the bargain.

At the time, the real estate slump was in full swing, the market awash in vacant warehouses. I looked at warehouses in East L.A., Studio City, Long Beach. Finally I spotted a vacant warehouse near Marina del Rey. It seemed ideal to our needs—it was close to the ocean, close to the marina, close to my home. The landlord, Jerry Cohen (who had never before rented to entertainment people), was anxious to have any sort of tenant. We settled on a 10-year lease, although the lease allowed us to quit the deal if the show was canceled.

During the winter of 1990–91, we had no money. At the same time we urgently needed legal assistance. We had set up a dozen deals-in-principle—Talbot's foreign deal; Hasselhoff's deal; the basic Berk, Schwartz, Bonann deal; the Gannett deal; Grant's deal—but could not finalize them without legal assistance. Michael Berk steered us toward a friend and associate, Peter Dekom, who was a partner in Bloom, Dekom & Hergot. Peter was one of the most respected, innovative entertainment lawyers in town, and certainly we would not have gotten past the security guard had it not been for Michael Berk.

As we sat in Peter's office and explained our legal needs, I could feel my feet practically disappearing into the deep carpet. Peter agreed to help. Then he immediately ushered us out of his

office room. We walked down the hall, toward a woman carrying a large cardboard box. "Gentlemen," Peter said, "meet Leigh Brecheen, your new attorney." Peter left us with Leigh and returned to his less financially challenged clients. We wouldn't see Peter again for months.

This just happened to be Leigh Brecheen's first day on the job and we were her first clients. Right from the start she proved to be a tough, competent, and altogether capable lawyer. She was also absolutely drop-dead gorgeous. It's sad to say, but beautiful blond women are often not taken seriously in business matters. I soon learned that whenever we walked into a room, we should make the deal as soon as possible, while the opposition was still staring dumbly at our attractive attorney. Leigh attacked the challenge with gusto, working wonders, taking our flimsy deals-in-principle and, through hard core negotiating, turning them into iron-clad contracts.

When it came time to work out the final details of the agreement with All American, Leigh and I met with their attorneys. Leigh, being new to Bloom, Dekom & Hergot, was very inclined to consummate the deal since it would help solidify her position at the firm. In general, it would be an enormous feather in her cap. The All American attorneys, however, were not so predisposed. Some attorneys in the entertainment business specialize in making deals *not* happen. Over the past year I had taken *Baywatch* all over town, and everywhere I went, I had come up against clever attorneys who always found a reason to block the deal. As we neared the finish line, I was worried that the small print—some minuscule detail—might derail the signing of the pact.

As Leigh and I walked into the room, I felt that we were jumping, fully clothed, into a swirling riptide. With us in the riptide were All American's well-dressed, ravenous attorneys. But one of All American's attorneys was quite different. He was pleasant, almost fatherly. His quiet confidence and professionalism set him apart from the others. This was Irwin Russell.

At critical points in the negotiations—with all sides present—Irwin said to his team, "Maybe we should consider their suggestion." He wanted to make the deal. He felt, as we did, that a deal involving compromise was better than a fabulous deal that falls apart.

Control was a major sticking point. All American wanted control of every aspect of the series, including the scripts, so that they could better control the costs of each episode. Of course, we wanted to maintain as much control as possible, since we were the producers and knew *Baywatch* intimately. Since both parties were adamant about their position, it seemed the deal was about to come apart. Then Irwin Russell and Leigh Breechen suggested a compromise: Berk, Schwartz, and Bonann would control the creative side of the show—just as long as we stayed within the budget. Should we go over budget, All American would take control. We all agreed. The compromise succeeded and the deal was closed.

Without Irwin Russell in the room that day, *Baywatch* never would have been launched. Soon afterwards, Irwin parted company from All American. They simply were not his kind of people.

While that meeting solidified the deal-in-principle, we still had to sign the legal agreement, which was drawn up over the next few days. Besides myself, a lot of people were anxious for signing to occur. All the cast contracts were ready; the Hasselhoff deal was in place; the line producer, Paul Cajero, had been hired; the production designers were hired. All these people and more were continually passing up other jobs while they waited to begin work on *Baywatch*.

On the night of Friday, May 10, 1991, I crowded into Myron Roth's tiny office at All American's headquarters on Pico Boulevard in Los Angeles, joining Myron, Syd Vinnedge, Tom Bradshaw, and Tony Scotti. All American was still worried. Could we do what we claimed? What if we went over budget?

One last time I showed them the schematic I had drawn up for our warehouse/studio. I went over the contracts that I had collected from the various actors, with agreed-upon salary reductions from the NBC year. I showed them the schedule for delivery of each episode. I showed them the construction schedule for the permanent sets. I showed them contingency plans, in the event an episode went over budget.

We bickered over the last few details, much of it having to do with the music for the show. Although it is rarely mentioned, a show's music can be worth a fortune. Much the same way that an actor is paid a residual each time his episode is rerun, the composer/owner/performer is paid a residual each time his or her music is used. The only difference is that the musician's residuals don't decrease over time, as do an actor's residuals. These music residuals are paid by the production company. For example, during the network year our main title song, "Save Me" by Peter Cetera, cost GTG $25,000 *per episode*.

For the new *Baywatch*, we wanted to create our own music. This would enable us to turn an expense—buying music from an outside source, guys like Peter Cetera—into a source of revenue.

All American had its roots in music, and not surprisingly they wanted to control this particular aspect of the show. We knew we would be left in the cold unless we were intimately involved. To satisfy both All American and Berk, Schwartz, and Bonann, we jointly created two new companies to oversee music usage on the show: Tower 88 and Regina Beach Music (for ASCAP and BMI respectively, the companies that tabulate music usage).

Eventually our in-house music team created the song "I'm Always There" for the *Baywatch* main title. Now, instead of putting $25,000 in Peter Cetera's pocket each episode, we could put $25,000 in ours. That's a $50,000 swing. Multiply that times 200 episodes, each shown dozens of times, and before long you have quite a chunk of money in the bank.

While the music business can be somewhat intriguing, the real lesson is in learning not to be intimidated by companies like All American, who can steamroll over a producer without missing a beat. A producer who is willing to learn about the intricacies of such matters as the music, and who can take on the big boys, stands to make a lot money. More accurately, he stands to be paid the money he is rightly due.

Finally, I initialed my name 100 times, once for each of the myriad of line changes. Lastly we all shook hands and the deal was sealed. After 14 months, *Baywatch* had been refloated. Where would it sail? I had lots to think about as I left All American's office on Pico, which has long since given way to their new, gorgeous building on Wilshire Boulevard—the house that *Baywatch* built.

On the drive home I called Doug and Michael from the car and together we cheered the signing of the deal. Tomorrow we would start focusing on our areas of responsibility: Michael with scripts, Doug and I with producing chores. Next I called David Hasselhoff. He, too, cheered our rebirth. We were back!

Now that we were back I could finally take the hard-earned lessons I'd endured during the NBC year and apply them to the new *Baywatch*. In the big picture, it all starts with the show's budget. NBC paid GTG a license fee of $860,000 an episode. GTG was also paid $75,000 an episode for the foreign rights. The show's budget was $1.3 million. Grant Tinker's company was deficit spending $365,000 a week, out of their own pocket. (A deficit is a planned loss, as opposed to an unplanned, unexpected one, such as the *Baywatch* pilot going $2 million over budget.)

After reflecting on the numbers, I said no way. If $860,000 is the license fee, then the show's budget should be $860,000. The premier thought in everyone's mind, from the trainee cable puller to the executive producer, should be, "We will not exceed that budgetary number!" It's like an architect designing your house. How big a house do you want? Can you afford five bedrooms, five

PAYMENT SCHEDULE-Director 1 Episode

7/2/98 thru 6/30/99 Contract Year (7/1/99 still in negotiation)

(Base Rate-$16,064.00)

DIRECTOR'S FEE	1st Run	13,473.00	
40%	2nd	6,425.60	19,898.60
30%	3rd	4,819.20	24,717.80
25%	4th	4,016.00	28,733.80
25%	5th	4,016.00	32,749.80
25%	6th	4,016.00	36,765.80
15%	7th	2,409.00	39,175.40
15%	8th	2,409.60	41,585.00
15%	9th	2,409.60	43,994.60
15%	10th	2,409.60	46,404.20
10%	11th	1,604.40	48,008.60
10%	12th	1,604.40	49,613.00
15%	For 1st	2,409.60	
10%	For 2nd	1,604.40	
10%	For 3rd	1,604.40	5,618.40
	TOTALS		$55,231.40

In the big picture, directing a Baywatch episode will earn a director more money than if he'd directed a network show.

baths? Or do you have less money? Can you afford only two bedrooms, one bath? Of course everyone wants five bedrooms, five baths, but if you only have enough money for two bedrooms, one bath, then that is what you should build.

When appropriate, the foreign and ancillary sales should be factored into the equation. But overall, why should a producer go into a deal knowing he is going to lose money? Not even a deep-pockets backer like Gannett could afford to lose $9 million a season. The new *Baywatch* would be different. We sold the show on the premise of a strict, no-nonsense budget. Now the trick would be seeing if we could we stick to it.

Right from the start I told the crew—many of whom had worked on the NBC *Baywatch*—that if we were going to survive in syndication we would all need to take pay cuts, beginning with the executive producers, the actors, right down the line. I called Monte Markham, who played Captain Thorpe during the NBC year. Over breakfast at Coogie's in Malibu, I said, "Monte, I'm embarrassed to tell you this but our budget is pretty limited." I explained to Monte that I could pay him a relatively modest percentage of his previous year's salary. But why would a veteran actor agree to such a dramatic pay cut? First, I could promise Monte that he would appear in 17 out of 22 episodes. The most appearances Monte could get during the NBC year was seven episodes.

Second, I knew that Monte wanted to become a director. For a guy who wants to break into directing, getting that first opportunity is always the toughest. To encourage his return I told him that he could direct an episode of the new *Baywatch*. Besides the big-break aspect of directing, the money he'd earn would more than make up for any initial pay cut as an actor. For directing two episodes, Monte stood to earn, in *net*, $110,000.

Finally, Monte and I were good friends. We had enjoyed working together during the NBC year. The agreeable prospect of working together again helped seal the deal. He took it.

Billy Warlock returned, but for less than half of his previous year's salary. Eleniak also returned, also for far less than her salary. I wasn't trying to cheat anyone—I simply couldn't afford to pay them network wages. The late Richard Jaeckel, an excellent actor, returned to play a senior lifeguard. We offered Parker Stevenson a part with a pay cut, but he turned us down. I'm happy to say that Parker and I remained close friends and eventually I gave him his first shot at directing. He has since gone on to become an accomplished director for many other companies in town, working on *Beverly Hills 90210*, *Savannah*, and *Melrose Place*. In the past two years he has directed three to four episodes of *Baywatch* per year.

Actors turned directors… (Top) Director Monte Markham, in blue shirt, white hat, firing up his actors. (Above) Parker Stevenson chats with David Hasselhoff between setups.

When it came to asking these actors to return with a pay cut, we had a powerful selling point, something unique to first-run syndication—guaranteed residuals.

While everyone on the team is paid a salary for each episode or day they work, some of the players—actors, director, and writer—are given an additional payment each time an episode to which they contributed is aired. This additional payment is called a residual.

First off, the series had a contractual guarantee to run for one full year—52 weeks. We were set to produce 22 new episodes. Those 22 episodes would be run twice, adding up to 44 weeks. Finally, 8 of the 22 episodes would be run yet again, to complete the 52 week year. One last, important factor has to be considered: The nature of first-run syndication calls for each episode to air *twice* during the week, as opposed to once on the network. For example, an episode might air on Friday evening and on Sunday afternoon.

Thus an episode would air twice its first time around. It would air two more times its second time around. Finally it might get two more airings—a total of six airings in one year. Because of the numerous airings (a minimum of four times and possibly six), an actor will eventually collect far more money through residuals than they would earn through their initial salary.

I applied this same argument when it came to hiring a director. At the time, DGA scale (minimum) for directing a network one-hour episode was $26,000. Scale for directing a non-network, one-hour show was $13,000.

When we offered to pay our directors non-network scale, they all considered it to be a grievous insult—in their eyes, a 50 percent pay cut. I had to explain to them (and their agents) over and over that any episode they directed would air at least four times during the year, guaranteed, and possibly six times. The director would not only earn his salary but at least four additional residual payments. (The money to pay for residuals comes from the additional advertising revenue generated when the show is aired again in reruns.) By adding in the residuals, our directors would be paid more than a network director whose episode would air only once, or, as in the case of many shows, such as NBC's *Wind on Water* with Bo Derek, which didn't air at all. Plus the monies earned from strip syndication will take residual income even higher.

Besides reducing salaries whenever appropriate, the other key to staying on budget was locking in the costs, so we could accurately calculate, to the nearest dollar, exactly what would be spent on each episode. A big part of that mission was accomplished by taming the monster that has haunted producers since the beginning of film-making time: overtime.

The moment the crew goes into overtime (after 12 hours on our schedule), a sudden shriek of happiness is heard throughout the set: "shing-shing," the cash register opens and the money starts pouring out. Grips, gaffs, guest stars, supporting cast, extras, transportation, they all go into double-time pay—gold overtime. This profitable passage of time is acknowledged by shouting out the international sound of a cash register opening, "shing-shing." When we went into syndication, we made a hard and fast rule: The work will get done in 12 hours. No exceptions. No overtime. None!

We also made flat deals with as many people as possible. I'd had an inspiration a few years earlier when we were filming a portion of our pilot in Honolulu. At the time, the city's trash collection was a disaster. The trashmen, paid an hourly wage, just couldn't seem to pick it up fast enough. Essentially it took them six days to pick up the whole city's trash. As you can imagine, with that hot, humid air, the place smelled to high hell. But the city of Honolulu didn't have enough money to buy more trucks or hire more trashmen. After weeks of dickering, a plan was floated: The trashmen would work for a flat fee, so that whether it took them seven days to pick up the trash or five days, they would make the same amount of money. With the deal in place, the trashmen starting working earlier and staying later. Before long they were picking up the trash in a mere three days. I say to the trashmen, if it's a fair wage for a week's work, good job. Keep it up.

I applied the same concept to some of our people. I said to David Hagar, our editor, one of my best friends and my oldest filmmaking compatriot, "I want to pay you episodically." That meant, for every episode, he would get a fee. I didn't care how long it took him to do the job. He took it. With everyone we could, we paid them a flat fee.

Actors, producers, writers, directors—we are all tremendously overpaid and we know it. As long as the cuts were equitable, across the board, practically everyone agreed to sign on.

The same philosophy applies to hiring outside concerns. At a network, a single voice—for example Brandon Tartikoff or Fred Silverman—could wake up one morning on the wrong side of the bed and decide to cancel your show. But thanks to Paul Talbot, Chris Craft, and NATPE, we had a 22 episode order, which meant that we could not be canceled mid-season. When we went around town with our 22 episode order, we were welcomed with open arms by every vendor, equipment rental house, post-production facility, catering concern. If we hired them, even at a discounted rate, they would have 22 episodes worth of work. Guaranteed.

Paul Cajero and David Hagar, two of our deal makers, knew the party line: We weren't going to pay the network rate—not when a network orders only six episodes. We had a 22 episode order. Paul and David had to explain the concept over and over, until finally the message sunk in.

We learned during the NBC season that the *Baywatch* audience liked the fact that the show was shot "exterior," on the beach, or in the surf, or underwater. With the new *Baywatch*, I wanted to shoot outside even more.

Not only was shooting outside good for our ratings, it was good for our budget. Daylight is the *only* light for outdoor shooting. A quick glance at the sunrise/sunset tables in the newspaper gives you all the information you need: You have exactly 11 hours, 8:00 A.M. until 7:00 P.M. Then it's going to get dark. The mythical "plug," which producers are always threatening to pull when their production is going over budget (but never actually do), is abruptly yanked out by Mother Nature. The day is over—you can't shoot any more. New directors always wanted me to give them a 6:00 A.M. call because they knew that if they got into trouble they'd have more time to finish the day's work. But it never happened—they'd always work until dark, venturing into golden time, $5,000 an hour. No way. I'd give the later call, 8:00 A.M., and just step back and let the setting sun work its magic.

The problem is that during the summer, when we shoot many of our episodes, the weather at the beach consists mostly of low clouds and fog, whereas we needed bright, bright sunshiny days. Since it is pretty hard to manipulate the weather, we sought out a different solution—a cover set—where we could shoot when the weather was lousy. (It's called a cover set because it is covered over, and thus impervious to bad weather.)

For the new *Baywatch*, we tried something altogether unique: We built our cover set on top of the *actual* lifeguard headquarters at Will Rogers beach. This cover set consisted of Mitch Buchannon's office, a hallway, and a communication room. On foggy, rainy, or freezing cold days, we no longer had to transport the whole production to the studio—and waste four hours and $20,000 in the process. By going upstairs, we suddenly had "Interior – office – day," ready to go. We could shoot for days and days on end without moving our trucks. And if you were to drive down Pacific Coast Highway on a Sunday afternoon, you'd pass this headquarters set without a glance. From the outside it looks like the usual county building, a nondescript gray box. To everyone's satisfaction, we kept it looking as un-Hollywood as possible.

The fact that I was a lifeguard was key to getting permission to build the Will Rogers set. They knew I would do my best not to jeopardize the safety of beach patrons. I also gave the chief lifeguard script approval. Other shows are scared to death to give script approval, and I don't know why. The chief's suggestions only served to make the show better. Like me, the chief didn't want to see guns and knives and police work, as in the NBC *Baywatch*. When he asked me, "What's the new *Baywatch* about?" I said, "We're going to show the lifeguards as heroes." He liked that. The chief still has script approval. If he has a problem, we fix it.

Will Rogers Lifeguard Headquarters underwent extensive changes thanks to Baywatch; we added a second floor and used it as our "covered set" when filming at the beach.

Overall, having our set at Will Rogers has been a huge success. We have saved a lot of money and it has kept us at the beach where the show was always meant to be. But it doesn't suffice for all our needs. To accommodate the other sets, the staff headquarters, and other divisions, we used the huge warehouse that I had rented in Marina del Rey.

With the signing of the lease, we entered the big time. Suddenly we had a modest studio of our own. Using a schematic of the building and a stack of Post-its, I arranged and rearranged the floor plan: Editing Room 1, Editing Room 2, casting, offices, writers' offices, music supervisor, production manager's office, props, set dressing, construction. I moved the Post-its around until it all fit together and made sense.

Putting a complete studio under one roof—from scratch—can be done the GTG way or the *Baywatch* way. At GTG, we paid $300,000 per month for three sound stages and all our office space. We shot an episode every eight days, three episodes a month. Dividing three episodes into $300,000 gives an over-head of $100,000 per episode.

In the new *Baywatch*, we rented the warehouse in Marina del Rey for $17,500 per month. The ware-house contained our sets (lounge, weight room, locker room, hallway), offices, everything. We shot four episodes a month—one every five days. Dividing four episodes into $17,500, gave us about $4,500 per episode overhead. By moving to Marina del Rey from GTG, we saved $95,500 an episode—in one line item.

But it is not enough to simply have a building. You need lights, camera, action. To back up for a moment, all the big studios, GTG included, have two distinct factions: studio-and-equipment rentals on one side, and the production group on the other. Both sides of the business are supposed to make a profit.

At GTG, the *Baywatch* production group had to rent its lighting equipment from GTG's studio and equipment rentals—for $60,000 a week. Then we hired one of the best lighting guys in the business, Gary Hazelbush, for a top fee. Altogether, we paid a lot of money for the lighting package. When I mentioned to Jack Clements, the head of production at GTG, that we seemed to be paying a steep rate for lighting, he said he

(Opposite) The second season cast, posing on the Scarab rescue boat. From left: Tom McTigue, David Hasselhoff, Billy Warlock, Erika Eleniak, Pamela Bach (Hasselhoff's real-life wife), Richard Jaeckel, Monte Markham, and Jeremy Jackson.

couldn't do it any other way—it was GTG's money. The exorbitant amount that Grant paid for overhead and equipment rentals was funneled into the GTG coffers through the studio-and-equipment-rental division. While Grant was going deep into deficit, the other side of the business was doing quite well.

Being new to the business and relatively impoverished in our warehouse scenario, I was immensely interested in the cost of the lighting package. I ended up paying Gary Hazelbush a smaller fee for his services, and I also rented his own lighting equipment for $8,100 a week—a third of what GTG was paying. Gary was happy. He was realizing much more money overall. I was ecstatic.

In the big picture, once all the numbers were crunched, Gannett discovered it could make far more money in the entertainment business *without* Grant Tinker. After Grant Tinker moved on to other challenges, Gannett rented out the studio on Culver Boulevard, 52 weeks a year, to various

motion picture and television production companies. In fact, until they sold it to Sony for a profit, it was a huge moneymaker for Gannett.

At the new *Baywatch*, we created a situation such that no one voice could be loud enough to alter our course of common sense. Any experienced person—Bochco, Tinker, Spelling, Cannell—could have done what we did if they had had the freedom. But they didn't. Grant had NBC looking over his shoulder. Spelling has ABC and Fox. Cannell has Fox and CBS. These men must play by strict corporate rules, which may or may not make sense. At *Baywatch*, we wrote our own rules.

Over the years, *Baywatch* has spawned its share of creative imitators: *High Tide*, *Key West*, *Acapulco Heat*, *Pacific Blue*. But those clones are insignificant compared to the business clones we have spawned, such as *Zena*, *V.I.P.*, and *Hercules*. We started a whole industry based around renting a warehouse and producing high-quality shows quickly, at low cost. No messing around. Now you can't find a vacant warehouse to rent in all of Southern California.

CHAPTER 9

Independence Day

On the Monday after the Fourth of July 1991, we began filming our first episode in syndication. Doug and Michael wrote the episode and I directed, which was our way of keeping a close hand on the show.

That episode, called "Nightmare Bay," was based on the Medal of Valor rescue I had made two years earlier. We flopped the facts, to make it more dramatic: Erika Eleniak's character, Shauni McClain, rescues a little African-American girl. Later Shauni visits the girl at home. On this visit Shauni realizes that the girl is drowning in the inner-city environment as much as she had been drowning in the water. I like episodes where the lifeguards become involved with the victims. In real life it happens quite often. You become vested in their well-being. You follow up, keep in touch.

At the beginning of production we encountered an unexpected problem, something almost unprecedented for Los Angeles in July—it started raining. Everyone came running up, asking what we were going to do. I said, "Line it up and shoot it." That's what we did, put a cover over the camera and marched on. Shooting that first scene in the rain set a standard for the next 10 years: Neither bad weather nor earthquakes nor fires nor riots has caused us to lose a day of shooting. To date we have never lost a single day.

(Opposite) Billy Warlock and Erika Eleniak were together for a time, both on and off screen.

The first scene involved Erika Eleniak arguing with her father about her staying on as a lifeguard, as opposed to going back to school. It was a dramatic sequence which Erika performed remarkably well. In the 14 months since I had last worked with her, she had been in heavy training, not in the gym but in acting classes. Her hard work paid off. When Eddie Morey, the camera operator, told me that an overzealous extra in the background had made the shot unusable, Erika performed the scene again with the same flawless execution. That's the sign of a good actor.

That episode, a two-parter, came in under budget and ahead of schedule. At last we were on our way.

Doug directed the third episode, called "The Trophy," in which an underage girl pretends that she has slept with a lifeguard. To her, this handsome lifeguard is "the trophy." She brags to her girlfriends about the supposed encounter, who then tell the girl's father. The father presses statutory rape charges against the lifeguard, played by Billy Warlock. He is arrested, sent to jail, suspended from his job, and yet the whole time he is innocent. This actually happened to a lifeguard friend of mine in the late 1970s.

Unfortunately "The Trophy" came in over budget. Also, the episode was much too long, 10 minutes too long in a 40 minute show. After all the plans and promises we had made to All American about staying on budget, it was downright scary. We sat around for a day grinding our teeth, trying to decide what to do. My strength is in keeping shows on budget, which ultimately comes down to saying no a great deal of the time. That is not necessarily a talent, but someone has to say no to night shoots, special effects, stunt men, crowded bar scenes, overtime, big dressing rooms, extra makeup and hair people. When I am shooting, the next show is prepping. It's during the prepping phase that a show either makes or breaks its budget, not when you shoot it. When shooting, you're only executing what has been prepared.

The solution for "The Trophy"? "To be continued..." We created another story line, shot for an additional two days, and turned the whole thing into a two-part episode. We took that episode out of the line-up and put it later, so that two two-parters didn't air in a row. Overall, we saved a lot of money.

You can explore unorthodox solutions if you are not a network supplier. If we had been

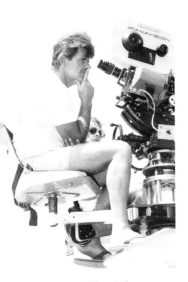

(Above) Cameraman Eddie Morey. (Right) Erika was certainly one of the most beautiful women we ever had on Baywatch. *Here she waits patiently for the next take.*

working with NBC, and they'd gotten wind that we were making a two-parter out of a single episode that went too long, they would have said, "You can't do that. You're economizing at our expense." But it made excellent business sense, and "The Trophy" turned out to be one of our best episodes that season.

During the NBC year, after we cut a show, we would send it to Grant and Stu for review. They would look at it, give us notes, and we'd make the necessary changes.

Then we would send it to the network for review—and wait. The network would usually get it back to us by Friday, with more suggestions for changes. They'd want to see the revised version the following Monday. Our editors, after sitting on their hands most of the week, would work on Saturday, at time and a half, and on Sunday, at double time. On Monday, we would send the revised show back to the network. Then our editors would wait again, Monday, Tuesday, on normal time.

I established new rules when we went into syndication: The editors were to go full speed ahead. If, for some reason, we were not available to screen an episode or a scene, they should proceed without us. That rarely happens because we make a point of making ourselves available to them. But the concept is clear: We appreciate their time and their skills. The editors are not simply "meat on the hoof," as at the network. The network didn't care that these guys had lives, that they had families. The editors don't want to make double time on Sunday, they want to make love on Sunday.

The whole idea of sending it to the network for review was absurd. I soon learned that they would inevitably suggest a dozen or so cuts, some major but most of them minuscule—"frame fucking" in the vernacular of the industry. After a while, I began to leave in obviously superfluous footage, knowing ahead of time that they would want me to remove it. This way, the final product would contain what I had originally desired—altogether a frivolous waste of time and money. This practice ceased immediately upon creation of the new *Baywatch*.

At our warehouse studio we had two main editors, each assigned to his own episode. Most of the time the editor assembles the show, and then the director comes in and takes a pass. Finally it is turned over to the producer. I'll make my changes and then lock the picture.

No more notes from Grant Tinker. It is not a matter of whether his notes were useful or not—his notes were always good. And given another day or two, I can always make incremental improvements in any one episode. But it's a business. Get the show to length and lock it. That's what we do, make the best show we can with the money we have.

This first season, especially, money was key. By contractual agreement with All American, if we went over budget, we would lose control of the show, something we were loathe to have happen. We—Berk, Schwartz, and Bonann—were also responsible for half of any overages. To maintain our creative control and to stay out of the poorhouse, we had to stay on budget. Besides, the audience doesn't watch an episode, they watch a series. Acquiring an audience is a building process. Without a doubt, certain things help the ratings, for example promotion and publicity. If we buy an advertisement in *TV Guide*, the ratings go up. If that ad promises something special, such as Connie Stevens playing the mother of the Pamela Anderson character, that's even better.

Inevitably, one or two episodes are dogs. You can't air the dogs at the beginning of the season, when the audience is sampling your series. We put a lot of money into the early shows to establish an audience up front. Then we put the dogs at the end of the season. Hopefully, by then we have gained a loyal audience and they will still watch it because they are fans.

Since the beginning of syndication, we have stayed true to the philosophy: If you are short, don't worry about it. We can always make it longer. We can always shoot more. If you are long, you have really screwed up. The network always wanted it long, 60-page scripts, which added *20*

Having a star like Connie Stevens on an episode will hopefully boost ratings.

minutes of extra screen time, so they could nit-pick it to death, cut this, cut that, cut out complete scenes.

"Throw money at it" is all they knew. Certainly everyone wants to be considered a great artiste, a master of the craft, willing to go to any length in order to make the best show possible. But ultimately the show is judged on its dollar. Does it bring in more than it costs? That is the fundamental equation in any business. And they just didn't get it. NBC would cut scenes that had taken me days to shoot. Why? Because they didn't like some minor aspect of it. It was an indulgence on their part that I still find astounding.

NBC, ABC, and CBS have had a monopoly for decades. Now they have competition: UPN, Fox, WB, HBO, Showtime. These new networks are filled with people like me, doing exactly the same thing: coming in short, making it longer if necessary, never wasting a thing. At *Baywatch*, our motto became simply: We make the best show we can with the money we have. Ultimately the best show is made by talented people who are utilizing sound business sense.

Midway through the first season, around episode 14, our domestic distributors, LBS, Henry and Paul Siegel, went bankrupt. No one in the industry was particularly surprised at their departure, nor did anyone mourn the event.

Upon the demise of LBS, All American decided to expand their company's focus. Now, not only would they guarantee the show, but they would also become the domestic distributors of *Baywatch*. It seemed like a natural evolution for them. They owned the copyright. They had arranged cash flow facilities. If they owned the distribution rights, they would control another pivotal piece of the whole formula.

Distribution, at that time, was a relatively low-risk business and the profits could be staggering. But All American's first duty to *Baywatch* was to serve as the guarantors.

By this time we had spent all of Fremantle's foreign advance money ($400,000 X 22) in making the first 14 episodes. All American, however, was not yet receiving its advertising revenues from these shows. The All American executives told us they were under a tremendous financial crunch. To relieve this burden, they asked the four executive producers to defer their salaries. Hasselhoff politely declined and demanded to be paid. The three remaining executive producers, Doug, Michael, and I, agreed. For 12 weeks we went without our salaries, which at the time amounted to $10,000 a week, each.

Twelve weeks later All American called us again. It happened that the All American executives were flying from Los Angeles to New York. The Berk, Schwartz, Bonann team and our attorneys were gathered around the speaker phone in my office. After the usual preliminaries, Tony Scotti, head of All American, told us that the loan facility his company had set into place had fallen apart. Would we, Berk, Schwartz, and Bonann, agree to defer our salaries once more?

After a brief exchange, our attorney Peter Dekom stepped to the plate. Dekom shouted into the speaker phone, "Your first priority is to supply the show with cash. Write a fucking check out of your own checkbook. That's what this business is about." Click.

Had the air conditioning broken down? This distracting thought entered my consciousness as I felt a solitary bead of sweat course down my back. Peter Dekom is a tough player, as tough as his All American opponents. Tony Scotti had probably been thinking, *Berk, Schwartz, and Bonann went for it once, maybe they'll go for it again.* Dekom kept telling us, "That's what All American is here for. They're supposed to 'cash flow' the business. Otherwise, you could do *Baywatch* without All American. They'll pay you. They must pay you!"

Dekom was right. All American, it turned out, did have the money, or at least access to it. They just didn't want to write the check. It was that simple. Good, clean, capitalistic, hard ball stuff. All American never forgave Leigh Brecheen and Peter Dekom. They still don't like Leigh, but by now it has been so long they can't remember why.

Now that we had the money to continue, Monte Markham, our veteran actor who played Captain Thorpe, directed his episode, "Sandcastles," about a 15-year-old runaway, played by Nikki Cox (her first big acting job), who lives under the pier. Through the course of the show, the runaway is finally convinced to return home.

Monte turned out to be an excellent director. On the set, he worked well with the actors, guiding them expertly through the scenes. Better yet, Monte wasn't hesitant about doing the massive preparation that is needed before the cameras started rolling. Actor-directors often don't realize that directing is mainly about preparation. Quite frequently when you tell an actor-director that he must take the preceding episode off in order to prepare to direct, they say, "What do you mean take an episode off?" It shows an ignorance on their part, although this was not the case with Monte. He had been around long enough to know how it really works.

In the prep phase, the director will study the script, looking at the broad issues: Is this an action episode or a drama? Is it character-driven or guest star–driven? Basically he studies the script to figure out where he'll want to spend his time directing. If he has an important guest star like Connie Stevens, her presence will dictate that he spend more time on her scenes. It follows that less important scenes will be shot more quickly. Then the director meets with the executive producer and the writer. The director will present his view of the script, and together they will sort out how it should be filmed. The budget rules the decision-making process— out goes the ocean liner. In comes the fiberglass fishing boat.

Next the director sits with Frank Conway, the line producer (Paul Cajero the first six years), and the assistant director assigned to this episode, and boards the show. Boarding a show means breaking the script into the most efficient shooting days we can arrange. Obviously we must ignore the actual, linear progression of the story in favor of grouping certain scenes together. If the script calls for three separate scenes to be shot in a Starbucks, we'll group them together. Or more likely, if the guest star is available for only two days, all their pages must be plucked out of the script and shot in rapid succession.

If, after thoroughly boarding the show, the director ends up with a half-day shoot at Will Rogers beach and a half day at the warehouse studio, the script must be rewritten to allow a full day at one set or the other. Our audience prefers beach scenes, so if possible we'll rewrite the script toward moving the warehouse scenes to the beach.

We often encountered a similar dilemma at NBC. The network solution was invariably to work a half day at Will Rogers and then move to the stage for the remainder of the day. That move costs $20,000, a huge sum. Worse yet, those dollars never end up on the screen, meaning the episode doesn't look any better for having spent the money.

Nikki Cox's first big acting role was in the episode called "Sandcastles." She's shown here being rescued by David Hasselhoff.

I n that first year of syndication, we managed to do our part creatively (producing shows that satisfied our standards and ITV's guidelines) and financially (staying on budget). All American, in their role as our distributor, was then challenged to do their part. You can challenge someone just by holding up your end of the bargain. This can serve as powerful motivation for the other members of the team, in our case All American.

Throughout the industry, an uneasy alliance exists between the producer and the distributor. The producer feels that the distributor, whether it's a big network like NBC or an independent like All American, considers the producer's beloved show to be nothing more than filler between commercials.

After spending months resurrecting *Baywatch*, the act of handing it over to All American was predictably difficult. Later it was even more difficult to sit in a meeting and hear them say, "Channel 9 in San Francisco has given us a bad time slot. They don't seem to understand the show." I said, "Wait a minute, let me talk to them." All American replied, "That's our business, not yours."

At the end of the first season, All American agreed to let us talk to the buyers. The buyers told us they wanted more "soap," more relationships, more love. When we lost Billy and Erika (who both set sail on a search for better-paying acting jobs), we recast David Charvet, who was younger than Billy, and Nicole Eggert, who was younger than Erika. We put them into a high school mode, and the buyers loved it.

The buyers said, "We noticed a lot of people tune out about halfway through." We said, okay, we will put the second action beat, which would usually come at the end, at the halfway point.

Most producers would have said, "I'm going to make the show my way, end of discussion." The network would have responded, "Okay, you're canceled."

(Above) Watching the water, or at least pretending to watch—Nicole Eggert and David Charvet (playing Summer Quinn and Matt Brody). (Opposite) Nicole emerging from the blue Pacific. Nobody looked better wet.

Getting renewed for a second year (a joint decision by All American and Berk, Schwartz, Bonann) was not a slam dunk. Overall the show was doing well, ratings were excellent; costs were under control. But the profits were not at the level we needed. In order to improve the profits, we had to get *Baywatch* distributed into a greater percentage of the country, in the mid–90 percent range. The only way to do this was through another visit to NATPE.

A producer in first-run syndication needs an intimate knowledge of production. He must also know marketing and distribution. I doubt if any network producers have ever sat in a room with a station manager from Little Rock, Arkansas, and listened to him describe his station's particular needs.

If he airs *Baywatch* at 8:00 P.M. and he doesn't get his audience, then he is screwed at 9:00 and he's dead in the water at 10:00. And then his local news show at 11:00, where he can actually make some money, will be history. He's taking a huge risk putting you on at 8:00 P.M. He tells you he wants a family show; he wants action; he wants big name stars to appear throughout the season; he wants soft-news items that he can use to promote *Baywatch*.

I sat in these meetings and I listened. If I had been an established, hugely successful producer, with a powerful network and studio backing me up, I would not have taken the time. But I wasn't. I needed to listen, and I needed to make a commitment to deliver the show each station desired. I fully understood that my passion, *Baywatch*, was another man's commerce.

At the time, the networks were not in 100 percent of the country. ABC has 95 percent, NBC has 92 percent, CBS has 94 percent, and Fox has 74 percent. (Fox must be under 75 percent so as not to be legally counted as a network, which allows them to play by different rules.) At the start of the second season, 10 NBC affiliates, 7 CBS affiliates, and 8 ABC affiliates decided that *Baywatch* would get better ratings than a show being offered to them by their respective network. These affiliates bought *Baywatch* and used it to preempt a network show. This rarely happens. It's a bad sign for the network, especially if the affiliates are in a top 10 market, but it was good for *Baywatch*. By the beginning of the second season we were being distributed in 94 percent of the country.

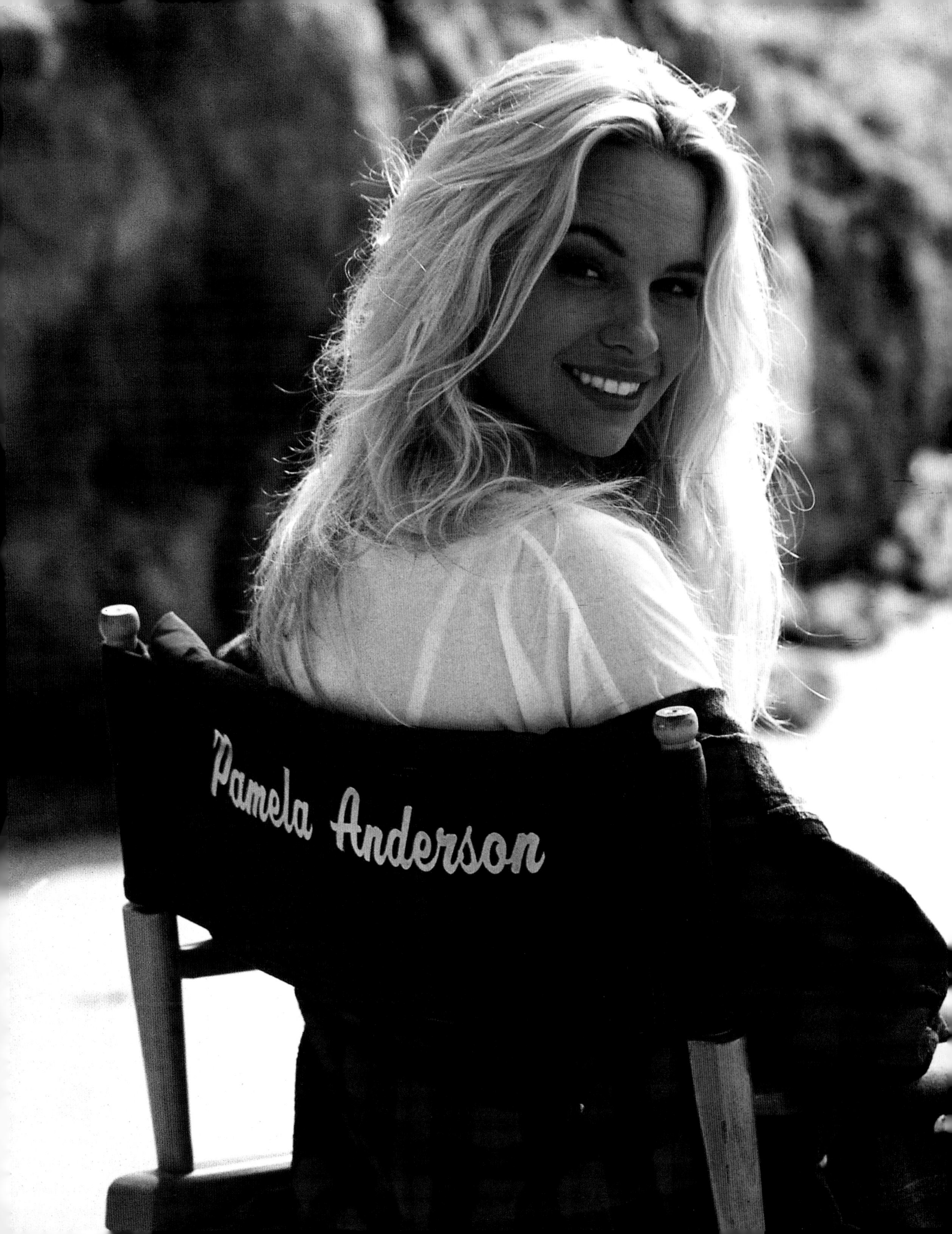
Pamela Anderson

CHAPTER 10

Second Season: Poor Man, Stuntmen, and the Catalina Flyer

Like hunters going on safari, several NBC network people, led by Perry Simon, drove through the not-so-nice areas of Los Angeles to visit our warehouse studio and see for themselves the source of their preempted headaches.

During lunch I took them on a quick tour of our offices, editing rooms, wardrobe, casting, and finally our newly constructed tank. At NBC, a trip to these various departments would have involved a bike ride across a sprawling lot or more likely a drive across town on a crowded freeway. The hassles that can be avoided by having everything in tight proximity are phenomenal.

At one point, an NBC person said, "Where are all of the producers?"

I said, "We have only four, Berk, Schwartz, Bonann, and Hasselhoff. Hasselhoff acts and produces. I direct and produce. Doug Schwartz directs and produces. Michael Berk writes and produces. We are all doing a bunch of different tasks."

At NBC we'd had 13 credited producers.

Perry asked, "How do you do it so fast?"

I said, "After the editors have assembled it and the director has had his pass, I go up, take a look, and lock the picture." They said, "Oh, that's right. You don't have to send it to a network. I bet that saves time."

(Opposite) Pamela Anderson came to us during the second season of syndication, ready to set the world on fire.

We shot Kelly Slater, one of our lead actors at the time, competing at the OP Surfing Championships in Huntington Beach. Later we used the footage in an episode.

(Above) Assistant Director Frank Conway and I conferring on a shot—or, more likely, discussing whose truck is parked in the wrong place and interfering with the shot. (Right) The day my appendix burst, Frank (with megaphone) managed to get us through the day.

Time? If it was about time, it wouldn't matter. We all have plenty of time. It's about money. They don't understand that in our business the old cliché holds true: Time is money, the only difference being time is BIG money. No one at the network really understands this concept because they are all on salary. For us, if more money is in the pot when the show is finished, that's more money in our pockets.

We shoot an episode in five days. The first season we delivered 22 episodes of *Baywatch* in 32 weeks. Most production companies need 42–46 weeks to produce and deliver 22 episodes. We have designed our whole system to move fast, and we simply don't have time—which translates into money—for network or studio people.

The networks employ dozens of creative development people, dramatic development people, comedy development people—these people just get in the way. They should hire someone like Grant Tinker, Steven Bochco, Aaron Spelling, Dick Wolf, or Chris Carter, and then get out of their way. All NBC needs is a solitary guy who can say, "Bochco, we have problems clearing your show in the south because they're so conservative. Don't use bad language. Everything else, go for it."

The network people left *Baywatch* without saying much. What could they say?

We all have our problems, our challenges. For us, problems occur when things happen that simply cannot be anticipated. When those things happen on the set, the best way to extricate yourself from the situation is to have a really good A.D., assistant director. I am fortunate to have Frank Conway.

During the second season I was directing an episode featuring our surfer/actor Kelly Slater. In this episode he was surfing at the national championships in Huntington Beach. About six hours into the day, I began to feel sick—really ill. But the show must go on, and the director must keep directing. Frank, seeing me come unglued, took me aside and gave me two "special little pills." I took them and almost immediately I felt fantastic. About two hours later I started feeling bad again. I said to Frank, "I've got to have two more of those pills." Frank said, "Okay, I'm going to give you two more but that is it. They're a heavy narcotic. No more after this." I took the pills and sure enough, I felt fantastic for two more hours. When those pills wore off, I felt worse than ever. As I was lying in the back of a flatbed truck, feeling awful, I said to Frank, "I need two more pills to get through the day's work." He said, "No way." I said, "Frank, give me those pills or you're fired." He finally relented, saying, "Okay. But absolutely no more. Period!" I took the pills and somehow managed to finish out the day.

The pills turned out to be aspirin. I had been taken in, hook, line, and sinker, by the placebo effect. Nothing like a good A.D. to help you get through the day.

Back home that night I called my father and told him how badly I was feeling. He immediately came over, took one look at me, and said, "Get to the hospital." My appendix had

ruptured two days earlier, but for some reason it was not tender to the touch, which kept the doctors I had seen from diagnosing it properly.

When I returned to the set, I saw Tai running on the beach. In a world of amazingly beautiful women, she stood out.

Once at the hospital, the doctors cut me open, took out my intestines, washed everything, and stuffed it all back in. Instead of finishing the episode, I stayed in the hospital for two weeks, where I passed the time reading the daily hot costs, which showed that episode screaming way over budget.

There was one silver lining—when I returned to the set I met my future girlfriend, Tai Collins, who had just recently joined the cast as one of our countless background people. She was running on the beach, and my eyes just kept going to her. With a person like Tai, incredibly beautiful, capable, fun, exciting, and just plain wonderful, it would be impossible for her to ever be in the background—not even for a moment.

When someone hires a producer to make a film or a television series, they are mainly hiring all the people with whom that producer works on a regular basis. I have Frank Conway, David Hagar, Stuart Asbjornsen, Gary Capo, Craig Kwasizur, and many others. The unknown ingredients, in many respects, are the starring actors. We have David Hasselhoff—a professional, consistent, steady performer. But unfortunately he is the exception. For a producer, if you want a lot of trouble, get a lot of stars.

Even if we wanted other stars, we could not afford them, nor do we need them. On *Baywatch*, our strength is in recasting. When we went from NBC to syndication, we recast Brandon Call, who played Hobie, with a young actor named Jeremy Jackson. Nobody missed

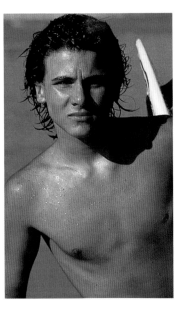
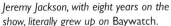

Jeremy Jackson, with eight years on the show, literally grew up on Baywatch.

Brandon. When we recast Billy Warlock with David Charvet, we didn't receive one critical letter. Later, we recast Charvet with David Chokachi—again, not one letter. And it is not because our audience can't write. We get sacks of fan mail each week from all over the world.

Jeremy ended up staying with the show for the next eight years. He literally grew up on *Baywatch*, going from a little kid to a mature adult. He was a natural when it came to acting, never missing a beat.

When Erika left the show at the end of the first syndicated season, she said, "I'm leaving because I don't want to be thought of as a *Baywatch* bimbo for the rest of my life." I said, "For all eternity, you're going to be Shauni, a lifeguard from *Baywatch*. Whether you're considered a bimbo or not is up to you to a large degree. The character you portray can be whatever you make of it."

No matter what, Erika will certainly be remembered as a *Baywatch* actor. How could it be otherwise? The show is watched by a billion people worldwide, every week. It will air in reruns forever. She could play Lady Macbeth for the rest of her life and never lose her *Baywatch* identity. She should have talked to Patrick Stewart, the great actor who mouthed the Bard's words for 20 years before taking on the role of Captain Piccard. On his first episode of *Star Trek, The Next Generation* he seen by more people than in all his on-stage performances combined. As with many actors, Erika was given bad advice, both from her agent and from her boyfriend at the time, Billy Warlock. Actors' rule No. 1: never leave a winner.

In Hollywood, a winner is defined as any show that continues in production. Certainly I can understand Erika's desire not to be niched as a bimbo. But in truth, the ratio of available actors to challenging roles is about a million to one. If I were an actor, and I had the choice between acting in a popular series or sitting home reading *Vanity Fair* and waiting for my agent to call, I would just as soon work.

Series television is a magical place, and that magic can be summed up in one word: residuals, the additional payment an actor receives when a show is rerun. The domestic residual formula pays 40 percent of the original salary. Suppose, Erika, for example, was paid $4,000 to act in an episode, she would receive $1,600 the first time that episode airs in reruns. The percentages decrease the number of times it is shown: from 40 percent, to 30 percent the next run, all the way down to 15 percent at the end of 10 runs. Also, it should be noted that a cap exists, which limits the residual payments for those stars who make astronomical salaries.

When I first hire an actor for one of our regular roles, I tell him, "We can only pay you this amount…" After he calms down and I explain to him the residual structure—which will eventually pay him 235 percent of his original salary—he cheers up.

Often an actor will say, "What if we get canceled?" I tell him, "This is first run syndication. We have a 22 episode order. We cannot be canceled, at least not until the order is filled." If, for example, Erika was initially making $4,000 an episode, she would eventually make $15,000 in total, per episode. Not bad for a week's work, especially when multiplied times 22, the number of episodes each season.

I discuss these figures with our actors and their representatives. I show them the percentages that would accrue from their staying with the show. Yet still, by the second season of syndication, two of our regulars were quitting: Erika Eleniak and Billy Warlock. Needless to say, for weeks on end we had a steady parade of potential replacements marching through my office.

Sex and money—it all boils down to one or the other. Billy Warlock thought he should get more money. Erika was worried that having the image of Playboy sex kitten/Baywatch bimbo would type-cast her for life.

To replace Billy Warlock, we narrowed the field to 15 men. My preference was for Dean Cain, who went on to star in *Lois and Clark*. David Charvet came in—five times. Each time, after he left, I said, "No way. He doesn't have the look we need." And each time our casting ladies, Susie and Fern, would storm over to my desk, saying, "What are you doing letting him walk out of here? This guy is awesome." I ultimately deferred to the experts. David Charvet was hired.

Susie and Fern were certain that they had found just the right woman to replace Erika. Unfortunately, this woman kept missing her audition, four times in a row. Usually this is the kiss of death. The last thing we need is an actor who cannot fulfill his or her most basic commitment—being on time for the audition. Still, our casting ladies told me to keep an open mind. This actor would show up soon enough and she'd blow my socks off. I knew to trust the judgment of our casting ladies—they understood exactly what worked on the show.

Why casting ladies? Why not "casting gentlemen"? The problem is the "casting couch," a phrase used to denote the age-old practice of trading sex for a role in a movie or on a television show. Reverse sexism be damned, the best way to steer clear of that abyss is to give the casting process over to women. Susie Glicksman and Fern Orenstein do an exceptionally good job finding the right people.

On one of the last days of auditions, we were scheduled to see about 40 women. In the days leading up to it, we had auditioned dozens more, including Paula Abdul (way too short) and Sandra Bullock (not the look we wanted).

From the beginning of *Baywatch*, my lifeguard friends have told me how much they envied my job on the day of auditions. In the abstract, it does seem great. But when you actually get down to it, the whole process is a strange and somewhat surreal ordeal. I came from a competitive swimming background—the winner of the race was the swimmer who touched the wall first. Landing a role on a series is exactly the opposite kind of competition, an utterly subjective test. Without glancing at the waiting room, I knew ahead of time that each of the 40 actors I would be seeing had great physiques, lovely smiles, a lively personality. But by the end of the day, 39 of those women were guaranteed to be extremely disappointed. The unpleasant part of the audition process was in having to tell those women that they had lost out. (It's clear, too, that an actor without a bulletproof ego is not going to last long in this business.)

Finally, the long-awaited actor showed up: Pamela Anderson. With all four executive producers in the room we asked her to read a page from the script. She stood up, pulled off her sweater, unwrapped her skirt—revealing a tight, one-piece bathing suit—and started to read. We hadn't asked her to wear the suit—she did it all on her own. I guess you could say Pamela was already into the part. And she read well.

Whenever we audition a new woman, we always ask a key question: "Will you have a problem performing 90 percent of your scenes in a red one-piece bathing suit?" The one-piece suit is our show's uniform. If they have a problem, we can't use them. (The question was

Pamela Anderson had a much softer look when she first came to the show.

somewhat unnecessary in Pamela's case, since she was already appropriately clothed.)

Pamela's response was straightforward: "If possible I'd work in the nude." She loves to show off her body. She is the most uninhibited actor we have ever had, male or female. It's obvious from the clothes she wears, both on and off the set, that the word "demure" is not part of her regular vocabulary. With Pamela, we knew we had something special.

You can measure a star's heat by the type of requests they generate from affiliate stations, magazines, tabloid television, print tabloids, even the Internet. Gradually, over a period of two years, Pamela began to generate a phenomenal amount of heat. In our society, heat has its rewards. Recently she was paid $100,000 to go to Australia to host their "Media Awards." She puts out a popular calendar each Christmas. Too bad she doesn't make any money from having her photo downloaded on the Internet—she would be the wealthiest woman in the world.

Because of her *Baywatch* fame, she made a small fortune away from the set. To some degree, this also holds true for our other actors. That's one of the reasons we feel justified in paying our actors a relatively modest wage. We know they are going to make a huge amount of money in other ways. Pamela sold her quasi-divorce story to *The National Enquirer* for $100,000. She sold her baby's pictures, worldwide, for $450,000.

Pam's passion for acting was
unexpectedly strong—not so surprising was her passion for David
Charvet, her boyfriend at the time.

Why is Pamela paid so much to memorialize these events, which for the rest of us are restricted to the annual Christmas card? *Baywatch*.

Her fame arrived in concert with a unique time in media history: the rise of the soft-news program, such as *Day and Date*, *Hard Copy*, *Inside Edition*, and the undisputed king, *Entertainment Tonight*. These shows don't want stories about famine in Zaire or the latest breakthrough in computer software. They need photogenic, harmless, puff pieces to capture the imagination of their mall-shopping, gossip-talking, middle-American audience. Tattoos are encouraged. Enter Pamela. She was tailor made for these shows.

Part of the producer's job is finding good people like Pamela Anderson. Then the director must figure out how best to utilize their relative acting abilities. As an actor, Pamela showed herself to be excellent at performing action scenes, particularly swimming underwater. Before long, we included a clip of her swimming underwater in the opening credits.

In general, when it comes to filming action scenes, the director has two choices: the expensive way or the "poor man" process. Early on, when a script called for David Hasselhoff to leap from the rescue boat to the bad guy's boat as they were speeding through the water, I shot it the expensive way. This meant shooting a master using a stuntman, who actually jumped from one boat to the other. The stuntman had to rehearse for two hours while everyone sat around and watched. (And besides paying him $1,000 to perform the stunt, I had to pay him a residual every time that episode aired or if I used the footage of the stunt again in another episode.) After piecing the sequence together, everyone said it was ridiculous. A stuntman was obviously doing the actual jump.

Only a seasoned, capable, competent lifeguard, such as Jim Doman, could row a dory through big surf intact.

The alternative is the "poor man" process. I shot Hasselhoff hanging onto the boat's railing, pretending to launch himself into the air, as though he was making the jump. Then I put him on the other boat—the one he was supposedly jumping to—and filmed him leaping from the gunnel onto the deck. Then I went to the beach, pointed the camera at the blue sky, and had David jump over me while looking down, so that his face was captured on film.

When I pieced it together using only the three Hasselhoff shots—omitting the stuntman/master—everyone agreed it looked better. Why bother with the extra money and time by using the stuntman, especially when it is better without him? The key is for the director to initially envision the scene using the poor man process, a skill I've had to develop because of our budget limitations.

Often we use real lifeguards instead of stuntmen. For example, when a scene calls for a dory to be rowed through the surf, I prefer to hire a lifeguard for $150 a day rather than a stuntman for $1,000 plus residuals. The stuntman would have to learn how to row a dory. And, when filming, I would have to surround him with real lifeguards to protect his safety. A lifeguard, who has been rowing a dory for years, would have no problem pulling off the trick.

From the beginning of syndication I said, "This isn't a stuntman show." Stuntmen look like stuntmen, they row like stuntmen, they swim like stuntmen. I wanted lifeguards who knew how to run, knees high, into the surf. My life became a lot easier when we hired Greg Barnett as our stunt coordinator. He understood that this was a series about lifeguards.

By the end of the second season I was coming into my own as "the king of the poor man process." But I began to realize that the real problem was unnecessary expenditures had a way of zipping past my desk so quickly that they went unnoticed—until the bills arrived. One such expenditure was a second-unit trip to Catalina (expensive), to shoot a sequence using stunt doubles for David Hasselhoff and Alexandra Paul (expensive), on Sunday night (very expensive), using a rented yacht for a prop (ouch). The few seconds of screen time they hoped to generate would cost $50,000, minimum. When I found out about this adventure—on the Friday afternoon before the trip—I called everyone into my office, Berk, Schwartz, Frank Conway, Paul Cajero, editor David Latham, for a meeting of the minds.

After the usual, "What the hell is going on? You guys want to spend $50,000 on a stunt? Are you crazy?" I went about telling them how to do it using the poor man process, which would look just as realistic and cost about $5,000. After laying out the whole scenario—using the real Hasselhoff and the real Alexandra falling through the air, day-for-night, I said to David Latham, "Can we do it? Can we do this stunt the poor man way?" Latham looked around at our expectant faces and said quietly, "Probably."

I immediately jumped up and yelled, "See? You heard what he said! He said PROBABLY!"

The trip was canceled.

Even with a boatload of second unit crew, Greg Barnett (below with Mitzi Kapture), keeps everyone safe when filming in the water. (Bottom) For "poor man" process we had David Hasselhoff stand on the gunnel, as though he was just about to leap off.

CHAPTER 11

Second Unit Rules

An action movie like *Lethal Weapon 4* can easily cost over $100 million. A talk-talk movie like *Gods and Monsters* rarely costs more than $40 million. The $60 million difference is due to only one thing: action. High-quality action sequences cost a phenomenal amount of money to record on film. *Baywatch* is an action show, but obviously we don't have the mammoth budget found in feature films. Our success comes from the ability to film action sequences for a relatively modest amount of money. In our case, the action is the exclusive domain of the second unit.

The first unit is like an army, with production trucks by the dozen and all manner of essential and ancillary players milling about. Like it or not, it takes an army to attend to the needs of the principal stars.

The second unit is our version of the Navy SEALS. It's far smaller—a dozen members vs. hundreds—more mobile, more likely to seek out the adventurous side of filmmaking. On most shows, the second unit is limited to shooting very simple items: establishing shots, drive-bys, inserts. And none of these shots includes principal actors. We developed a new definition of second unit for *Baywatch*: The second unit could shoot anything on the water. Anything underwater. Anything dangerous. Anything needing special preparation. Anything set to music. Anything

The **Baywatch** *main unit takes over in the sunshine while Gary Capo does masterful work with the camera—so masterful, in fact, that he has gone on to shoot some of the biggest films in Hollywood.*

exploding. These shots can be done with or without principal actors. Car chases, fist fights, explosions are all second-unit work. Additionally, the second unit must do the boring stuff found in the old definition—establishing shots, drive-bys, inserts.

The most vital part of our second unit's domain is water work. By its very nature, water work is very difficult to film. *Titanic*, *The Abyss*, *Waterworld*, *White Squall*, *Wind*—all these movies experienced mishaps during the filming of their water work.

Since we film so much of our show on and under the water, we have had to write the book on the subject. It starts off simply: prep, prepare, preparation. In a scene where the rescue boat is trying to pick up Hasselhoff and a victim, we want the cameraman to shoot from the water. But it's not so easy. Due to the tide, wind, and current, all three entities—boat, actors, and cameraman—are in a constant, swirling flux.

Now we have it down to a science. We rehearse on land, get it choreographed just right. Then we head to the water for one more rehearsal. Finally we shoot the sequence. Also, we have learned to always have the camera running while doing the in-the-water rehearsal. Who cares if an actor forgets a line? Knock it off, even if it's sloppy. If the footage is at all serviceable, we will use it for the master shot. Then we shoot the close-ups. When the actors and crew are in the water we want to move quickly, to limit their risk of hypothermia.

Besides preparation, the other key is location. We choose our locations carefully to remove the most difficult elements: strong winds and big waves. When they were filming *Waterworld*, we tried to tell them that building a million-dollar floating set on the

(Above) Filming on and under the water is the essence of second-unit work. That's me on the surfboard, directing. (Right) Our key second-unit guys: Stuart Asbjornsen, Chilli Jackson, and Matt Berner. They can shoot on land, on water, underwater. (Opposite) Having our own tank allows us to shoot a variety of water work in a tightly controlled environment.

windward side of the island might not be such a good idea. They passed on our advice, being more concerned with the set's proximity to the best hotels, the best restaurants, and the airport. Not long after it was completed, the set sank in a storm and had to be completely rebuilt.

We film most of our water work in our own "sweet spot," a place where the wind is almost always calm, the water is clean, and no buildings interfere with the background. For us, the sweet spot is just north of Marina del Rey. Here the jetty keeps the ocean swells down to a minimum. We take great advantage of the fact that the ocean looks essentially the same whether you are 50 yards off shore or 500 miles.

The other option for water work is to shoot in a tank. When we were at NBC, the only

suitable tank in town was owned by Warner Bros. To film the underwater work in our episode called "The Drowning Pool," we packed up and headed across town.

On Day 1 we put the set piece into the tank; on Day 2 we filled the tank with water and filtered it; on Day 3 we heated it; on Day 4 we shot; on Day 5 we drained the pool and pulled out the set piece. The Warner Bros. tank rented for $7,500 for prep/wrap days and $15,000 for shooting days, altogether $45,000 for the week.

In syndication, we decided to build our own tank next to the warehouse. Sometimes, smaller is better, as is the case with our tank. Our whole contraption can be drained, cleaned, refilled, filtered, and heated in just one night. We recouped the tank's $60,000 cost after two episodes.

For tank work, we rehearse thoroughly in the parking lot. First, an outline of the set piece that is underwater in the tank is drawn on the asphalt. Then, on my cue, the actors, in bathrobes, walk through the motions that I want them to perform underwater. Of course it looks hilarious, but it is essential. Otherwise they will be lost once they are underwater in the tank.

Greg Alan Williams did a great job portraying the real beach cop, Bob Aliniz.

Besides water work, our second unit films all the montages. I came to appreciate the artistic value of montages while making the Olympic documentaries. The challenge when making a documentary about something as familiar as the Olympic Games is that the outcome is already well known. Even worse, our primary subjects, American athletes, rarely won medals at the Winter Games. To keep the viewer's attention, I needed a different approach, something unlike the usual, linear, fact-filled progression. I experimented with matching certain pieces of music to the action, as was done so beautifully in *Chariots of Fire*. It worked remarkably well, greatly enhancing the competition footage. Also, I learned that using a conventional voice-over to dispense facts and figures wasn't necessary. In fact, it could often be intrusive. If we were showing a hockey match, for example, the audience gained the necessary information by flashing to the scoreboard, USSR 2 – USA 3.

Eventually we sold *Baywatch* on the strength of a montage presentation, and by now montages are an integral part of the show. Montages, when they work, really work. They give *Baywatch* a unique look, which, when added to our realistic portrayal of lifeguarding, gives the show a strong identity. I have had to work with our writers very closely to educate them as to the nature of what makes a good montage. The montage must move the story along in a definite manner. The writer cannot put the whole cast into a montage. At most, one or two of our regular cast members will be featured. The problem with our montages is that they are sometimes too long, which happens if we are using the montage to bring a short episode up to length.

One of the big fallacies about montages is that they are a way to save money. They are not. Per minute of screen time, montages are some of the most expensive things we do. They can contain expensive elements: several background actors, special effects, large wardrobe with literally dozens of changes. We need a mountain of film stock since we often shoot in slow motion. Three to five times as much film is needed to shoot an actor running down the beach in slow motion as compared to regular speed.

Also, we must buy the worldwide rights in perpetuity to the song we are using, which can cost $25,000. For Seal's "Future Love Paradise" we had to pay $15,000 for the synchronized rights, to the person who wrote the song, and $10,000 for the master rights, to the individual or group who actually performed it. Few shows in the history of television have had to contend with worldwide, long-term matters. Needless to say, it gets very expensive.

For one of our better montages, we had Pamela Anderson and David Charvet reenact the famous scene from the movie *From Here to Eternity*, where Burt Lancaster and Deborah Kerr embrace on the sand as surf sweeps over them. The energy of that particular scene hasn't diminished in the slightest over the years. I was worried that the recreated version might be too sexy. I always imagine a grandmother and her little granddaughter watching the episode together. Is anyone going to blush?

Episodic television is a collaborative art, but a dozen different opinions wouldn't work. Doug, Michael, and I have an iron-clad vote rule. We argue a point, we yell, we scream, and then we vote. Once the majority is established, the tally is final. No more arguing, no more screaming. The issue is finished. After David Hagar and I cut the Pamela Anderson–David Charvet montage, I screened it for Doug and Michael. They both loved it, and neither man thought it would offend any delicate sensibilities.

Our ensemble cast evolves over time. Below are our cast line-ups for (from top) season 3, season 6, and season 9. Following pages: in our montages, the song comes first, then the visuals, wardrobe, and finally the setting. Lastly, we shoot!

We have an ensemble cast, 11 regular actors altogether. The great advantage in having so many cast members is that we can play up an actor's individual strengths through their *Baywatch* character.

Also, we can introduce romantic themes by pairing up certain members of the ensemble, for instance David Charvet and Pamela Anderson. For a time they were boyfriend–girlfriend in real life, which made it even better. No faking required—they were truly passionate about each other.

During the NBC season our full cast appeared in every episode, even if they just walked through and said hello. The network thought someone in the audience might be a big fan of a certain character, and they didn't want to disappoint that particular member of the audience.

The payment structure for actors is important in terms of the overall budget for a series. To begin with, an actor gets paid his full episodic salary if he appears on screen, whether it's for three seconds or thirty minutes. (Also, if an actor's contract calls for him to appear in ten episodes, and for some reason he appears in only five episodes, he still gets paid for all ten episodes.) When we recreated *Baywatch*, we avoided the huge expense of having each actor appear in every episode. For new actors, our contracts call for them to appear in only 12 of 22 episodes. By their fourth year they are guaranteed to be in 16 out of 22 episodes.

Having an ensemble cast gives us more options. If the first unit is shooting two people talking on stage, the second unit can shoot another actor in an action scene. If an actor says, "I don't feel well," they are out. Search and replace, C.J. instead of Caroline.

With 11 actors, someone is always leaving the show and new actors are coming on board. When Brandon Call left, we kept his character, Hobie Buchannon, and simply brought in a new actor to assume the role. More often, when an actor leaves, a new character is created for the incoming actor.

We sign our new actors to five-year contracts. They are always tickled pink to scratch their name on the dotted line. They want to have their picture taken as they sign it. They want to keep the pen they used. We start each actor at $2,500 an episode, with a 20 percent raise each year. No other crew member gets that large of a raise.

In many cases, this is the biggest thing in the actor's career. If, after a few seasons, they walk into my office and demand more money, I tell them, "If you are unhappy, leave. But we can't pay you more. The money is not in the budget."

As long as the actor is under contract to us, we have a legal right to keep him or her from working in other film or television projects. This holds true even if we are not using the actor, just as long as we keep paying them the required amount as stated in their contract. We could also force the actor to work.

The *Baywatch*
Montage
"Silver"

Silver is coming down / Silver is washing over us

Silver is falling down / Silver all over this blue town

Silent night holy night / Winter is come behind the sun

Silver is coming down

Silver is washing over us

The heavens break the heavens break

And my soul away let this soul can take

Rising above the lonely lake

A frozen hand opens holding a flame

Bringing us peace and sweet belief

Silver is coming down / Silver is washing over us

Silver is falling down / Silver all over this blue town

If they sign the contract, they must come to work. Yet we have never done that. If an actor is unhappy and wants out, we let him or her go. We don't need any whiners.

If we hire an actor who does not have a manager or agent, I recommend they get one. The representative can sort out the legalese contained in the contract. I also recommend to the actor that he or she pay this manager or agent a percentage of their income, in the 5 percent range, to keep everyone vested and happy. If the manager/agent is not making any money because the client is on *Baywatch*, he or she might encourage the actor to leave the show.

The main problem I have with agents is that on occasion they have convinced an actor to leave the show. The agent tells the actor how much they are doing for *Baywatch* and how much more money they should be making. Then the agent tells the client what actors are making on other shows, a figure that is invariably grossly inflated.

It is a long, slow evolution, the process of becoming unhappy, one that takes place over the course of a season. I hear the pay-me-more-money blues ringing in my ears every day, either on the phone or in person. I have learned to anticipate it, recognize it, and combat it. I tell the actor

what the show is doing for them. Hopefully this will neutralize what the agent is saying. But when it doesn't, when the water is poisoned to a fatal degree, then it gets serious. The phone rings and it is the actor or the actor's agent, saying, "Give us more money or we are out of here." Once I tell them no, they are stuck. They can't backpedal and say they were just kidding. Now the actor is doubly unhappy, and soon they are gone.

I tell the actors, don't let your agent persuade you to do something you don't want to do. Ultimately you are going to take the fall. The agent represents the actor, not vice versa. Erika, Billy, Nicole, and David Charvet all left the show because ultimately they drank the poison served up by their agents. And later on, all these actors called and asked for their old jobs back. I had to tell them: "Sorry, the position has been filled."

hen you are sitting in front of the tube, remote control in hand, depressing the channel-changing button at a rate of two stations a second, what causes you to halt the progression from Channel 2 to infinity? Is it the clever dialogue, an interesting character, a fascinating story? No. You stop for the visual. Television is a visual medium. I would often sit in my tower and visualize how something would "look" on camera, set against the blue sky, the lifeguard towers, the jetty with waves crashing against it, shimmering late afternoon light, on a deserted winter's day. How could I best capture that image on film?

When we are filming an "interior - headquarters" scene, I always ask myself, "If someone were to zap the show at this particular scene, would they stop?" Probably not. That's why we try to keep the non-beach scenes to a minimum. Once a viewer stops, you can keep their attention with dialogue, character, story, and action. But if they don't stop at all, you are lost. For the average viewer, myself included, it is all in the visuals.

The world of the beach and lifeguarding is a great subject for the visual medium of television.

I'm fortunate in that I tend to "see" scenes. I have been taking pictures all of my life—not the Kodak variety but pictures in my mind's eye. I think in terms of visuals, as opposed to more literary-verbal terms. When I read a book or a script I see what I'm reading: What's in the background? What's in the foreground? Is the camera moving? Sometimes I'll glance at a picture in a magazine and I'll see it moving, as though it is a solitary frame out of a continuous film.

To broaden my visual world, I make a point of regularly visiting big magazine racks. Magazines are great for inspiring new visual ideas. If I see a picture in a magazine that somehow stimulates a creative impulse, I buy the magazine and file the page in a "visuals" binder I keep in my office.

On one visit to the magazine stand, I noticed that every magazine, whether it was *Playboy*, *Cosmopolitan*, or a general interest magazine such as *People*, featured a woman on the cover. A television show like *Baywatch* is similar to a general interest magazine. Women watch men, and women also watch women. Men only watch women. Our viewership is 65 percent female. We have learned to put lots of women in the show.

During the NBC year, when I said to the network, "We want to cast this actor. She is perfect for the part," NBC would respond, "But she can't act." That may be true, but like it or not, a certain amount of television is pure modeling. It is a visual medium. People don't tune into *Baywatch* each week to evaluate the acting skills of our cast. They want to see handsome men and beautiful women in action, not necessarily performing Globe Theater–quality acting.

NBC, after agreeing to cast Erika Eleniak (*Playboy*'s Miss July '89), said they didn't want any more "Misses,"—Miss USA, Miss October, Miss Universe, Miss Nude Nicaragua. But that is exactly what the *Baywatch* audience wanted to see. When you look at our show today, you see many novice actors, but they all look great and overall it works quite well.

Part of the secret is in the writing, which Michael Berk has perfected. He keeps the dialogue short and simple. All soliloquies and expositions are left to David Hasselhoff. Let him describe the physiological ramifications of the bends. He can do it and make it work.

Unlike some shows, we are not married to the words. If Chokachi has a line of dialogue that causes him problems—"Her swimsuit had a red leather top and a yellow leather bottom"—we change it on the fly. Until the actor is on his feet delivering his lines, and the scene has been rehearsed, we can't know if he is capable of making it work. We have learned that it is easier on everyone if we simply change the dialogue to match the abilities of the actor. If we do alter any dialogue while on the set, the script coordinator, Tom Moore, takes center stage. It is his job to make sure that any information that is essential to the story is preserved once the changes are made. Tom has gotten so good at anticipating the effects of various changes that we rarely have a problem.

Quite often our novices become good actors. Acting on *Baywatch* should not be confused with working on the atom bomb. A certain amount of talent is helpful, but it is an achievable skill. Do it every day, and you will get better. David Charvet and David Chokachi (we mostly hire Davids) are good examples. They were print models. As actors, they are fine. Pam Anderson had been on *Home Improvement* as the Tool Time Girl. Her essential line was "Hi."

Hasselhoff is the undisputed king of *Baywatch* actors. He rarely reads the script before we shoot. He will come in, grab a cup of coffee, and by the time we have rehearsed it twice, he will know his dialogue, word for word.

For five years David was on *The Young and the Restless* where they did massive amounts of dialogue, then on *Knight Rider* for 90 episodes, and now *Baywatch* and *Baywatch Nights* for over 200 episodes. In addition to being experienced, he is a sharp, talented man with an almost photographic memory.

Hasselhoff's last-minute technique doesn't cost us any time. But once, when another actor tried the same strategy, it caused huge problems. After this actor's fifth consecutive send up (forgetting his line), I took him aside and said, "Okay, I'll start the clock right now. We will see how long it takes you to learn this scene, which you should have learned last night." By the time he mastered it, 20 minutes, 40 minutes, an hour later, I told him what that time cost us. He never did it again. An actor must come in prepared.

David Charvet proved to be a modest challenge for whoever was directing his episodes. We had to write, shoot, and edit especially for him. He memorized his dialogue, which is the wrong technique. An actor should internalize the dialogue, so that besides knowing the words, he knows the meaning and intent of the scene. Charvet would even memorize the other actors' lines. He

Hasselhoff in deep meditation in the moments before I shout "Action!"

would silently mouth the words while they were being spoken to him. Needless to say, it bugged the other actors to distraction.

Two years after he left *Baywatch*, David Charvet landed a role on *Melrose Place*. I received a call from their producer one day who said, "What the hell is going on?" I said, "Sit down for a minute. Here is what to do: no expository dialogue, no speeches over four lines, no business (a term used to describe any secondary activity that an actor is doing as part of the scene, such as eating, pouring drinks, folding laundry. Charvet could never duplicate the action at the same point of dialogue). Keep the blocking (movement within a scene) to an absolute minimum. Most of all, emphasize his athletic ability. The guy is a tremendous athlete."

Actors want fame and adulation, which is why they go through all the nonsense, the rejection, the general bullshit. I know that is true for Hasselhoff. Countless times he has said, "When I'm up on stage, I'm alive." Acting touches the very core of their being. Our women actors especially love performing. The loss of anonymity, the occasional hassle with a fan, or a run-in with an obnoxious photographer is a small price to pay. Actors love the limelight.

Having an experienced actor like Hasselhoff leading the charge works well. I have miles of footage showing him swimming to the rescue, always wearing red trunks, always with the harness of a rescue can draped over his right shoulder. I have him swimming left to right; I have him

The never-ending hair wars, Pamela vs. Nicole.

swimming right to left. And now, with our new editing machines, I can "flop" the negative, so that left–to–right action becomes right–to–left.

Basically, I never again need to shoot Hasselhoff running into the surf, diving through waves, coming up, seeing the victim, or swimming to the rescue. I have it all in stock. All I need is the victim-of-the-week yelling, "help, help," and then Hasselhoff connecting with the victim.

Since *Baywatch* is a "uniform" show, I can use the stock footage to fill a hole. We have one basic costume: a red bathing suit. We use the same sunglasses, wet suits, swim fins. And fortunately, real lifeguards don't wear jewelry. We have saved quite a lot of money by being a uniform show, not to mention the fact that it has eliminated any squabbling among the actors about what they are going to wear.

Hair is another matter. The "hair wars" began the first day that Pam Anderson and Nicole Eggert saw each other. With their similar size and body types, they both assumed that only their hair could differentiate them for the audience. Before coming to the set each morning, each one checked on the other woman's hair. More than once they both changed their hairstyle only to have it match perfectly a second time.

ow that *Baywatch* was established, I said to All American, "Do you want to save some money? Maybe a million dollars? Give me a pickup now. If you tell me now, in January, that you want to go another season, I'll have six months to prepare. We will be able to write the episodes ourselves. The show will have more continuity.

The industry is traditionally built upon a May pickup. When you get picked up in May, and you air in September, you have to start shooting in July or August. This gives you only a few weeks to prepare to go into production. Hundreds of pieces must be assembled, from solidifying deals with the actors to scheduling the sound stages. One of the most important pieces is the writing of scripts. Suppose you wanted to write a novel in two months. You would need an army of writers to complete the project, which is exactly what happens on network shows. They hire a huge writing staff. All American agreed to a January pickup, which allowed us to eliminate six writers.

The early pickup also gave us another option: the chance to sell a big, two-part episode as a movie. Blockbuster Video loves *Baywatch* movies. They know they are getting a good family show. Blockbuster gives its patrons three choices: a hot movie like *There's Something about Mary;* a straight-to-video movie, which is usually awful; or specialty movies, such as an episode of *Baywatch* called "Forbidden Paradise," six months before it airs on television. Blockbuster patrons know *Baywatch*. It is an established commodity. And the patrons rent *Baywatch* movies.

The production of "Forbidden Paradise" required the whole crew to work in Hawaii for 13 days. Doug handled the logistics, which was an impressive feat considering the complexity of taking 150 people to Hawaii. The trip was a raging success, thanks in part to a paparazzo with a long lens. During the filming of a montage, he took some racy photos of Pamela Anderson and David Charvet kissing under the famous Waimea Falls. Their passion was not all make believe since Pamela and David were a hot item at the time. This chemistry made for some great scenes. In this instance, when I yelled "Cut," they kept right on going.

The photos found their way into the tabloid *Star*, and the subsequent publicity was worth millions.

(Right) The covers for the home video versions of our two-part episodes. (Below) The breathless layout from the Star. Pamela Anderson and David Charvet just kept on kissing, even after the director called "Cut."

For More Information
1-800-WHY-MILK

When I'm not
giving
mouth-to-mouth
or consoling
a fellow
lifeguard
with
sun-damaged
hair,
I worry about
real-life
things like
getting
osteoporosis
when I'm older.
You know,
men
and women
are both
at risk when
they don't
get enough
calcium.
That's why
I drink
lots of
milk now.
1%.
And
depending
on how
much I drink,
I wait
a half hour
before
saving a
life.

MILK

Where's *your* mustache?℠

CHAPTER 12

Happy Baywatch Nights through Happy Days

By the beginning of season five we had a new personality-star emerging, Yasmine Bleeth. Yaz came on for one episode, playing Caroline Holden, the sister of Alexandra Paul's character, Stephanie Holden. she performed so well, we brought her into the cast full-time. It worked out well. Her whole look and demeanor served as a nice contrast to our other actors.

Back home at our warehouse studio, we had a serious matter to resolve: what next? It made incredible financial sense to hustle along 22 episodes of *Baywatch*, and finish them in record time. But then what should we do? The warehouse studio was sitting idle. Our crew needed more work. Hasselhoff did not want to wait seven months for next season's *Baywatch* production to begin. David Hasselhoff is the James Brown of television, the hardest-working man. He simply cannot tolerate being idle. The only way to take advantage of all our hard-earned resources, from warehouse studio to distribution system, was to mount another series.

Stop. Wrong. Very wrong. Having had time to reflect on it, that was not the ideal premise from which to begin a major undertaking.

As the legendary director Sidney Lumet writes in his book *Making Movies*, "Good work comes from passion." He is right. I had wanted to do *Baywatch* because I was passionate about telling the lifeguard's story. Passion, I believe, should lead the attack. I suppose you could have a

(Opposite) Yasmine got a milk mustache, the ultimate sign of success. She left at the end of season seven (1996) to pursue a career in feature films. You may have seen her in Baseketball *and later* Nash Bridges.

passion for making more money, and certainly the whole industry is built on turning a profit, but at this stage in our *Baywatch* life, we were already making decent money.

Nonetheless, we were a small company looking to expand. The reality of the market dictates that it is much easier to get a second series on the air while the first one is still ongoing. (An analogous theory applies to finding a new job—it is easier to find a new job when you already have one.) We marched ahead.

All American put up the money for us to produce a new one-hour dramatic series. Our job was to deliver the goods, starting with the basic script. After much discussion, in which Hasselhoff played a big part, we decided that the best way to capture a decent audience would be to carry over the Hasselhoff–Buchannon character from *Baywatch* into another series.

With that decision made, we then spent weeks arguing about the show's basic premise. Finally we settled on a series where Hasselhoff's *Baywatch* character, Mitch Buchannon, would moonlight as a private detective working out of a jazz club. Behold *Baywatch Nights*.

Right away *Nights* ran into problems. Hasselhoff wanted his *Nights* character to drive a hot car. He wanted him to wear snappy clothes. Michael Berk, who had the task of writing the initial script, kept saying, "Guys, this is not working. The audience will reject it. If he is still playing the character of Mitch Buchannon, a lifeguard, how can he drive a hot car? How can he afford these clothes? How can he leave Hobie at home while he goes out and solves some stupid crime?"

I kept saying to Michael, "This is not like *Baywatch*. This is *Baywatch Nights*. Think of it as basic commerce. We want the series to go ahead. Make it work, please."

The script was due before Christmas '94, but we missed that deadline. We truly were, at this point, in a riptide. No stopping possible. We had to deliver a show. That meant we had to conceive it, write it, cast it, build the sets, and shoot it. The clock was ticking.

Michael was still writing the script when NATPE '95 rolled around in January, held that year in Las Vegas. As I was preparing to leave for the conference in order to sell *Nights* to independent distributors (as we had done with *Baywatch*), Michael said, "Why should I sit here, racking my brain on this stupid concept while you and Doug go to NATPE and have all the fun?" I said, "Okay, take two days off. Come to NATPE and bring your lucky dice. We'll have a ball."

But at the same time All American, our parters for *Baywatch Nights*, was expecting to read a script. When they saw Michael wandering around the floor of NATPE, they hit the roof. We realized our mistake right away, but it was too late. All American, rightly so, went ballistic.

Hindsight being so excellent for one's vision, I realize now that Doug, Michael, and I had made a mistake coming to NATPE. We should have stayed in L.A. and worked on *Baywatch Nights*. That was the show that needed immediate attention. We were the driving force behind it. To shirk our responsibilities, even for a few days, was an error on our part.

Other incidents of a similar nature (not all of them emanating from Berk, Schwartz, and Bonann) served to disrupt the working relationship between All American and Berk, Schwartz, and Bonann. As mentioned earlier, the inherent relationship between producers and distributors is tenuous and prone to disagreement. It didn't take much to put our relationship with All American into a tailspin. We, Berk, Schwartz, and Bonann, found ourselves acting out of suspicion rather than mutual cooperation. We should have maintained the attitude: we could never have made it this far without All American; let's not sink the ship that brought us here.

Due to the deteriorating relationship, we wanted, more than ever, to hold up our end of the *Nights* bargain. Part of that bargain was that we find an actor, someone in addition to Hasselhoff, to cross over from *Baywatch* to *Baywatch Nights*. The logical actor was Gena Lee Nolin, who had been doing great work on *Baywatch*. To my surprise, when I offered her the part, she said she didn't want to do it. She was happy doing *Baywatch*, she said, but she did not want to do *Nights*. I thought it sounded peculiar: Why would anyone turn down such

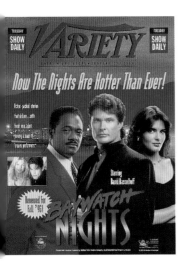

Look out world, here comes Baywatch Nights. *An advertisement in the* NATPE *edition of* Variety *promised big things.*

a great opportunity, not to mention the money? Finally we hired Donna D'Errico for *Baywatch Nights* and let her then cross over the other direction into *Baywatch*.

Four months later Gena called and said she wanted to talk. This time she came in with her husband and then-manager, Greg.

Gena said, "I don't want to be on *Baywatch* next year."

I said, "You're kidding. First you turned down *Nights* and now you're quitting *Baywatch*. What's wrong?"

She hemmed and hawed, but she wouldn't say. Obviously something major was going on in her life, but I was at a loss to figure out what it might be.

Finally, to get it out in the open, I asked her: "Are you willing to give up working in the industry for four years to get out of doing *Baywatch*?" Her contract stated that as long as we paid her, she could not get another acting job anywhere in the industry. Also, I could put her on the call sheet every day— on hold. That meant she would have to stay near the phone, all day, waiting for a call that she knew would never come. Those stipulations are in every actor's contract—not just *Baywatch*—and many producers exploit every clause at their disposal. At *Baywatch* we've never chosen to go that route.

Gena said, "Yes." She was willing to give up working in the industry.

To not work for four years is a serious matter. What exactly was the deal? She squirmed in her chair, obviously uncomfortable. For a moment I thought she might even bolt from the room. As she started to cry, she said, "I have a fear of the camera."

I couldn't believe it at first. After her years on *The Price Is Right*, and then all her *Baywatch* episodes, having a fear of the camera seemed impossible. She went on to say, "I study the script, I memorize it, and then, when I show up the next day, someone wants to change my dialogue or change a cue word. I have a nonstop stomachache. I live in fear. I can't do it anymore." Her husband nodded in agreement with everything she said.

I was stunned. I begged her to give it one more try. We had to fix this problem. As a possible solution I suggested to Gena that we try taking it one episode at a time. I would give her the scripts early, which we never do for anyone because they usually change so drastically. That way she could study the script thoroughly. Most of all, she would only act in the episodes that I directed, so that she could know with certainty that nothing would be changed on her at the last moment.

She said okay. The next season she acted in only the episodes I directed, and she did fine. Clearly she had not had a fear of the camera so much as a fear of changes being made that she couldn't handle. I gained a great deal of respect for her that year, knowing her fears, watching her meet them head on. She conquered them all. She is a real winner and I am very happy for her.

Gena Lee Nolin, red suit, yellow door, remarkably beautiful.

*An advertisement in
TV Guide told viewers
they'd see Donna as
only Playboy magazine
readers had
seen her.*

n real life, just about everyone is glad to be at the beach. Beach patrons might have driven from as far away as Grand Rapids or as close as Glendale. Everyone is happy when their feet touch the warm, clean sand.

When guarding, I particularly love the morning shift. I enjoy seeing the beach gradually fill up with patrons. A midweek summer day is like heaven. You can see an accountant playing hooky from work, an older couple letting the sun warm their bones. When I walk the beach, rescue can in hand, everyone waves and says hello. They know I am on the beach for only one purpose: to protect their well-being. I couldn't so much as write them a ticket. I am on the beach to guard lives. To me, the beach embodies the best of our modern life. It is an extraordinary, wondrous place, one that should be respected, appreciated, and enjoyed by all.

With that said, as much as I hate to do it, each season on *Baywatch* we show the beach in a somewhat less than realistic light. We feature episodes about gangs and sharks. I dislike gang shows and I particularly dislike shark shows because neither reflects the real beach life. I have never seen a shark while on duty in 30 years of lifeguarding. As long as I can remember, we have never had a shark attack at any Los Angeles County beach. A few years ago, when a kayaker was killed while paddling a mile offshore, everyone initially thought she had been attacked by a great white shark. It turned out she had been murdered by a fellow kayaker, who then disappeared.

Gang shows and shark shows receive good ratings because of the sensationalism and danger factor, which people inevitably find so intriguing. The *Jaws* theme lives on in the hearts of many swimmers.

But why do some episodes get good ratings and others do not? It is impossible to know the exact reason. Was it the show the week before? Was it the promotion for that particular episode, like an ad in *TV Guide*? An ad in one issue of *TV Guide* read, "Donna poses for *Playboy*. Sends shock waves through the beach." To some extent that is false advertising since the *Playboy* connection was only a "C" storyline, accounting for only 10 minutes out of the whole episode. Yet that type of promotion usually helps an episode to rate well because, as we all know, sex, on any level, sells.

Promotion is an enormous part of first-run syndication, something I didn't realize when we first started producing the new *Baywatch*. On a weekly basis, we must do battle against the networks, who have huge promotion, publicity, and public relations departments linked up around the country. If they have a show airing on Friday at 8:00 P.M., they can buy ads nationwide. We cannot. Our show airs on different days and at different times in various markets. To get the word out, we use other promotional strategies.

One of these strategies requires our featured actors to devote six weekends per season to promote the show. With a cast of 11 actors we can collectively send them to the top 66 markets. Basically they work until 8:00 P.M. on Friday. Then they take the red-eye or an early flight the next morning. They attend a party where they meet the buyers and sponsors in that market. Finally they get back to Los Angeles on Sunday evening. Monday morning they are at work, 6:00 A.M. It's a tough schedule, but at least they get to fly first class.

If we hadn't made *Baywatch* an ensemble show, only Hasselhoff would be available to do this sort of traveling promotion. The world is too big for one man to go everywhere, although he did visit Thailand last weekend to open a Hard Rock Cafe. He left on Friday night and came back on Sunday.

The promotion *Baywatch* has derived from *Playboy* magazine has been invaluable. Without a doubt, *Playboy* photographs women better than any magazine in the world. Pam Anderson has been on the cover six times, a record. We have had *The Girls of Baywatch* photo spreads. It's a good relationship. Playboy executives Gary Cole in Chicago and Marilyn Grabowski in Los Angeles have steered us toward some of our best people. And on occasion, we have returned the favor.

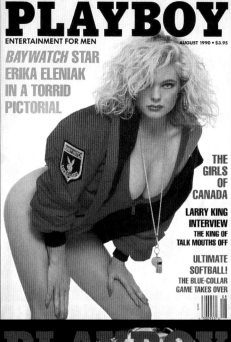

PLAYBOY

ENTERTAINMENT FOR MEN

AUGUST 1990 • $3.95

BAYWATCH STAR
ERIKA ELENIAK
IN A TORRID
PICTORIAL

THE
GIRLS
OF
CANADA

LARRY KING
INTERVIEW
THE KING OF
TALK MOUTHS OFF

ULTIMATE
SOFTBALL!
THE BLUE-COLLAR
GAME TAKES OVER

Over the years,
Baywatch and
Playboy
have been very
good for each other.

PLAYBOY

ENTERTAINMENT FOR MEN

DECEMBER 1993 • $5.95

Gala
Christmas
Issue

PLAYMATE
ERIKA
ELENIAK
BECOMES
A STAR

HOW MARLON
BRANDO
DESTROYED
PARADISE

AMERICANS
TALK ABOUT LUST:
THE HOT NEW
BOOK ON SEX

INTERVIEW:
RUSH
LIMBAUGH
GETS
IN OUR
FACE!

SEX STARS

PLUS
BRANFORD
MARSALIS,
BRUCE JAY
FRIEDMAN,
CARL HIAASEN,
THE COLLEGE
BASKETBALL
PREVIEW AND
MUCH MORE

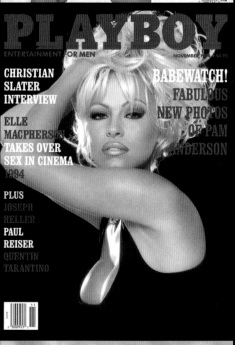

PLAYBOY

ENTERTAINMENT FOR MEN

NOVEMBER 1994 • $4.95

CHRISTIAN
SLATER
INTERVIEW

ELLE
MACPHERSON
TAKES OVER
SEX IN CINEMA
1994

PLUS
JOSEPH
HELLER
PAUL
REISER
QUENTIN
TARANTINO

BABEWATCH!
FABULOUS
NEW PHOTOS
OF PAM
ANDERSON

PLAYBOY

ENTERTAINMENT FOR MEN

JANUARY 1996 • $5.95

*Holiday
Anniversary
Issue*

THE ULTIMATE
PAM ANDERSON
PICTORIAL

IN DEEP WITH
JOHNNY DEPP
A SURPRISING
PLAYBOY
INTERVIEW

THE NBA'S
BADDEST BOY
DENNIS
RODMAN

VOTE IN
THE 1996
PLAYBOY
MUSIC POLL

A TUMULTUOUS
YEAR IN SEX

PLUS: ANAIS NIN
CONAN O'BRIEN
ROBIN QUIVERS
HAROLD ROBBINS
A FABULOUS
REVIEW OF THE
PAST DOZEN
PLAYMATES
AND
PLAYBOY'S
COLLEGE
BASKETBALL
FORECAST

PLAYBOY

ENTERTAINMENT FOR MEN

NOVEMBER 1996 • $4.95

DONNA
D'ERRICO
THE HOT
NEW
BAYWATCH
BABE

SEX IN
CINEMA
STRIPPED
BARE

SCOTT TUROW
A SHOCKING
THRILLER

CHRIS O'DONNELL
ANSWERS 20 QUESTIONS

LIAM
NEESON
INTERVIEW

RALPH REED
SMART AS
THE DEVIL

CAN YOU
PASS THE
PLAYMATE
TEST?

PLAYBOY

ENTERTAINMENT FOR MEN

MARCH 1998 • $4.95

THE NEW
BAYWATCH
BABE
MARLIECE
ANDRADA

KEVIN KLINE
INTERVIEW

CRITICS'
CHOICE
THE 25 BEST
RESTAURANTS
IN AMERICA

SWIMSUIT
ISSUE,
PLAYBOY
STYLE
(we left out those
annoying suits)

THE REAL
BOOGIE
NIGHTS
THE LIFE AND
DEATH OF
JOHN HOLMES

PLAYBOY

ENTERTAINMENT FOR MEN

JUNE 1998 • $4.95

COLLECTOR'S SPECIAL

Speed Thrills! Nascar Rules
The Funny Girls of Saturday Night Live
Mad About Paul Reiser Interview
20 Questions With Yasir Arafat
The Torrid History of Sex in
the Sixties—Everybody Was Doing It
Great Ideas for Summer
The Minidisc Takeover

*The Babes
of*
BAYWATCH

NAVY
FLIER
SHOWS
HER
STUFF
BREAKS
THE
PLAYBOY
BARRIER

Baywatch is similar to *Playboy* in some respects. Hugh Hefner, by charting his own path, created a whole new industry. At *Baywatch* we have done the same thing, charted a different course, and because of it we have found success. When I eventually met Hefner some years ago, he said, "You're probably the second luckiest guy in the world."

With *Playboy*, it is all about being on the cover, preferably the cover of an issue that can do us some good. Donna D'Errico, our newest star, was scheduled to be on the cover of *Playboy*—but the issue was supposed to hit the stands in the middle of summer, when *Baywatch* was in reruns. No good. Since Donna was not even in those episodes, I asked the people at *Playboy* if they could schedule Donna's cover for later in the year. Sorry, summer or nothing. Then, through sheer good luck, *Playboy* bought some photos of Uma Thurman topless on a beach, probably taken with a 600-mm lens. You could barely tell it was Uma—it may have been Uma's grandmother. Uma's spread bumped Donna to the November issue, which was perfect because it hit the newsstands in October, during our launch month. Long live *Baywatch* karma.

Relationships are vital for our success, relationships with publicity generators like *Playboy*, with affiliates, with the actors, and with a whole variety of business entities.

One of the more difficult relationships has been with the L.A. County Department of Beaches. The county oversees the locales where much of *Baywatch* is filmed. The original agreement between *Baywatch* and L.A. County, negotiated by me with the NBC and GTG attorneys, was extremely advantageous for us. We paid the county $50,000 a year for the right to use their name, official patches, badges, uniforms—everything.

In addition to this $50,000, we also agreed to pay all fees, permits, and parking. This final item, parking, sounds innocuous but it can amount to an astronomical sum. A solitary production trailer takes up five spaces in the parking lot. We are charged one-and-a-half times the daily rate, since that trailer will be parked in the same place all day, rather than in-and-out as with most beach patrons. A standard Will Rogers shoot requires dozens of these production trailers. Altogether these items—fees, permits, and parking—earned the county over $600,000 during the NBC year.

Then *Baywatch* was canceled. As I was mounting the new *Baywatch*, I went back to the county and said, "I can't afford the old deal. I'm considering going to New Zealand or Australia or San Diego because it's too expensive here." They said, "What do you need?"

I said, "I can pay only $15,000 a year. And I want to build our set on top of Will Rogers lifeguard headquarters." They said okay, but only if we got permission from the Coastal Commission and the building department. That took some doing. We ended up adding a lot of structural steel to the headquarters so that it would support another level.

Jump cut to several years later. We have the most popular show in the world. We now pay $800,000 a year to the county in fees, permits, and parking, an amount second only to Gladstone's Restaurant in Malibu as the top contributor to L.A. County coffers. Overall, the best thing that ever happened to the L.A. County beaches was the creation of *Baywatch*. Besides the money we pay, other shows have followed behind us. They pay even more money to the county.

Most importantly, *Baywatch* has brought tremendous awareness and respect to the whole county-beach scene. The real county lifeguards love *Baywatch*, and to me they are the ultimate arbiters of the show's validity and importance.

I made my original deal with Ted Reed, the head of L.A. County Department of Beaches and Harbors. When Ted retired, he was succeeded by Eric Berdon, who was then succeeded by Stan Wizniewski. Stan started as a fee collector at a beach parking lot and worked his way to the top. Quite an impressive feat.

Unfortunately, Stan was not a fan of *Baywatch*. For years he had felt that we should be paying more money to the county. Apparently Stan was on the board of directors when the original agreement was negotiated, and he recommended that the county not make the deal. (One of Stan's bosses, a member of the citizens advisory board—and also a William Morris agent—constantly pestered Stan to get more money from *Baywatch*.)

Now that Stan was in charge, he could control all future deals. Worse yet, he could attempt to manipulate the old ones. Soon after taking over in 1994, Stan announced that L.A. County had a proprietary right to the word "Baywatch," and since we had used that word for years, we owed the county a huge amount of money.

We created our own patches to better establish our show's unique identity and to distance ourselves from the L.A. County Department of Beaches.

Wrong. *Baywatch* was never a part of L.A. County's official lexicon; it did not even appear in the county's training manual. It had been used merely as a nickname for the rescue boats, Baywatch Hermosa, Baywatch del Rey, depending on the beach associated with that particular boat. But the word "Baywatch" wasn't even painted on the transom of the rescue boats.

Thanks to the education provided to me by Will Maguire, our trademark attorney (who is also a lifeguard buddy), I have learned that two things signify ownership of a word or mark: First, you must use and register the word or mark, which we did in 1991. Secondly, you must defend your ownership of that word or mark.

During the last five years we have spent over a million dollars defending our ownership of the word Baywatch.

When someone opened a Baywatch Beach Restaurant in Florida, we sued them and had it shut down. When someone published an illegal *Baywatch* Fan Club magazine, we sent them a cease and desist leter, and the magazine folded. The money we spent added up to our defense of the ownership. By all measures, including those of L.A. County's own legal counsel, Stan did not have a leg to stand on. After months of pursuing this dead end, he finally dropped his claim.

Because of this incident and other hassles with Stan, we decided to sever all nonessential relations with the county. We started by dropping any reference to L.A. County within the show. The *Baywatch* beach became a mythical beach rather than an L.A. County beach. We removed the county seal from the Scarab rescue boats and lifeguard trucks; we removed the official patches, badges, and embroidery from the lifeguard jackets and bathing suits. Everything associated with L.A. County disappeared.

Taking the place of the county seal was our own logo: the *Baywatch* tower with the setting sun in the background. Not only did it make us less reliant on Stan, it also increased the asset value of everything we owned.

Things quieted down until the inception of *Baywatch Nights*. Since we were already using the Will Rogers headquarters for *Baywatch*, we had hoped to build the *Baywatch Nights* set right next door. With *Baywatch Nights*, the county would have had a production company in place for 44 weeks a year, which would have earned them another $800,000 in fees, parking, and permits.

We have been using these Baywatch surfboards since the first season, yet Los Angeles County claimed that they "owned" the Baywatch logo. Get real!

Then Stan became involved. At last, through *Baywatch Nights*, he could extract his pound of flesh. He wanted an outrageous amount of money for the right to build the *Nights* set on county property. We tried to negotiate, but he held fast to his price.

Finally we dropped the whole idea and moved the *Nights* set to Paradise Cove, a private, gated community in the northern end of Malibu. We then spent $330,000 building a new *Nights* set in Paradise Cove.

Oddly enough, the day before production began on *Nights*, Stan called and suggested we get together to work something out. We had a brief meeting where I offered to fold the set at Paradise Cove and move it to Will Rogers, if he would cover the cost of the move. He declined my offer. Paradise Cove became the home for *Nights*.

Stan was left with little to do regarding *Baywatch*. But he still had his authority over the actual L.A. County lifeguards, or at least until 1996. At that time he was being forced by his superiors to make budget cuts. Rather than make his cuts across the board, he recommended reducing only the lifeguard's budget, since the lifeguards did not generate revenue, they only saved lives. The lifeguards called an emergency meeting. As a former member of the board, I was invited to attend. After a brief discussion, we voted to join the fire department.

Stan lost the crown jewel of his administration, the lifeguards. Now he has nothing to do with lifeguards. We are part of the L.A. County Fire Department, with our own Lifeguard Division.

It has worked out well. The fire department has an excellent infrastructure, elite training, top equipment, and great leadership. Just last week, as I was driving home from work, I saw a rescue under way near Will Rogers headquarters. I turned into the parking lot to see what was going on. A young woman had been swimming 100 yards offshore, and suddenly she disappeared. The ensuing rescue effort—lifeguards and firemen—was massive, with three rescue boats, 10 SCUBA divers, three helicopters (including a Coast Guard and police helicopter), and a mobile command center complete with media liaison. This impressive army searched well into the night, until the quest was finally halted. As it turned out, the woman was later found, unharmed, at a nearby gas station. She had been angry at her family and decided to disappear for a while. Still, a rescue effort of this size, scope, and professionalism was a stunning example of what could be expected now that the firemen and lifeguards were working together. The very next week we put a script into production, "Missing," that was based on this incident.

Every year the *Baywatch* production company had donated money to the county. We sponsored an L.A. County women's lifeguard team to compete in the National Championships. After the TWA Flight 800 crash off Long Island, we sponsored one of the best search and rescue men in the world, lifeguard Mickey Gallagher, along with two of his crew, to work on the salvage operation. The people who had been diving on the wreck, in their haste to make some progress, had developed a habit of coming up with a bad case of the bends.

Now we give our money to the lifeguard association. I am afraid that if we gave it to the county, it might never find its way to the people we are trying to assist.

Incident Report CS 94127
Narrative

At approximately 13:10 hours, we, Baywatch Santa Monica, Lt. Tom Estlow and Ol B. Hogue observed an individual dog paddling seaward and not using any armstrokes to be almost 300 yards from shore. We proceeded to advise him to swim parallel to the beach and swim closer to the beach.

Once on the scene, we noticed the suspect staring constantly into the sun and ignoring our advice. The subject stated that he "was swimming to Jesus" and didn't need our help. Due to the subjects inability to talk to us coherently, his constant wide-open eyes gazing directly into the sun, and his very poor swimming ability, we decided to place him on the rescue boat and return him to the beach. We requested additional personnel from the beach to assit and 201 for manpower. Due to the subject's behavior, we determined that he may be under the influence of an unknow substance or drug, so we requested a P.D. unit.

At about 13:15 hours BW Topanga (Lt. B. Robinson/ O.L. D. Shenbaum) arrived and were utilized to return the subject to the beach. Once the subject was brought aboard BW Topanga, he was hand-cuffed for his safety and that of the lifeguards. BW Topanga backed into the surfline where the subject was dropped into the water with the support of two OL deck hands, and brought to the Santa Monica P.D. unit waiting on the berm.

Major Incident Reports cross my desk each week. When appropriate, we work the incidents into an episode.

Incident Report CS 94190
Narrative

At 20:45 hrs., L.A. County Sheriff, Marina del Rey dispatcher notified CSH of a car that had driven off the Venice Pier. L.A.P.D. were on the scene, and requesting our assistance. Unit 201 responding with Thomas, Boiteux with unit 420, and Lt. Gallagher due to the nature of the call, and on scene supervision. Upon our arrival L.A. City Fire #63 informed us that the driver had been extracted, with no other occupants found. Driver drove vehicle across the sand on the North side of Venice Pier and came to a stop at the surf line. The vehicle did not drive off the Pier. At this time we double checked the vehicle for occupants, including the trunk, with no one found. Extrication of the vehicle from the surf commenced, with dual wrench operation from both units, 201 and 420. Vehicle was pulled to high sand, and released to private tow truck.

Vehicle information: Nissan Maxima four door, license plate CA 3CTH958

Entertainment WEEKLY

NO. 191 ◆ OCTOBER 8, 1993

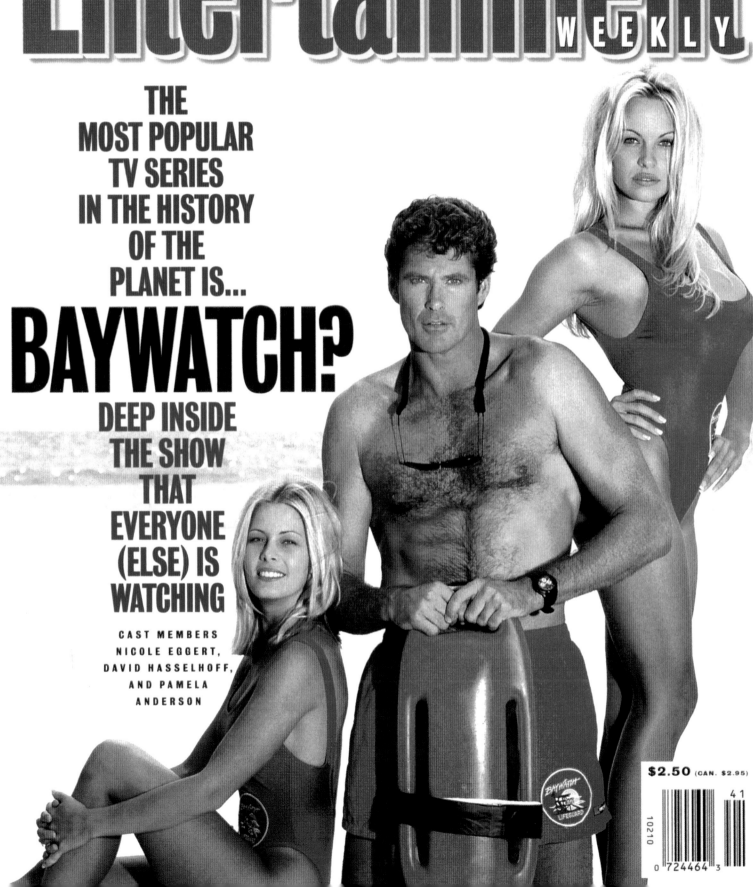

THE
MOST POPULAR
TV SERIES
IN THE HISTORY
OF THE
PLANET IS...

BAYWATCH?

DEEP INSIDE
THE SHOW
THAT
EVERYONE
(ELSE) IS
WATCHING

CAST MEMBERS
NICOLE EGGERT,
DAVID HASSELHOFF,
AND PAMELA
ANDERSON

$2.50 (CAN. $2.95)

CHAPTER 13

Seeing Baywatch Red

(Opposite) Entertainment Weekly *honored us (I think) with a cover in October '93. (Below) Katie Couric visits David Hasselhoff on the set.*

O ur hassles with L.A. County seemed to fade into insignificance one morning in April 1994. On the *Today Show*, Katie Couric did a segment about *Baywatch*. She stood in front of a giant map of the world and said, "This is the coverage of *Baywatch*." With a red pen she proceeded to color in all the countries where *Baywatch* was shown, 145 altogether. The whole world was covered in *Baywatch* red. The next closest show was *I Love Lucy*, in about 100 countries. She said, "More people know David Hasselhoff than Lucille Ball."

Thanks to the *National Enquirer*, *People*, and our own stellar promotions department headed up by Paul Nunn and the Lippin Group, *Baywatch* was now garnering a mountain of media attention, good, bad, curious, envious, absolutely none of it indifferent. In tandem with the media attention came viewer attention. Viewers by the millions sampled *Baywatch*. Lo and behold, they liked what they saw. They liked it so much they came back to watch more episodes, week after week. The ratings surpassed even our most optimistic predictions.

All manner of major and minor touchstones showed our growing popularity. On an episode of *Friends*, Joey and Chandler are sitting on a couch watching television.

Joey asks, "What are we watching?"

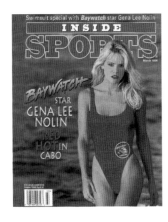

Getting on the cover of
TV Guide *is bound to
give the ratings a bump.*

(Above) Over the years
we've had an excellent
relationship with Inside
Sports. The key to a
cover is having it come
out when it can do us
some good—at the begin-
ning of a new season or
during sweeps, when
ratings are tabulated.
(Below) Jasmine Bleeth on
the cover of an Australian
magazine, Inside Sport
(no relation to Inside
Sports). (Bottom) David
Chokachi, a competitive
swimmer in college, made
the cover of Swim.

Chandler responds, "*Baywatch.*"

Joey replies, "What's it about?"

Chandler says: "Lifeguards."

Give that boy another raise.

The domestic recognition, while phenomenal, paled in comparison to *Baywatch*'s interna-
tional popularity. Certainly a resident of Newport Beach, California, might not consider
Baywatch to be so remarkable. But to a citizen of Helsinki, snow-bound for 39 weeks of the year,
Baywatch is a one-hour glimpse of pure heaven. All the key elements of *Baywatch* translated
beautifully into Finnish, Mandarin, Romanian. Music doesn't need dubbing. Action is action.
The good guys wear red. The victims are flailing in the water. Imagine taking *Cheers* to China.
No way. Cliff's post office humor simply would not translate. Imagine showing Pamela Anderson
or David Charvet in Shanghai. Words only get in the way.

Just when we thought the wave of popularity had crested, it surged again. We were featured
on a cover article in *Entertainment Weekly*: "*Baywatch*, the most popular show on earth." Then
TV Guide ran a cover article in the August 13, 1994, edition: "*Baywatch*, The Amazing Appeal
of TV's Billion-Viewer Beach Show."

At the same time, Pam Anderson caught fire. For her first two years, Pam had been just
another member of the cast. Then her heat index shot through the roof. For 81 weeks, nonstop,
you could not walk through the check-out line at the supermarket without reading another
installment in the up-down, on-and-off-camera saga of Pamela Anderson. One week she battled
hubby Tommy Lee, the next week she was caught on camera planting one of her Gucci-clad feet
into the groin of a disagreeable photographer. Never a dull moment.

The planets had aligned. *Baywatch* was king. In four years, the producers of *Baywatch* had
become worldwide exporters of entertainment goods. In one week, more people watched an
episode of *Baywatch* than saw some of Hollywood's biggest blockbusters in the total life of the
film, and the audience watched our series 52 weeks a year.

Our popularity went far beyond that of an ordinary television series. *Baywatch* had become
an established part of the American culture. My sister Kathe, with her Ph.D. in Modern English

Literature, began sending me articles from all manner of learned epistle, from the *Harvard Quarterly Review* to the *Utne Reader*. All these articles included a reference to *Baywatch*, such as: "A character in Proust's *In Search of Lost Time* could have had a starring role on *Baywatch*." It implied that everyone who read the article knew the show. All that was left was a *Baywatch* entry in *Webster's Dictionary of Global Culture*.

A few years ago Disney made a movie called *The Program*, about a high school football team. In one scene the players lie down in the street and play chicken with oncoming traffic. After seeing the movie, some kids imitated that scene. Tragically, a boy was killed.

Nationwide this caused a big outcry, a denouncement of the negative effects of television and movies through imitation, mostly by kids. Fresh examples of this imitation were brought forth daily, from girls being raped to people being murdered.

To offer another perspective on the argument, we bought a full-page advertisement in *Variety*, in which we reproduced a letter we had just received from a fan of the show, Mariano V. del Rosario, III.

Mariano describes how his wife, Bettina, discovered their son, Nico, at the bottom of the family pool. Bettina pulled Nico from the pool and immediately realized that he wasn't breathing. She

Baywatch saves lives! We've received dozens of letters from thankful parents and relatives, whose children have been saved by using CPR that was learned from watching Baywatch.

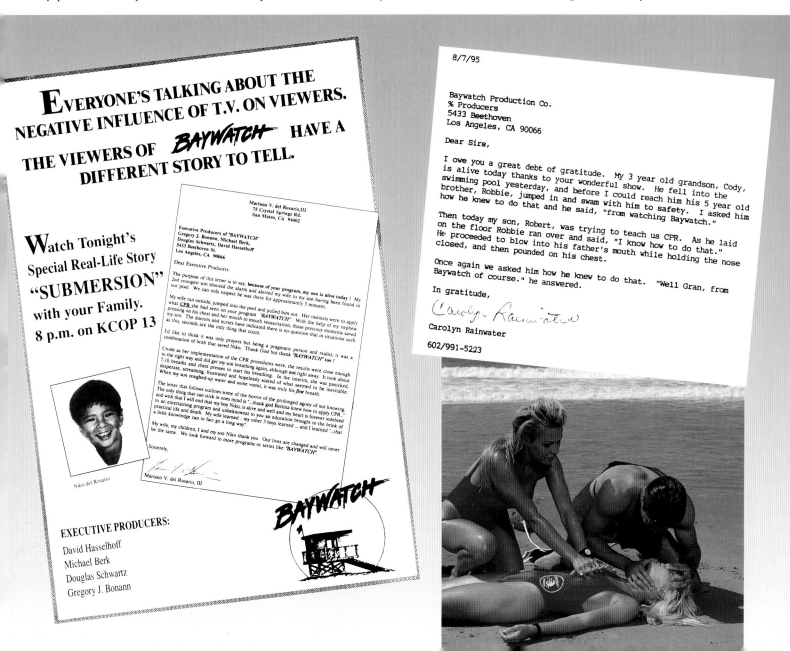

then applied CPR, which she had learned from watching an episode of *Baywatch*. Bettina revived her son, actually saved his life, by imitating what she had seen on our show.

At the top of the ad, we wrote, "Everyone's talking about the negative influence of TV on viewers. The viewers of *Baywatch* have a different story to tell."

This has happened literally dozens of times, people performing hands-on, mouth-to-mouth resuscitation, and reviving the victim. Afterward, the paramedics will ask, "Where'd you learn to do this?" They will say, "I saw it on *Baywatch*." We try to include at least one mouth-to-mouth resuscitation scene in every episode, and we take special care to present it correctly.

The collective Hollywood mentality usually tries to deny that its movies and television have an influence on people. That's wrong. It must be wrong, or else why would advertisers spend millions for a one-minute commercial? When commercials cease to influence viewers, that'll be the end of commercial TV. And it follows that if a one-minute commercial can convince you to buy a certain brand of detergent, the 40-odd minutes of actual episode will have at least some effect on your psyche. The power is undeniable. Rather than pretend this power does not exist, I believe we have a keen responsibility to do something useful, productive, and positive with the medium. This is especially true in the case of *Baywatch*, where we have the attention of billions of people.

Because of *Baywatch*, the American Heart Association has changed their CPR guidelines. Formerly, it was recommended that if you could not do it exactly right, you shouldn't touch the victim. Now it has changed: Do anything. Pound on him. Breathe into him. Clear the airway or not. Pinch the nose or not. Do something. People had previously been afraid to do anything. They would stand back and yell for help and subsequently the guy would die. Now they get down and do the best they can. The Good Samaritan Law has eliminated concerns about being sued for using less than doctor-certified procedures while trying to save a person's life.

When we had our 100th Episode party, David Hasselhoff flew in Nico, the boy who had almost drowned, and his family so that they could celebrate with us.

A long with our worldwide popularity came the inevitable slings and arrows of harsh criticism. When people knock *Baywatch*, I immediately ask if they have seen the show. Many times they have not. If they have not seen the show, I get a little bit pissed off.

If they have seen the show, I want to hear their criticism. I want to discuss the points with them. I listen carefully and take notes.

Most of the criticism we hear comes from professional television critics, as opposed to viewers. I am leery of these professionals. It seems they often have a built-in preference for *Masterpiece Theatre* or *NOVA*. Frequently the professionals wish they were producers, actors, or, at the least, reviewers of feature films.

Some critics, professional and otherwise, have said that *Baywatch* lacks substance. I find this comment intriguing. If you are looking for a broadly developed story, with nicely fleshed out characters, a clever subplot, and a subtle message intermingled throughout—then read a book. The medium of one-hour episodic television is surprisingly limited. After you have subtracted the time given over to commercials, credits, next week's preview, you are left with only 37 minutes in which to tell the story. That is equal to 37 pages of script, which wouldn't get Melville's *Pequod* out of Nantucket Harbor.

Jack Warner, the celebrated producer, said it best: "Give me a page out of the Bible and I'll make you a great movie." He didn't say, give me the whole Book of Mark. If a two-hour, big budget movie can handle only a solitary page from a thousand-page story, then it follows that a one-hour episode can barely tell the story contained within a paragraph.

I am the first to admit that *Baywatch* is not for everyone. To a sophisticated audience, it may seem simplistic. I say, for every viewer let a channel (or at least a show) shine forth, one that will capture his or her imagination. Long live *Crossfire*, *NOVA*, *Dateline*, *Beverly Hills 90210*, *Seinfeld*, *Law and Order*, The Home and Garden Channel, the Travel Channel, the Weather Channel. Long live *Baywatch*.

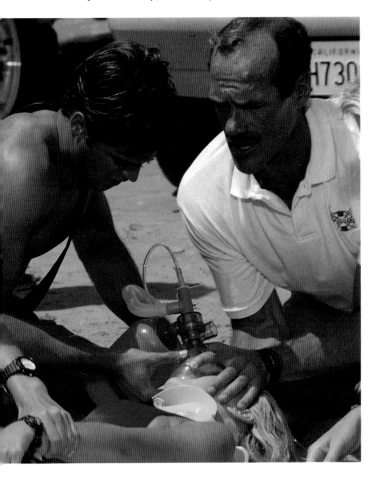

Critics have repeatedly commented on the tits–and–ass character of our show. From my years at the beach, I know that many of the patrons on our Southern California beaches, the mythical home of *Baywatch*, wear skimpy bathing suits. Of course, our beaches are quite tame compared to European beaches, where clothing is optional. Skimpy suits tend to reveal breasts and buttocks. We are depicting the real people found on our beaches. If you find this hard to believe, I strongly recommend a walk on the beach on a nice, summer day. I'm certain you'll find the experience enlightening.

We have had criticism that *Baywatch* promotes an unhealthy body image for women, specifically, large breasts on skinny bodies, a combination not often found in mature females. The image criticism can be broken into two distinct problems: eating disorders and breast enhancements. Eating disorders are a very serious, complicated matter, and at *Baywatch* we recognize this. Through the years we have done episodes about the dangers of bulimia and anorexia. And in nearly 200 episodes of *Baywatch*, no character has ever said, "Only thin people are attractive." Anyone who has ever known a sufferer of either bulimia or anorexia will know that it is a tragic, complex, awful illness that confounds everyone involved— friends, family, and especially the victim.

Breast enhancements are another matter. *Baywatch* has undoubtedly contributed to the increase in these operations. Erika Eleniak already had implants when she came to the show. After her first year, she surprised us by going under the knife a second time, getting yet another set of enhancements. This made her huge, practically circus big. She was so big, she couldn't run. She looked awkward on camera. Her new breasts hurt her physically. They also caused a change in her attitude. Rather than wanting to show off her new body shape, she suddenly became quite

Only one of the countless CPR scenes through the years. This one, from "Sky Rider" in 1994, features Pamela Anderson, David Charvet, and Mike Newman.

shy, never allowing herself to be shot in a one-piece bathing suit. I told her, "Erika, that's the job." Even on the hottest days, she always found an excuse to wear a jacket.

Nearing the end of the second season, she quit the show. Erika said she was leaving because she was unhappy with her growing bimbo image. But how much did she contribute to that bimbo image by getting these ridiculously large enhancements?

Gena Lee Nolin had a second breast enhancement last year, as did Pamela Anderson. Time after time I've seen these women get enhancements and, surprise, they don't necessarily feel any better about themselves. So they go in again, get them even bigger, hoping that this time they will get what they are after, self-esteem. Here's the truth: Self-esteem cannot be found in the operating room of a plastic surgeon.

I had three separate, lengthy discussions with Alexandra Paul as she was trying to decide whether or not to get breast enhancements. One time she came in with a *Playboy* magazine, the one with Stephanie Seymour on the cover. She put it in front of me, opened it to a dog-eared page, and said, "What if I got this size?"

Alexandra, with her naturally long, lean body, has modest-sized breasts in comparison with our other actors. I kept telling her, "It won't make any difference in what you can do for the show. We think you bring an ability, a character, something that's not measured by the size of your breasts."

She was skeptical, but fortunately she opted not to get the implants. As I came to know well over the years, Alexandra is an exceptional person, truly unique in body, spirit, and soul. Nothing about her needs changing. She is simply wonderful.

Big fake breasts aside, we have always made a point of presenting the women characters as equals to the men. Pam Anderson did not play an ancillary character, trotted out in a skimpy suit just to say "Hi." She played a working lifeguard of equal rank to the men. Alexandra Paul's character actually outranked Hasselhoff's character. The point is often overlooked: Unlike many shows, we give our women characters something to do besides standing around like mannequins.

Fortunately Alexandra never went under the knife. If I had a daughter and she wanted breast enhancements, I would spend the $5,000 on professional counseling for her. If she had a boyfriend who wanted her to get enhancements, I would tell her to get a new boyfriend.

It was a sad day for me when Alexandra left *Baywatch*. She had a great attitude—very gung ho, always ready to plunge into the chilly Pacific. She was one of our best athletes, as good as the real L.A. County lifeguards. She even competed in the tortuous Ironman Triathlon in Hawaii. After *Baywatch*, Alexandra went to *L.A. Fire*, which was canceled after a few episodes. She calls occasionally and we chat about whether or not she can come back. But I usually remind her that we killed off her character.

The success of a television series can be measured in a variety of ways: Emmys won, prestige earned, stars launched. For a producer, all these things are secondary to the ultimate measure: having completed 100 episodes.

The majority of television shows never reach 100 episodes. Many never get beyond the pilot. During the 1994–95 season, *Baywatch* reached this 100-episode milestone. (In order to achieve this vaulted number, we included the 22 episodes produced during the NBC year.) Not bad for a show that had been discarded by NBC only a few years prior.

At the end of the season we threw ourselves a huge 100th Episode party at the Ritz Carlton in Marina del Rey. The whole cast zoomed up to the Ritz Carlton dock on the Scarab, looking great, decked out in black tie and elegant dresses. For an hour the cast wound their way from the dock to the main ballroom, taking their time, chatting up the worldwide media representatives who had shown up to cover it.

Besides the cast, everyone associated with the show attended, from the completion bond people

Alexandra certainly could have been a real lifeguard, had she not been portraying one on Baywatch.

Thanks for 100 Episodes

Notes from my speech given at our 100th Episode party:

Perhaps for more than most, the past 100 episodes are especially significant to me.

My dad gives me articles, poems, anything he thinks is important for me to read. I find them in the mail, on my car, under my door, now by fax. But I want to read one that he gave me 26 years ago as we were driving toward the beach. It is by Ralph Waldo Emerson. It is called "What Is Success?"

"What is success? To laugh often and much; To win the respect of intelligent people and the affection of children; To earn the appreciation of honest critics and endure the betrayal of false friends; To appreciate beauty; To find the best in others; To leave the world a bit better, whether by a healthy child, a garden patch or a redeemed social condition; To know even one life has breathed easier because you have lived; This is to have succeeded."

It wasn't just any trip to the beach, we were on our way to the lifeguard tryout swim.

He knew that becoming a lifeguard would keep me in good company and he told me when he left me at the headquarters' gate: "Remember, you are only as good as the people you compete against, and make it or not, you are competeing against the best today."

From that moment on lifeguards were tremendously influential in my life—tangible heroes—in Emerson's words, really successful men and women.

It was then that I knew that there were lifeguard stories worth telling, but what I did not know was that they would someday be told to the largest audience in history.

For the past 26 years, I have shared countless hours and days on the beach and in the water with some of the most interesting, heroic, and successful people I have ever known—lifeguards.

As lifeguarding did for so many

who had been torturing me for years, to my lifeguard friends who supported me from early on.

David Braff brought his wife Joanne and their kids. He continues to play a key role on the show, as the man in charge of the story department. I met David in Palms Springs—in the Jacuzzi at Two Bunch Palms Spa. He was sharing the hot water with a woman I had dated years earlier, Joanne Butler. To my complete surprise, I found out that Joanne was now married to David.

David was already a successful writer of such shows as *Night Rider*, *Miami Vice*, and *Simon and Simon*. David came in, beginning as a writer. Soon he was running the whole story department, and doing a great job. He has proven himself over the years as a steady, hard working, utterly dependable guy.

There were speeches, champagne, more speeches, several of which pointed out that the best revenge against NBC was going 100 episodes. We showed a fantastic "best of" clip, which included all the amazing stunts we could never afford to reuse on broadcast television because of the cost of residuals.

As I watched the video, I found myself wondering, *what next*? Early on, we had been forced to utilize every ounce of innovation and creativity that we possessed in order to refloat the show and to make it thrive on a worldwide scale. Now that *Baywatch* had reached this milestone, I wondered if we would still be able to tap into the wonderfully motivating role of underdog, the Rocky Balboa who lives within us all. Fortunately I still loved the show as much as ever, particularly the people with whom it has allowed me to work. The best goal I could imagine was to keep *Baywatch* up and running until it reached 200 episodes.

When it came my turn to speak, I thanked my family and the lifeguards, all of whom had supported me through the early days, the dark days, the tough days, and the good days. Finally I read a passage written by Ralph Waldo Emerson, "What Is Success?" My dad had given it to me 25 years earlier as we drove to the beach for the lifeguard tryouts. I had kept it with me ever since.

At our 100th Episode party, we had a great time celebrating an important show milestone. (Opposite) The executive producers celebrate at the 100th Episode party. From left: David Hasselhoff, Doug Schwartz, Michael Berk, and myself. The Hollywood Reporter did a special issue for the event in which many people took out congratulatory ads—even NBC, who humorously acknowledged a costly error in judgment. (Below, left) That's me with Tai, and (right) me with my folks.

years, Baywatch has done for the past five years—put me in the company of many, many great people. But there was a time when I thought it was over. I can remember the Saturday in June, five years ago, when I sat in my tower, when the boat went by my tower, and waved. It made me cry.

The next day was Father's Day. My partners and I were gathered at my parents' house and we decided to try to resurrect the show—you all know the rest.

To all the people who have taught me so much and worked with me so hard, and challenged me to be the best I can be. I thank you from the bottom of my heart.

My partners Doug and Michael, who grabbed onto the idea with me and crafted it into what it is today.

David Hagar, for sharing his creativity and dedication with me—220 montages.

Cory/John for the composition of the music.

Ev/Paul for taking the montage concept to world acceptance by bringing their taste in music to me.

CTK, and those in my office. I revel in their growth in the industry as well as their growth as people.

Editors who have crafted the 100 shows (25 of which I have directed) into much more than they were when they got them.

To Mom for naming Baywatch, and for her example of selflessness and dedication throughout my life.

To Dad for living what he teaches.

To Tai for Camp Baywatch, something I am especially pround of.

To the guys at AAT: Tony, Myron, Tom and Syd, who gave us the means to go on and earned my repect and admiration on the way.

To David Hasselhoff, who defines real Success, every day, with his outlook on life, focus on what is really important, and without whom my dream could not have come true.

CHAPTER 14

Baywatch Universe

hen the party is over, it's back to work. We had a lot to do if we were going to reach 200 episodes. The prospect of reaching even 100 episodes of our other show, *Baywatch Nights*, did not look good at this stage in its life. In a word, *Nights* bombed. Certainly, for a relatively small company, we were attempting a major coup: to produce a total of 44 one-hour episodes (22 of *Baywatch* and 22 of *Baywatch Nights*), in less than a year. But that is no excuse for not turning out better work.

At the end of the first season (1995–96), our Los Angeles and New York stations declined to buy more episodes of *Nights* for the following year. At this point, All American should have canceled the show immediately. Instead, All American renewed it for a second season (1996–97). The reasons were somewhat valid: All American did not want to damage the overall *Baywatch* franchise; they didn't want Hasselhoff (nor All American television) to be perceived as having failed. Lastly, All American didn't want their new executive in charge of *Nights*, David Gerber, to be perceived as having failed.

At All American's request, Berk and Schwartz both left *Nights*—yet another conflict of interest, similar to the NBC hassle. That left only me to run the whole *Nights* show. I couldn't do everything, so All American brought in their own man, an experienced writer/producer, Maurice

(Opposite) **Baywatch** actors Alexandra Paul and Pamela Anderson pose for the world's press photographers.

Hurley—or simply "Mo" to most of us. Any objective observer might rightly assume that Mo and I would butt heads from the start. But for some reason we didn't. In fact, Mo and I became very good friends. At first, Mo ran the script department for *Nights*. Soon he was serving as the show's executive producer. While I went off to prep *Baywatch* for the next season, Mo became the show runner for *Nights*, the person who actually creates the show by having a hand in every aspect of its production. We were lucky to have Mo's competent leadership, which kept the show on budget and on schedule. While *Nights* might not have fulfilled its overall ratings promise, it introduced me to Mo, and that was practically the only silver lining.

In order for *Nights* to air in Los Angeles and New York during the 1996–97 season, All American had to buy it onto the air, much like an infomercial. It is a risky concept, one that has the potential to lose huge amounts of money, which is exactly what happened.

The end of the line came in typical Hollywood fashion. On a Sunday morning in April 1996, I met with All American's Syd Vinnedge at the Starbucks in Malibu. We had several things on the agenda. Finally, toward the end of our meeting, I said to Syd, "Time is running out. If All American wants a third season of *Nights*, you must commission new scripts right now. Do you want new scripts?"

He thought for a moment and then said, "No." No new scripts translates into cancellation. The white flag had been hoisted. *Nights'* overall ratings were awful, a 2.2. In Los Angeles, the show aired at 11:00 P.M. Sunday and 3:00 A.M. Tuesday. You could put up the test-pattern and get a 1.0 rating, simply because people fell asleep with the television on.

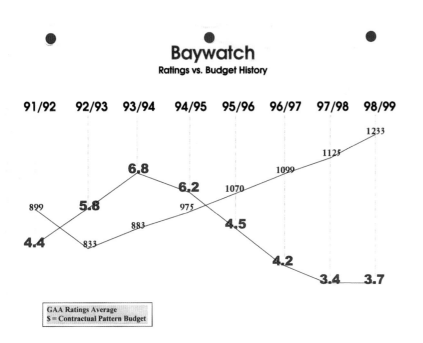

Baywatch
Ratings vs. Budget History

91/92   92/93   93/94   94/95   95/96   96/97   97/98   98/99

1233
1125
6.8
1099
6.2   1070
899   5.8   975
                           4.5
883
4.4   833
                                4.2
                          3.4   3.7

GAA Ratings Average
$ = Contractual Pattern Budget

Ratings went up and down through the years while the budget mostly went up.

Still, it was sobering news. We managed only 44 episodes, not enough for strip syndication unless we could slip it into the *Baywatch* package. Unfortunately, *Nights* was so different from *Baywatch* that the buyers did not accept it.

We did many things wrong with *Nights*. For starters, when the star is the executive producer and has a strong voice in the running of the show, conflicts can arise. Hasselhoff was tired of running around with his shirt off. He's my age, I can relate. He was sick of driving the rescue truck. I can understand that too. He wanted to surround himself with sexy women. Who doesn't? But then he wanted to solve assorted crimes using previously unknown detective skills. Basically, he wanted to be James Bond, Matt Helm, and Thomas Magnum rolled into one. Certainly that wouldn't have been so bad—detective shows have been on television forever and continue to succeed—but Hasselhoff's Mitch Buchannon character was already established as a lifeguard.

Nonetheless, we ended up producing the show Hasselhoff wanted. Hell, we figured, it might work. The audience then responded with a resounding: bullshit. This is lifeguard Mitch Buchannon. How can he afford these snappy clothes, the red car? How can he mess with babes when Hobie is left at home by himself? They were watching *Baywatch*, and they totally rejected *Baywatch Nights*. It was the worst-tested show in history, but by the time we received the results from the focus group, we were already down the road. We had shot nine episodes at $1,070,000 each.

Nights was filmed indoors, which allowed us to control the elements. No foggy mornings or big surf to contend with. But when you are shooting outdoors, as with *Baywatch*, and you know the sun goes down at 5:00 P.M., you find a way to complete the day's work. Filming *Nights* on a sound stage was like being in a Las Vegas casino. Suddenly you would ask, "What time is it?" only to find out you had been shooting for 16 hours.

I won't miss *Nights*. It was not my sort of show. Toward the end it had more ghosts than *The X-Files*. The ratings were nonexistent. It had a nagging habit of being named among the worst series of the season. Now, for all of eternity, it is relegated to the television trivia books. Good riddance.

With the cancellation of *Nights*, we became even more attentive to the costs of *Baywatch*. Starting at the top with the executive producers, we strove to maintain a functional, frugal, filter-down philosophy. Functional and frugal, top to bottom. We have learned that you can't send mixed messages. You either give everyone a raise or no one a raise. You either give everyone paid holidays or no one paid holidays. If someone wants new furniture in their office, let them buy it themselves. If you do things selectively, you will piss people off. In any industry, pissed-off employees will find innumerable ways to spend the company's money until they've gotten their perceived due.

We have about twenty-five offices at our Beethoven Street headquarters—offices for writers, producers, directors, casting people, set designers. This army has brought in Ikea particle board desks, steelcase file cabinets dating from WWII, used leather sofas on which their second and third children were conceived. The overall decorating scheme would make Martha Stewart run for the hills. But it works.

For our everyday correspondence, we buy envelopes in bulk from Costco, and then we stamp our return address with a cheap rubber stamp. More than a few people have commented on this hyper-low-budget method. But besides saving a little money, it tells the whole company that the executives think that every dollar counts. Believe it or not, these seemingly minor things make the difference between being able to do the show or not.

I always come back to the essence of what we are about: creating 22 original episodes of a one-hour action adventure show based on the lives of lifeguards. The key is not to compromise the essential points. Each story line and script must be strong. Our actors must be up for the challenge. Production values must be good. Each episode must deliver the inherent pact it makes with the audience—an audience that isn't going to care if we spend $1 million per episode or $20 million. The audience wants a good, entertaining, original, unique show.

My goal is to make it happen, and to do it in such a way that it can happen for years to come; that is, stay in production. As long as we can find a sufficient audience, and as long as we can keep the costs under control, that's how I want to spend my working day. Over the years I've gotten pretty good at it. Fortunately I've been able to work with people whose company I enjoy a great deal. The hours are long, but I know that I'd be putting in long hours no matter what job I was doing—the long hours I work says more about my own personality than about the job.

In just the last 12–24 months, however, the business of distributing independently produced programming such as *Baywatch* has changed dramatically. Whereas before it could be a cash cow of heroic proportions, lately it has become a risky business, particularly when launching a new show.

Despite all the talk about 57 channels or 500 channels, most Americans still get the same number of channels as when I was a kid. In Los Angeles, those channels are familiar to everyone: 2, 4, 5, 7, 9, 11, and 13. CBS, NBC, and ABC own three of those channels. Fox, WB, and UPN have taken over three more. All six networks have their own shows: Fox has *King of the Hill.*

WB has *Felicity*. Our original partner, Chris Craft, now has a bigger partner, Paramount. Together they have created United Paramount Network (UPN), a new network with its own original programming. Rather than promote *Baywatch*, UPN now promotes its own *Parkers* and *Star Trek Voyager*.

That leaves only one channel in Los Angeles for a company like All American to approach, and through the process of elimination, that channel has found its own niche: local news and sports. At the same time, a dozen independent shows are competing for any open slots: *Stargate SG-1*, *Xena*, *Hercules*. It's like having nine dories trying to race on an eight-lane course. Somebody is going to miss out.

All American's other option is to approach a network in hopes of filling one of their slots. When pitching a show to NBC, for example, the network will ask All American, "How much money are you willing to put into your show?" All American will respond, "zero." But a real player, like Warner Bros. or Carsey-Werner, will deficit spend hundreds of thousands of dollars per episode, much the same way Grant and GTG deficit spent $400,000 an episode for *Baywatch*. Essentially, if the network invests a million dollars as a license fee, in return they want an expensive series, costing $1.5 million or more.

The only other revenue source is foreign sales. For certain shows, like *Baywatch*, this money can make all the difference in the world. But for shows that don't translate well, the only money they can expect to earn is in the domestic market. The lesson for today: Only produce shows with foreign licensing potential.

Not every actor is suited for Baywatch. When the director yells "Action!" they hit the water, no matter how cold.

he most difficult part of *Nights'* cancellation was breaking the news to the people who worked on the show. We had added to our staff in order to produce *Nights*, and now I had to tell a lot of good people that they would soon be needing a new job.

In 1990, the new *Baywatch* started with three people: Doug, Michael, and myself. Now, just for *Baywatch*, we employ around 250 people, and that doesn't count the people who work for us in various production facilities around town.

Our people are composing music, making costumes, creating masks, doing hair. Hair people love to work on hair. Allen Payne, our department head, stopped by my office and said, "Come out and see this wig I did." Giving these people a canvas on which they can perform their craft is one of the most satisfying aspects of producing *Baywatch*.

Everyone respects that we must do the best we can for the dollar, or we are not going to be around much longer. I had a long conversation with our casting ladies. They were concerned that they might have to take a pay cut next year.

I told them that I honestly didn't know. It all depends on the ratings. The ratings are lower than they were two years ago—therefore we generate less revenue, which means less money can go into creating the show. That doesn't mean we cannot keep making *Baywatch*. Each episode now costs $1.2 million to produce, and generates a 7.0 rating. With a 5.0 rating, we would need to make the show for $950,000. Given the choice between continuing at a reduced budget or not continuing at all, we will continue at $950,000. Obviously it would mean asking everyone to take a pay cut if they wanted to remain with *Baywatch*.

(Top) The director and actors engage in a serious discussion.
(Above) The actors concentrate on the upcoming scene.

Between shots, David Hasselhoff and I discuss a point of contention. What's best for the show always wins. David challenged me, as he does all directors, to do my best.

People respond to equality and honesty. The key is to make sure everyone understands the reasons we are asking for the cuts in pay, and that the cuts be made equitably, across the board.

Besides making a salary, I think of the other aspects of work. What are we going to take away from this experience? How has it enhanced our lives? Have we made good friends? Have we challenged ourselves to do the best work possible? Good friendships and ongoing challenges are the keys for me. Over the years, a sincere, exceptional trust has developed among the crew, a trust that is altogether unique in this industry.

This trust allows us a lot more freedom, more leeway, more experimentation, more fun. Blow-ups on the set are remarkably rare. Ask any athlete: A tense, pressure-filled contest nearly always results in a sub-par performance. The same premise holds true on the set. If everyone stays loose and relaxed, from the director on down, and stays focused on the work at hand, everything will go well.

Also, it's a lot more fun. Once Mike Newman complained that he didn't have his own trailer, as did the other actors. We responded by providing him with a trailer—a horse trailer—complete with a half-door and a bale of hay.

The standard wooden clothes pin is the tool of the on-set prankster. The trick is to attach a clothes pin to the victim's back without that person knowing about it. At any given time, a half-dozen clothes pins are dangling off the back of Hasselhoff's shirt. If a funny note is likewise attached, all the better.

Hasselhoff and I have a special fondness for testing the boundaries of each other's sense of humor. Once, while filming at the beach, Hasselhoff mentioned that one of the extras looked familiar to him. He asked if I knew her name. I told him that her name was Gretchen. Hasselhoff, when standing next to her, said, "Hey Gretchen." She didn't respond. He said again, "Gretchen, hi." After a few more attempts, she turned to him and said, "My name is not Gretchen." Gotcha. Hasselhoff looked at me with fire in his eyes.

The director (especially when I'm directing) is a frequent instigator as well as a target of on-the-set mischief. During a recent episode, I told Jim Pergola, our director of photography: "I want the camera to open on Hasselhoff. Then pull back to a two shot of Mitzi and him. Have the camera come around to a single of Mitzi. Spin the camera to catch Hassel standing up and moving toward the door. Dolly back to see Mitzi getting up and following Hassel outside. Then come alongside for a two shot as Mitzi catches up and they walk side by side."

Pergola paused, adjusted his neckerchief, and thought for a moment to digest what I had just proposed. Then he shouted to the crew: "Okay, guys, Greg wants a No. 3."

Director of photography for the first eight seasons, Jim Pergola.

n January '97, after the last episode was finally delivered, I took my first real vacation in seven years, a week at Ski Paradise, Gordon Rathbun's world-class water skiing resort near Acapulco. Hands down, the best water skiing in the world!

Before I left, I cleaned up my desk, resolved any loose ends, made sure all the cast deals were signed and sealed for the next season. But no sooner was I out of the country than Pamela Anderson quit the show. I was surprised she decided to leave. She did not give any indication leading up to her departure. In fact, countless times, after a long day of shooting, she told me how happy she was to be part of *Baywatch*. We were having a good time on the set, and it was making her a star.

She was poised to make a small fortune next season. Over the years she had become the most famous dyed-blond, silly-married actor since Marilyn Monroe. We were going to reward her next season with a handsome raise, to $40,000 an episode. Then she quit.

The No. 1 rule for actors, mentioned earlier, is worth mentioning again: never leave a winner. The list of people who have walked away from winners is not a pretty sight: Shelly Long, Lisa Bonet, Ken Wahl, McLean Stevenson, Chris Noth, David Caruso.

Pamela is not a movie star, at least not yet. Her movie, *Barb Wire*, showed up on several worst-film-of-the-year lists. I saw it. It was in focus. A lot of the blame for *Barb Wire*'s financial failure should go to the film's producers. They made *Barb Wire* into an R-rated movie, yet Pamela's biggest audience is boys and young men, 12–18 years of age. Thanks to the R-rating, they couldn't get in to see the film (which may have been just as well).

Her parting kiss to us was a little disappointing. After five years with *Baywatch*, Pamela's method of telling us she was quitting was to feed the story to the *Los Angeles Times*. We learned that she was quitting by reading it in the newspaper. When we phoned Pamela to verify the story, she would not take our call. Finally her agent confirmed the story. By quitting in this manner Pamela hurt the show, since the episodes featuring her character would not air for another three to six months.

Why did she leave? Time may or may not heal all wounds, but it certainly works wonders to sort out various mysteries, such as why Pamela walked away from her *Baywatch* role.

Originally Pamela had a first-rate agent, Ray Manzella. Then she dumped Ray and signed with another agent, Nick Stevens. Then she dumped Nick and got a third representative, Henry Holmes. Then she was sued by a man who claimed that he had been her agent before Ray Manzella. This man won the lawsuit and was awarded a percentage of all Pamela's *Baywatch* earnings, plus interest. Each of the other three agents also received a percentage of her *Baywatch* earnings. And she was taxed in the 50 percent bracket. That left her with about nine cents on the dollar. The only way for Pamela to cut her losses was to quit *Baywatch* and try to find new work, where only one agent would be involved.

Pamela is a rock. She will get along fine. But I, for one, will miss her. She could do water work, especially underwater work, better than any of our actors. And during the years when Pamela was enjoying *Baywatch*, she was fun to be around.

One time we were shooting a montage of Pamela. Before we started, David Hass, our long-standing stand-in for David Hasselhoff, was "chumming for birds"—flinging crackers into the water to attract seagulls (using his patented cracker whacker). We wanted some birds to make the shot a little more interesting. Our cameras were loaded and ready. Pamela was ready. Everyone waited patiently for the birds to arrive. After a minute, Stuart Asbjornsen, the director of photography, tapped me on the shoulder and pointed toward Pamela. She was dancing, posing, gyrating to some enchanting muse that only she could hear. We shot this impromptu dance and then wrapped for the day. Who needs birds when you have Pamela?

Bonann's Angels. From left: Alexandra Paul, Pamela Anderson, and Yasmine Bleeth.

CHAPTER 15

Feeding the Beast

A day in the life of a producer is scary, fantastic, frustrating, fulfilling. The trick is to get an early jump.

4:30 A.M.

I awaken to find a script lying on my chest. I get up and on the road in short order.

5:00 Swim workout

I arrive at my old high school swimming pool for a master's swim workout. The meat of today's workout is a brutal series: 12 X 200 yards, on the 2:40. Our coach, Paul Henne (an L.A. County lifeguard), walks along the pool deck right next to me, cracking the whip, giving me splits every 50 yards.

In the pool swimming furiously are John Montanaro, Bob Janis, Eric Shargo, Jeff Strnad, Chuck Locko, Terry Henderson, Tim McNulty, Woody Gair, Barry Stein. In the lane next to me is John Fletcher, a good friend (lifeguard, of course), and a phenomenal master's swimmer. If you happen to finish ahead of John early in the workout, he'll make sure you suffer later on. John was on fire today. That's when you swim your fastest, when the guy next to you is having a great workout.

I've learned a lot about life in this pool. Back in high school, I gradually figured out the

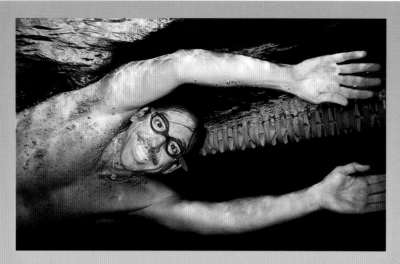

The *Baywatch* Swim Test

We have a swim test for all our actors, to make sure we don't get burned. They must:

- Swim 100 meters freestyle
- Swim 50 meters freestyle all-out
- Swim 25 meters back stroke
- Swim 25 meters breast stroke
- Swim 25 meters butterfly stroke
- Swim, water polo style, with head out of water (wearing fins)
- Swim underwater, eyes open, looking up at Greg
- Dolphin kick 25 yards underwater with fins
- Freestyle kick 25 yards underwater with fins
- Do a racing start off the block

difference between baseball and swimming. Baseball, essentially, is a game. I loved to play baseball. But no one plays swimming. Swimming is a discipline. The difference between a game and a discipline is immense. No doubt you can learn valuable life lessons from playing baseball. I, personally, didn't do it long enough to find out. Swimming, I know, teaches priceless life lessons: Discipline. Persistence. Dedication. Unbending devotion to one's goal. If you can stay with competitive swimming long enough, you will develop these characteristics. Later, you can carry these characteristics over to any arena of your choosing.

7:00 Swim test

At the end of our workout, an actor, Brooke Burns, showed up for her swim test. Ever since getting burned by the actor Pam Bowen, who said she could swim when actually she had a debilitating fear of the water, we've made our actors go through a swim test before we hire them for the show.

For some reason, the pool is always packed on the mornings of a swim test. Guys who I haven't seen in months—since the last *Baywatch* swim test—show up. Everyone loves it. On my cue, Brooke jumps into the pool and swims two lengths, up and back. After she completes that modest effort we move on to the next phase of the test. In truth, having done this for so many years, I can usually tell a person's swimming ability before they've finished the first lap.

Usually, at the end of the test, my fellow master swimmers give me a thumbs up or thumbs down, based on the actor's appearance and swimming ability. Today I get mouths agape. Brooke blew them away. John Fletcher was absolutely speechless. He even came to coffee with us afterwards, which he never does. That's a good sign.

Swim test aside, through thick and thin, I've always taken the time to work out. Always. It might sound corny, but swimming gives me my balance, my center. It's absolutely essential to my physical and spiritual well-being.

7:45 Set visit

While driving to the office, I get a call on my cell phone. An emergency has arisen at the Will Rogers set. I go straight to Will Rogers to help sort it out.

Frank Conway is the Line Producer. It's his job to open up the company at 6:00 A.M., making sure all the equipment is in place and that everyone shows up on time.

Today he has encountered a UPM's worst nightmare: The actor didn't show up. Suddenly Frank is faced with the prospect of 150 people standing around, waiting, everyone wondering if they'll be able to shoot the day's work. Our actors are told from Day 1: If you're going to be late, call and let us know.

The call goes up—where in the world is Carmen (Sandiego) Electra? No one knows. She doesn't answer her phone, pager, cell phone. (As it turns out, Carmen stayed out until 4:00 A.M. She woke at 1:00 P.M., thought it was 1:00 A.M., and went back to sleep. And Carmen was supposed to be on the set at 7:00 A.M. She completely lost a whole day.) To keep everyone working, we ask Kelly Packard if she wouldn't mind doing Carmen's dialogue along with hers. She said no problem. This meant Kelly had to quickly learn Carmen's lines, adding them to her dialogue.

Kelly is really sharp. She's a good actress—one of our best—and she can deal with challenges like this.

8:30 Morning briefing

First off, I get with Craig Kwasizur, Peter Hoffman, and Chris Celentano at the office. They play a huge part in my day. In detail, we go over the work ahead of us for the day. With so much going on—meetings, phone calls, unscheduled drop-in visits—the headquarters can easily become a madhouse. Without Craig, Peter, and Chris to keep order, I know for a fact that nothing would get done. They deal with the impossible. They each wear five or six hats—finance, promotions, publicity. Peter is the ratings king. He tracks down the ratings for the show, something that not even All American manages to get. I'm lucky to have capable people like Craig, Peter, and Chris helping me get through it all. And they do it with a calm, reassuring demeanor, which puts everyone at ease.

8:45 Review outline

One of my first tasks is to go over the outline for "Shark Fever." Here we discuss the action: How expensive can it be? How broad can it be? Can we afford a real shark?

Through our discussion we establish the executable elements of the show. For example, can we have a real shark in the open ocean? No. Can we have a shark in our tank? No, our tank is fresh water. Can we use a mechanical shark, as in *Jaws*? Probably. Can we film the shark scene at Sea World? Possibly. We've done it before but it's expensive.

"Feeding the beast" is a term we often use. The beast is the series. The beast continually feeds on fresh scripts. For years now the beast has been swallowing scripts at a frantic rate. Occasionally a writer will be late in finishing his script. You'd better believe sparks will fly if the beast is allowed to go hungry.

9:05 Music meeting

This is the meeting I look forward to the most. From the start, the music we showcase has been our own little island of creativity. I think it's fair to say that you don't see a lot of shows on television, other than *Baywatch*, that regularly use new and interesting music to such an extent.

The music supervisor, Kevin Edleman, comes into my office, along with David Hagar and the music producers, Evyen Klean and Paul Broicek. Over the last three years I have grown to trust Kevin's ability to bring me the music that's appropriate for the show. At some point I had to accept the fact that he was young, hip, cool, in touch. I, on the other hand, am 46 years of age. Once we're all settled in, the CDs start flying across the room like Frisbees. Cut No. 4 on one disc, cut No. 9 on another disc. The goal is to find a song that's appropriate for a montage we have scheduled. Kevin often employs an age-old salesman's technique, purposefully playing some music that he knows I'll hate and then hitting me with his best song. Once we've agreed on a song, Kevin types up the lyrics and gives them to me. I then create the visuals in my head. David Hagar usually gives me some ideas, too. We've done so many, the main challenge is figuring out how to make it different. At the same time the music department is left with the more mundane task of negotiating and acquiring the rights to the song.

Lastly we listen to Kevin's newest creation, an in-house version of Randy Newman's classic, "You Can Leave Your Hat On." That song was made famous in the movie *9¹/₂ Weeks*, with Kim Basinger performing a serviceable striptease in front of a leering Mickey Rourke. We're going to re-create that scene with Carmen Electra stripping for David Chokachi.

We considered buying the rights to the song as performed by Joe Cocker—no way. Cocker wasn't interested, not to mention it would have cost $50,000. Kevin Edleman bought the sync for

The *Baywatch* Montage
"You Can Leave Your Hat On"

Baby take off your coat real slow / Take off your shoes

I'll take your shoes girl / Take off your dress yes, yes, yes

You can leave your hat on / Go over there turn on the lights

Come over here, stand on that chair / Baby that's right

Raise your hands in the air / And now shake em

You give me reason to live / You give me reason to live

$2,500 and then hired singer Alex Fox to record it. The final mix was excellent, even sexier than Cocker's version, and it cost about one-tenth the price. We will recoup the cost of the song within six months—after that, it will start earning us income whenever it is shown in reruns.

10:00 Review script

For "Lifeguardian," I'm concerned that the episode is going to be too expensive. I say to script supervisor David Braff: "We must get rid of the night work."

David says: "How can we have a romantic scene, with people skinny dipping, in the broad daylight? It doesn't work."

I say: "Maybe we can do day-for-night. With the right filters and at the right time of day, the sun on the water looks like moonlight. Check out the movie *Point Break*, where they did a day-for-night surfing scene. It looked pretty good. Now, about this unicorn you have chasing an inner tube down the beach..."

The creative quality depends on the show holding true to the lifeguard's world. That starts with the scripts, which come from the writers. I get pissed off when our writers don't go to the beach to stay current with that unique world. They must get their feet in the sand. The temptation for some writers, with their years of experience doing shows that have nothing in common with *Baywatch*, is to sit around all day and create the most idiotic stories you can imagine, horrendous fantasies about drugs or guns or kidnapping or something they read in the newspaper. They'll sit in the office, pulling out their hair trying to think up a story, when all they need to do is get off their asses, drive down to the beach, and walk into lifeguard headquarters. They'll find stories that are better than anything they could ever dream up.

10:50 Production meeting

It's time for the week's major production meeting. Here we'll deconstruct, analyze, and evaluate the episode that will begin shooting next week, in this case "Buried."

Part of the producer's art form is in putting the dollars on the screen. This art is demonstrated during the production meeting, where the whole company, every department head, sits around a table and goes through the script, page by page, line by line. What's the episode about? What problems can we anticipate?

I especially like this part of the process, sitting with the people who make the show come to life. A line of script is read: "Caroline and Cody sit down to dinner at a fancy restaurant." Then the hands go up. Wardrobe supervisor Karen Braverman asks what she's going to wear. Special effects guys, Matt and Leo, ask if the fireplace is working. If yes, they will ask, "How big is the flame?" If the flame is working, it'll affect how the sound guy records his dialogue.

Quite often I'll answer a question by saying, "That's a separate meeting." I use this response when I feel the eventual answer won't impinge on the other departments. Action sequence? That's a separate meeting. Music, FX? Separate meeting.

We spend three hours working our way through the whole episode. And when the meeting breaks up, nobody moves. They all have more questions. Sporadically, for the rest of the day, I'll be fielding questions from the different department heads. My door is always open.

1:45 P.M. Lunch

Over lunch at my desk I meet with Kelly Packard. She's going to NATPE week, in New Orleans, to sell next season's *Baywatch*. I'm pretty sure she'll be good at meeting and greeting

Brooke Burns and Kelly Packard lightening the mood on the set.

(Above) Our soundman, Hal Whitby. (Below) Product placement at its best. We receive hundreds of items from wristwatches to sunscreen through product placement.

the various station managers and owners. I give Kelly and Brooke specific instructions not to talk about *Baywatch* moving to a new location next season. The station managers might not like the idea that they weren't consulted before we decided to move. I know they'll love the new *Baywatch* once they see it.

2:00 Editing update

After lunch I head to the editing department to sit with the editor who's leading the charge on this episode, David Latham. Together we look at a rough cut of "Chance of a Lifetime." This episode is requiring a huge, post-production effort, six weeks altogether. The scene where Alexandra's character dies was shot in the pouring rain, which made the sound track unusable. Everything has to be looped.

Action shows, in general, necessitate a great deal of looping. If we're filming a storm at sea, we create wind using a huge Ritter fan. We create rain using a special rain machine. We make the water rough by having speed boats zoom around. Between the fan, the rain machine, and the speed boats, it's a sound man's nightmare. He can't even hear the actor yelling "help, help," much less record it with any degree of clarity. Everything said by the actors in that sequence must be rerecorded in the studio, which is called looping.

After meeting with David, I stop by an adjacent editing room and say hello to Tom Erwin. A familiar name? Twenty years ago I rescued Tom Erwin and his sister, Jacey, at Will Rogers State Beach. This rescue then led to my meeting their father, Stu Erwin Jr., which eventually led to Grant Tinker, which, in a wildly roundabout way, led to NBC buying the show, which finally brought us here. Tom Erwin is a great editor and a good friend.

2:50 The cume

With Craig Kwasizur, I work on a new idea regarding double runs, which may eventually affect our actors, writers, and directors. (Craig was a young kid when I met him nine years ago at GTG. In fact, he was Stu Erwin Jr.'s Production Assistant. Now he's a producer on our show.) All over the country *Baywatch* airs twice a week, known as a double run. For example, it airs at noon on Saturday and at midnight on Sunday. Most importantly, the same commercials run in both airings. If *Baywatch* earns a 3.0 on Saturday and a 2.0 on Sunday, the ratings are combined, called "cume," as a 5.0.

As it stands now, each time the show airs, the actors are paid residuals. Since *Baywatch* airs twice a week, they make out like bandits. But if it's cumed as one airing, and it's paid for as one airing, why should we pay the actors for two runs? The actors should be paid as though it has run only once, and receive one residual.

Initially, the actors will hate it. But if it makes the difference between being able to do a show or not, they'll go for it. The key will be convincing the actor's union, SAG. Suppose it truly did make a difference, and the union turned it down. I'd tell the actors, you could be working today, except your union wouldn't give us a concession. The actors would go nuts.

The other unions would also have to agree—DGA, WGA. I happen to be a member of both those unions, so in a sense the producer side of me will be fighting against the writer and director side. In general, it's hardball stuff, but if you're right, you can play hardball. You have to be open, honest, respectful, and right.

3:30 Product placement meeting

Doug Schwartz has worked out a million-dollar bit of magic, which he briefs me on this afternoon. He has arranged for us to film an episode on a Princess Cruise Line ship while it's cruising off Alaska. If it goes as planned, we'll realize a million dollars in goods and services. Good job, Doug. He's great at attacking massive, unwieldy projects and seeing them through to completion.

When we ask a company to do business with us, from Body Glove wet suits to Wellcraft Scarab boats, they almost always say yes. It's a good deal for everyone. They give us the product and we showcase it on the show. And since we work without network hindrance, we can turn it into an extravagant puff piece.

Joining with Scarab boats has worked out especially well. During the NBC year, we rented the L.A. County rescue boats. Now we have two beautiful, sleek Scarab racing boats, painted in *Baywatch* colors. The real county guards are jealous as hell, since compared with our Scarabs, their rescue boats look like tired old tugs.

4:00 Final delivery

I meet with Cathy Dwyer, the producer in charge of post-production, to go over the final delivery of "Talk Show." She mixes all the sound elements together. Generally I don't get too critical at this stage because when I do, it costs a lot of money to go back and fix it. By now, after dozens of episodes, the editors know what I like. I do insist on hearing the playback through the television speakers, which is how the audience will hear it. The editors always want to play it back through their $10,000 speakers. No doubt it'll sound great, but often the whole bottom end will be lost when the average viewer at home hears it through a two-inch speaker.

5:00 Starbucks break with Newmie

I order a Grande Frappuccino with whipped cream. I'm practically the only one in Starbucks without a cell phone and beeper. Who wants to be tied to that stuff? Besides, if the office needs me, they can find me.

Newmie is going for the chocolate-chip scone and a double Grande Frappuccino with extra whipped cream.

Not only is Mike "Newmie" Newman a SAG-card carrying member of our cast and a full-time lifeguard, he's one of my best friends. I've known him for years, long before *Baywatch* was anything more than a fanciful dream reserved for quiet afternoons at the lifeguard tower.

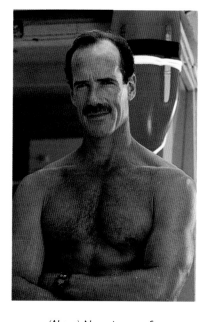

(Above) Newmie, one of my best friends, has been with Baywatch from the beginning. It's always good to know that he's there when things get hairy for the second unit, such as when they're working in the surf line (below).

Besides Newmie, we employ five real lifeguards on our second unit. They're great guys, and having them around keeps us safe. More than once, Newmie or Scott Hubble has tapped me on the shoulder and cautioned me against doing a dangerous shot. I'd been too wrapped up in the filming to appreciate the danger. At first, when they did this I'd get annoyed. Now I just thank them and take their advice. In the history of *Baywatch*, we've had only one injury. During the NBC year a stunt girl broke her ankle while jumping out of an armored car. This is especially amazing considering the amount of water work we do. Our stunt coordinator is the man behind that success, Greg Barnett.

Filming in and around water, whether it's *Titanic*, *The Abyss*, *Waterworld*, or *Baywatch*, adds an extra dimension of risk, as confirmed by our hefty marine insurance premiums. A hundred novel ways to injure an actor or crew member are as close as the water's edge. The guy in *The Abyss* suffered the bends because he was sent too deep. For underwater work, no matter the sequence, we never dive below 33 feet, one atmosphere. That way we eliminate the risk of the bends. Besides, we want our real actors to do it. Who in their right mind would want an actor going below 30 feet?

Going back to work is not something I dread. Quite the opposite. I love my job. I especially love giving people the tools and the opportunity to do their best work. The highest success I can realize is when a person comes up to me and says that they're doing their best work at *Baywatch*.

6:30 Budget meeting

Jane Williams, Frank Conway, and I go over the episodic budget for the show, which is running $30,000 over.

I say to Jane, "What are the expensive elements for this show?

She says, "The horse."

I say, "Lose the horse."

She says, "Then we don't have a show—it's about a horse."

"Okay, what else?"

Frank Conway will say boats or location or extras or cast.

"Who's in it?"

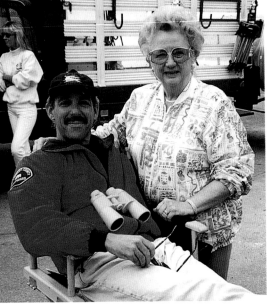

It's always a treat when Mom visits me on the set.

He'll tell me.

"Let's take one of them out—the most expensive cast member—search and replace."

Some way or another, we'll get it down to the budget. Not all episodes threaten to go over budget. The less expensive ones are truly welcome. We can use the money saved on those episodes for the more expensive shows.

7:00 Final walk-through of the set with Robert Henderson

Tomorrow is a big day. We're going to film a rescue scene for our episode "Search and Rescue." In this instance, the first unit will do the filming because the second unit is busy shooting water work. I'll be directing. A good director should see the set well before he shoots the scenes—several times if necessary. If I show up the day of the shoot and tell Robert to move a wall, he'll look at me and say, "Then why the hell did we build it?" We'll talk about how many walls we'll need, and in general how much effort he should put into the set. I've seen Robert build huge, magnificent sets, only to have the director come in and shoot only one wall. It's a waste of time, money, and effort.

The most essential point is that everything must be ready to go—absolutely everything: lighting, sets, wardrobe. In this instance we're using storyboards to outline the action. The storyboards serve as an outline, so that we can know, to some extent, where to place the cameras, lights, extras, props, etc. We can't afford to stop while a wall is moved or some other foreseeable problem is corrected.

7:30 Debriefing

Once again I sit with Craig, Peter, and Chris to evaluate the day's efforts and to plan for the day ahead.

8:00 Heading home

I leave the warehouse around 8:00 in the evening, usually with a few scripts in hand. The news of my departure, often broadcast with great fanfare over the intercom, serves to tell everyone that they too are now free to leave.

I'm usually on the car phone most of the way home, calling Mom and also dealing with the not-so-urgent matters that I wasn't able to resolve during the day.

Monday through Friday, I give over a few more hours to *Baywatch* in the evening, watching dailies (parts of an episode shot the day before) and reading scripts and outlines. The day is arduously long, to say the least, but it's never the same and it's never, ever boring.

More often than not, I fall asleep with a script on my chest.

Make no mistake: I have the utmost respect for the difficulties involved with filming around water and the ocean. By carefully planning every shot, often with storyboards like these, we have been able to film quickly, and safely.

CHAPTER 16

Pearson Buys All American

COMPANY TOWN ANNEX

All American in Talks to Sell Company

All American Communications Inc. said it is in preliminary talks to sell the company, whose television shows such as "Baywatch" could be attractive to a number of production companies, analysts said. All American, which also produces "The Price Is Right" game show, didn't identify the other parties in the talks. The company could fetch about $350 million, or about $28 a share, in a sale, said analyst Art Rockwell of Yaeger Capital Markets. The television and music producer has been benefiting from rising revenue from its TV operations in the U.S. and abroad. Its stock has jumped about two-thirds since the beginning of the year. Shares of Santa Monica-based All American slipped 13 cents to $22.50 on Nasdaq after trading as high as $25.25.

(Bloomberg News)

came to work on Tuesday, September 2, 1997, the day after Labor Day, and was met at the front door by Craig Kwasizur, who held the business section of the *Los Angeles Times* in his hand. The headline said succinctly: ALL AMERICAN IN TALKS TO SELL COMPANY.

The heart of the article can be summarized in one brief line: a major British corporation, Pearson, had commenced the process of buying All American Television.

Pearson, a multibillion-dollar media conglomerate based in London, is run by an energetic, very talented American woman from Texas, Marjorie Scardino. Pearson's purchase of All American was in keeping with its recent acquisition of other promising media companies.

I was ecstatic at the news. The relations between All American and Berk, Schwartz, and Bonann had been strained over the last few years. Now with Pearson we would have an opportunity to start fresh with a new owner. Fortunately, some of All American's best people, including Syd Vinnedge and Myron Roth, would stay with the new owner to help make the transition fairly smooth. In the big picture, my hope was that Pearson would take a liking to the *Baywatch* franchise and continue supporting it well into the future.

(Above) The first notice of All American's impending sale to Pearson TV. (Opposite) The women of Baywatch for the 1997–98 season. From left: Kelly Packard, Carmen Electra, Donna D'Errico, Marliece Andrada, Tracy Bingham, and Angelica Bridges. All but Kelly were soon to be gone.

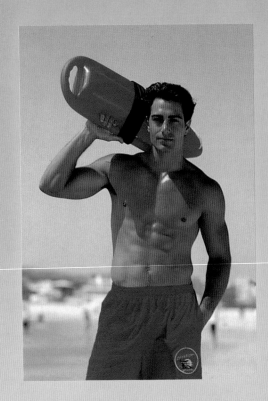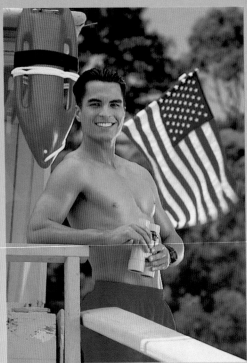

At the end of the 1997–98 season, the producers took a long, hard look at our ensemble cast. It seemed as though our men were holding their own—Jose Solano, David Chokachi, Michael Newman, Michael Bergin, Jeremy Jackson. Over this last year, Bergin, in particular, had improved tremendously as an actor. Parker Stevenson also played a strong role. Not only did he act in several episodes, he directed four episodes, performing both tasks with alacrity. As a director, Parker has an affinity for the whole process: preparation, on-set directing, and the often tedious post-production, where the episode is cut together, scored, looped, recut, on and on.

For a variety of reasons, however, our women actors weren't getting the job done. Gradually, one actor at a time, we created a *Baywatch*-red bloodbath—Gena Lee Nolin, Donna D'Errico, Tracy Bingham, Carmen Electra, Angelica Bridges, and Marliece Andrada were asked not to return for the following season.

Gene Lee Nolin was probably the biggest name to retire the red one-piece suit. Gena's character had recently married David Hasselhoff's character, which made her departure from the show a challenge for our writers. It seems that Gena never really conquered her fear of the camera. Her distress was simply too much, an unwieldy tension perhaps exacerbated by the fact that her husband was also her manager—always a bad idea. I hope she finds a way to get back into the business. When everything's right, Gena's a very good actress.

Donna D'Errico was another lead actor we decided to let go. Donna had been hired for *Baywatch Nights*, then brought into *Baywatch*. Following the lead of Pamela Anderson, Donna married a rock star while on *Baywatch*, in her case Nikki Sixx, a band-mate of Tommy Lee's from Mötley Crüe. Somewhere along the line, Donna became very unhappy. Also, she had been behaving disrespectfully to our wardrobe people, our hair people, our makeup people. That is some-

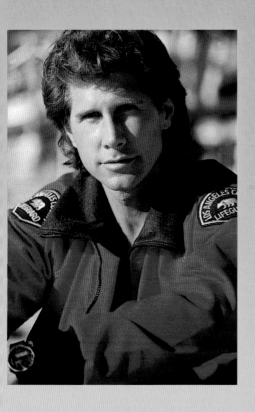  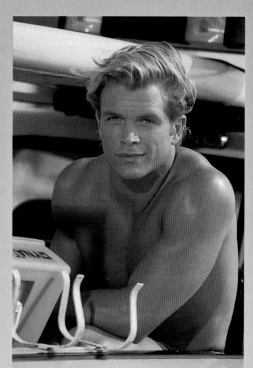

(Opposite and above) The men of
Baywatch during the 1997-98 season.
From left: Michael Bergin, Jose Solano,
Michael Newman, Parker Stevenson,
Jeremy Jackson, and David Chokachi.

(Right) The decision to write Gena Lee
Nolin out of the show was an agonizing
one for all of us. Her tearful departure
was emotional but friendly.

thing we cannot tolerate. Our actors, if they're legitimately nice people, are always sweet to me. But if the actor is a jerk, he or she is *also* always sweet to me. I, personally, can never see what's really going on. I have to find out through assistant director Lewis Stout, or fellow producers Craig Kwasizur and Peter Hoffman, or line producer Frank Conway, who does all the hiring and firing. Inevitably, either Louis, Craig, Peter, or Frank will know exactly what is going on at any given time.

Interestingly, Donna's distress coincided with her losing weight—too much weight. I have no idea if the two events were related but I'd be surprised if they weren't. Actually we were going to cut Donna loose a year earlier, after the 1996–97 season. I had even called Donna into my office along with her agent, Dennis Brody, a longtime associate of mine who formerly worked with Ray Manzella (who had represented Pamela Anderson). I told Donna straight out: "We're dropping you from the show." Donna was shocked. When she asked why, I said, "You're never happy with your wardrobe, your hair—you're making everyone around you miserable." She asked for another chance, and, after a long discussion, we decided to give it another try. We also decided to reduce her guarantee (the number of episodes in which she would appear) for the following season, and that, of course, meant a significant cut in pay.

I told her, "Forget about your makeup. Forget about your hair. Instead, work on the craft of acting. Get an acting coach. Go to classes. Work hard!" The next season Donna could have played it one of two ways: She could have grabbed the chance by the balls and run with it. Or she could have given up and just gone through the motions, which unfortunately is exactly what she did.

e also fired Tracy Bingham. Her main problem, to put it bluntly, was that she simply could not act. I'm well aware that we're talking *Baywatch*, not *Macbeth*. But still, she was so bad it was embarrassing. The other actors were always upset whenever they had to be in a scene with her because it inevitably made them look bad. We'd hoped she would have worked hard in the off season to improve her acting craft but it never happened.

One day, before the start of her second season, her agent called me and said, "Is there any way you can advance Tracy two episodes worth of salary? She's destitute. She's getting kicked out of her apartment. She's losing her car. She needs the money right away." I said, no problem. We sent her the money. As we neared the beginning of production, I called to see if she was still working out and still in acting classes, as she had been asked to do. Tracy said she hadn't been able to do anything because she had been ill. We didn't hear from Tracy again for several weeks. As we neared the beginning of the season, her agent called me and said, "I've got some bad news: Tracy lied to us both. Remember the money you gave her? She used it for breast augmentation." When she finally reappeared on the set, one look told me she'd gone from having a beautiful, all-natural body to getting a very major upgrade.

Fake breasts and lousy acting aside, the most disappointing aspect of our association with Tracy was her failure as a role model. She never participated in Camp Baywatch functions or charity

(Opposite) Donna D'Errico in her suit before and after her weight losses. (Right) Tracy Bingham after her breast augmentation.

opportunities—unless, perhaps, a camera was somewhere in the vicinity. This failure on her part disappointed me, personally. She could have done so much good—here she was, a beautiful African-American actress, being seen by a billion people a week—and she just turned her back on the opportunity to be a role model.

armen Electra was the third actor to go. Looking back, I have to admit that her presence on the show was a mistake from the very beginning. She was one of the few actors who actually had some degree of notoriety before getting to *Baywatch*. Because of this, she expected to be paid more than our usual beginner actors. But $40,000 an episode? Get real! But that's what her agent demanded. We battled back and forth for months. In fact, her contract wasn't signed until episode 10, for approximately 20 precent of her asking price. (Actually, a late signing isn't so unusual in our business. We've had actors work through the whole season while their contract was still being negotiated. In fact, I was presented with Mitzi's unsigned contract two months after we wrapped the last day of shooting for the season.)

Carmen's agent was a pill. He always made me feel that Carmen should be doing something other than working on *Baywatch*. He told me a hundred times that she had a thousand other offers, all of them incredibly lucrative. He insisted that she could rule the world, if only she wasn't doing *Baywatch*.

By episode six we knew it was over. Carmen was a pleasure to work with—a nice, energetic, relatively capable actor—but her management made life too rough for us. As time wore on, I realized that all of Carmen's decisions were being made by her management. I told her, "Carmen, you should get a hold of your career. Make your own decisions. Your management works for you, not the other way around." It never happened.

From the beginning, Carmen was not exactly the-most-likely-to-succeed *Baywatch* actress. Inevitably, she looked as though she was from Manhattan, not Malibu. When Alexandra Paul stood ankle deep in the ocean, you felt she could complete a rescue. Kelly Packard was the same way. Carmen, no

Carmen Electra is beautiful but she didn't have the Baywatch look.

way. In ankle deep water she looked as though she was over her head. The strange news: When Carmen married Dennis Rodman, every newspaper article referred to her as "former *Baywatch* star, Carmen Electra," even though she'd only been in 12 episodes.

hen Angelica Bridges came in to audition for a role, we, the executive producers, immediately saw that she wasn't right for the part. But we all agreed that Angelica was magnificent. Absolutely charming—a stunning presence. But we had no role for her. We resolved to find a place for her on the show. That's how we got ourselves into trouble, diverting from our usual process of writing a role first and then casting it. On occasion, however, we've done it the other way around and with success. That was the case with Alexandra Paul. We saw Alexandra, knew she wasn't right for the part for which she had auditioned (Pam Anderson was eventually hired), but we liked her so much we created a role for her in the show. In Alexandra's case it worked out extremely well.

Angelica Bridges was truly striking. But when I tried to shoot her, I quickly discovered that I could never make her look as beautiful on screen as she was in person. I simply could not do it. Very frustrating. As an actor, she wasn't any worse than the other women, but the unique "chemistry" she had off screen never made it on screen. She lasted one year. I hope she someday finds a role that will capture her exquisite beauty.

(Above) Angelica Bridges looking good, as though she's modeling, and looking not so good, as was often the case when I tried to film her. (Below) Marliece Andrada, who rose from background to feature player.

f you were to watch *Baywatch* over the course of the season, you'd see dozens of male and female extras in the background. They're paid a modest sum to strut back and forth—giving a little extra visual stimulation to the snow-bound viewers in Homer, Alaska.

From out of this relatively anonymous cast came a young woman, Marliece Andrada. In this group of extremely beautiful people, she stood out. Her role on the show was upgraded to montage girl. The next year we were looking for a woman to play a mermaid. Naturally the actor would have to be a good underwater swimmer. (It's more difficult than it sounds—take my word.) Marliece came up and said, "I hear you're looking for a girl to play a mermaid. How about if I audition?" With about 20 other candidates, Marliece auditioned in the tank. She was clearly the best. I noticed, too, that she'd been in heavy training. She'd lost some weight, toned up. By any measure, she looked altogether fantastic, and on shoot day she performed magnificently.

Finally, as we were casting regulars for the following season, Marliece asked if she could again try out. I sent her to Suzie and Fern, our casting ladies. Some weeks later, Marliece walked back into my office, evidence that she'd survived Suzie and Fern's rigorous casting process. Marliece read for the executive producers—and read well. Not only had she been working on her body, but she'd been in heavy acting training.

Eventually she came back to read a couple of more times, and ultimately she survived the final cut, thus accomplishing something no other actor had done—rising from background girl to montage girl to guest star (mermaid) to regular cast member. Unfortunately, we had so many other women actors at the time, that Marliece simply kept getting put at the end of the line and was never given much of a chance to shine. We let her go.

By the time we were done, the executive producers has retired *all* our women actors with the exception of Kelly Packard. When Paul Talbot asked me to visit our European stations, I invited Kelly Packard to accompany me. Together we visited ITV in England, Kirsch Group in Germany—we also visited the international lifesaving headquarters in Belgium, where I was awarded a medal for promoting good lifesaving techniques throughout the world. Kelly was the best possible actor to bring along. She is intelligent, witty, pleasant, talented, capable. She can handle a crowd; she can handle one-on-one. Kelly's happily married, which makes everything easier.

For our ninth season, 1998–99, we would need three women actors altogether. We hired Mitzi Kapture and Brooke Burns.

Mitzi was an actor on *Silk Stalkings*. She came to *Baywatch* with a different look—dark hair, smaller stature. Mitzi proved herself in our run-and-gun trip to Hawaii. She had to carry the whole show, and she did great.

(Above) Kelly Packard, who survived the departures. (Opposite) Kelly again, in between two new Baywatch women, Brooke Burns and Mitzi Kapture.

I first saw Brooke on *Ally McBeal*, as a guest star on a three-episode arc. Both on and off screen, Brooke is an elegant, statuesque woman with a confident manner and a winning smile. I also found out that her father, a great swimmer at SMU, had a good friend who was also a friend of mine—an Olympic swimmer in '72, Jerry Heidenrich.

Brooke had to win the role over Julia Schultz, a recent *Playboy* Playmate of the Month. With her sexy-nasty, biker-chick style, everybody went nuts for Julia. They could see all sorts of great story lines utilizing her rough look. Finally it came to a showdown: big bad biker chick vs. blond beautiful Brooke.

The *Baywatch* brain trust gathered on a darkened stage to see the battle—Michael Berk, Doug Schwartz, David Hasselhoff, Kimmer Ringwald, David Braff, Suzie, and Fern. Also in attendance were Syd Vinnedge and Pearson's own man, Tony Cohen, whom I hoped would be an ally of mine. From talking to him, I figured he'd prefer that our newest *Baywatch* actor have a more traditional *Baywatch* look.

An initial balloting showed Julia winning the day by an overwhelming margin, seven to one, with my vote being the only one for Brooke. I immediately got up out of my chair on the verge of outrage—how could we be making such a lousy choice after having just made a similar mistake the year before with Carmen Electra? We didn't need the quick fix—the immediate, in-your-face answer, one that suffices for two or three episodes and then promptly runs out of steam. Hadn't we learned anything from the previous year? Were we going to make the same mistake? I did my best to convince them that Julia was not what *Baywatch* needed. She didn't convey the image we'd spent a decade developing—strong, healthy, capable, beautiful.

After speaking my piece, each actor then came in and read a scene with David Hasselhoff—Julia going first, Brooke next. With her winning enthusiasm, her great attitude, her stunning physical presence (including a pre-fitted, one-piece red suit), and my torrid preamble, Brooke won the day. This time the voting went seven to one in her favor. Brooke was hired.

It should be noted, too, that Brooke's family background served to provide a great comfort factor for me. I knew she would be a disciplined person, with good work habits and a strong sense of teamwork. I knew she'd bring a positive spirit to the show. From experience, I've learned that a person such as Brooke stands a far better chance of making it in this business. Believe it or not, Pamela Anderson was much the same way. She came from a strong family. Pam had other issues that interfered with her success, but at her core, she was an extremely focused, goal-oriented, hard-working actor.

Having Brooke, Mitzi, and Kelly on the cast makes me want the show to go for another five years.

CHAPTER 17

Camp Baywatch

Our campkids learn the
basics of lifeguarding.

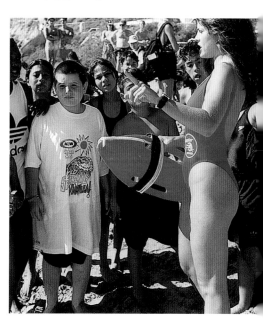

t was over 10 years ago, fall 1989, that we filmed our first episode at Will Rogers lifeguard headquarters. The building itself has changed quite a bit since then. We added a second floor, landscaped the whole area, remodeled and painted the building several times over.

The most recent change was the creation and installation of a Whaling Wall, a 50-foot-long, 10-foot-high mural that shows a vivid underwater scene, a full-size blue whale swimming among schools of fish, pods of porpoises, seals, and seaweed. The mural was painted by the renowned artist Wyland. But he wasn't alone. He had help in the form of 25 young kids, all of whom come from homeless shelters in some of the most dangerous parts of Los Angeles.

We worked the creation of this masterpiece, and Wyland, too, into a *Baywatch* episode—one of our best, called "Dolphin Quest," written by Tai Collins. Tai has written several episodes. The episodes she writes seem to generate the most letters from viewers. Her stories are inevitably heartfelt, often involving a child and his or her family. Tai is a good writer, willing to do the work, the reworking, the re-reworking. She's in for the long haul, which is absolutely key when it comes to writing for television. She does the complete job. Many do not.

(Above) We were thrilled to help put Wyland's Whaling Wall on Will Rogers Headquarters. (Below) A souvenir program for Team Baywatch.

Besides writing the episode, Tai arranged for the kids to be brought to Will Rogers Headquarters and to participate in the creation of the mural—all of this done under the auspices of our ongoing Camp Baywatch.

Because of *Baywatch*'s success, we have been able to explore some new challenges. Last summer we gathered together the best lifeguards in the United States and formed Team Baywatch. The team's first competition was the World Lifeguarding Championships, held in Durban, South Africa. One member of Team Baywatch was Ingrid Walters, an African-American lifeguard, who is now on the show. That trip, which we filmed and used in an episode, was remarkable. Team Baywatch finished fourth in the world. Not bad for the first time out.

In the future, we would like to take Team Baywatch to underprivileged areas to give demonstrations and teach the kids how to swim. It would be great: Team Baywatch comes to town. Have fun and learn to swim. A lot of kids don't know they have a community pool at their disposal.

My great passion is Camp Baywatch. Some people say that if you took all the money in the world and divided it equally, pretty soon the same people would have all the money. I doubt it. I believe many people with great potential never get the opportunity to realize their abilities. Some of these kids in the inner city could be great scholars or lawyers or doctors, but they never get the chance.

During our first year of syndication, I often talked to my good friend and lifeguard, Richard Mark, about helping underprivileged kids. Eventually Tai Collins, who is not only one of our best writers but is also my girlfriend, grew weary of hearing us squawk. She said, "Enough talk. Let's do something."

With our support, she started Camp Baywatch. We took under-privileged and homeless kids to the *Baywatch* set where they met the stars and rode on the Scarab. We also brought in inspirational speakers, such as a professional football player and an Olympic gold medalist. For five days we treated them like kings. For the first two years, the camp went ahead with very little fanfare or star support. I didn't want people to think we were using the kids to promote the show.

Gradually, through doing the camp, Tai discovered that a greater need existed for these kids, a need for ongoing education and support. Now, besides the camp, we are broadening our efforts. We sponsor a little league team, give scholarships to piano, dance, and computer schools; give swimming lessons; and offer college scholarships. One summer we sponsored eight kids to a sportscaster's camp. By the end of the camp they could write their own copy, work off a TelePrompTer, do interviews. One season we took six kids to Hawaii for a week. They all had a great time playing with the dolphins and zipping around on the rescue boats. Some weeks after we got home from Hawaii we received thank-you notes—the kids said they mostly appreciated simply having adequate amounts of food, clean sheets, and a safe place to stay.

Ultimately Camp Baywatch will become a funding source for people who have worthwhile projects but who don't have the money. I am hoping the book you are holding sells a decent number of copies because the profits are going to The Camp Baywatch Foundation.

Helping these kids is as important to me as having a successful show. Actually, it is more important. Shows come and go, but helping someone achieve a goal, a better day, a better life, a walk on the beach, a chance to see within themselves the person they might become, lasts forever. That is success. After eight years, the camp has definitely made a difference.

(Above) Camp Baywatch kids hit the high seas. (Below) Anthony Medina, "Baywatch Camper of the Year," 1998.

CHAPTER 18

A New Beginning

sometimes imagine how different this book would be if I'd written it five years ago, two years, even one year ago. By waiting until now, January 2000, I can write the definitive final chapter on *Baywatch*.

In mid-May 1998, we organized a party to celebrate the beginning of production for our ninth year of syndication (1998–99). One of the people attending the party was Klaus Hallig, president of the holding company that represents Beta Taurus, our distributor throughout Europe (with the exception of Great Britain). Essentially Klaus holds the key to our distribution in Europe. Without his support, which has been enthusiastic over the years, *Baywatch* would be dead in the water.

Klaus and I have been friends and business associates for many years now and I can always count on him to give me the straight scoop. He had already agreed to buy the ninth season—the one we were about to begin filming. I was curious if he was going to buy the following season (1999–2000), which would be our tenth season of syndication. I asked him, "How does it look for next year?"

He raised his eyebrows a little bit but otherwise didn't respond.

(Opposite) Stacy Kamano showing off our new Baywatch Hawai'i *suit.*

I immediately offered, "What if we were to recast? What if we change locations? What if we give the show a whole new look and feel?"

Klaus responded, "Well, you've got nothing to lose because we're not going to go beyond a tenth year here. But if you do those things at least you'll have a chance."

If Klaus wasn't going to buy the show for Europe, we would not have enough money to continue production. Insufficient money would mean the show would inevitably be canceled.

The reason Klaus wasn't going to buy more *Baywatch* was simple: the series had lost its "mojo" in Europe. It had run its course. Ratings were down. Advertising revenue was down. The story was the same in the U.S. In many ways the situation was analogous to our cancellation by NBC a decade earlier. The only difference was that Klaus had done me a huge favor by telling me when he did that he wasn't going to buy the show as it was beyond the 1999–2000 season.

I immediately made a decision: I did not want the franchise to die. Therefore I would not allow a tenth season to be filmed under the present incarnation. Luckily I had a whole year to prepare *Baywatch* for a radical evolution. Some precedent existed for what I had in mind: over the years *Star Trek* became *Star Trek, The Next Generation*, which evolved into *Deep Space 9*, which became *Star Trek Voyager*.

The usual riddle presented itself: how to reinvent the show in such a way as to solve the creative, financial, and technical challenges. The most important of the big three is the financial side. But the financial is thoroughly intertwined with the creative and technical.

Finding the right location would go a long ways in terms of resolving the big three. We had to find a place where lifeguarding was an essential part of everyday life. That fact alone eliminated whole countries and continents. We had to find a place that was relatively exotic (sorry, San Diego), capable of giving us the technical support we needed (adios, Mexico), and not ultra-expensive (bye-bye, Biarritz).

Rather than have a mythical, undefined beach as with the old show, I wanted the new *Baywatch* to have a real home, one that would be readily identifiable. At first it seemed as if we had many options: Bali, Rio, Cape Town, Gothenberg, Trieste, Kyoto—but in reality only a few places made sense financially: beaches located in Florida, Australia, Hawaii, and Canada. I soon ruled out Florida (too expensive), and the beaches in Canada were just too damn cold. When the dust settled we were left with either Australia or Hawaii.

My first choice was Sydney, Australia. During the '70's, I competed in lifeguard competitions in Sydney, Melbourne, and along the Gold Coast. For some reason I got along very well with the Australians, and over the years I made many friends Down Under. I was even "knighted" after my Medal of Valor rescue and for what *Baywatch* had done worldwide—save lives. With the 2000 Olympics on the horizon, I couldn't imagine a better time to be heading to Australia.

We decided to shoot the last two episodes of our ninth season of *Baywatch* in Australia, to set up the transition to the new location. We found an appropriate base of operations, the Avalon Beach Surf Life Saving Club, on beautiful Avalon beach, just north of Sydney. I came back to L.A. very excited about the prospect of moving the whole show, lock, stock and barrel, down to Australia.

I figured we'd be liberating the best of *Baywatch*: blue sky, warm sand, white rolling surf, exceptionally good looking men and women, dramatic rescues, romances between the lifeguards. We would have our characters confront a whole new set of water-related problems. For example, instead of riptides and gangs, the Australians have salt-water crocodiles along with blue-bottles, nasty little jelly fish that sting like wasps and injure scores of people each year.

Best of all, Australia made financial sense. The unions in Australia are weak and were keen to have work for their members. The government was also willing to invest some money to help us secure the infrastructure. A show like *Baywatch* is one of those non-polluting industries that employs scores of people. I figured we had it all worked out, right down to the shiny new yellow uniforms for our actors and the title: *Baywatch Down Under.* Then the problems began.

Before filming the two transition episodes at the Avalon Beach Surf Life Saving Club, we painted the exterior of the main clubhouse. Of course we obtained permission before a single brush was dipped into paint—and we promised to re-paint the headquarters its original color if the majority of members preferred the old look. When all was said and done, most members preferred the new look. Unfortunately a few members did not.

Specifically, three men raised such a ruckus about the violation of their clubhouse—and about the assumed upheaval *Baywatch* would soon be bringing to their little stretch of sand—that a community meeting was called so that the concerns could be addressed. I asked to meet privately with these three hypervocal opponents of *Baywatch* before the community meeting in hopes of addressing and possibly allaying their fears.

I introduced myself and began to detail our hopes and expectations for bringing *Baywatch* to Australia. About two minutes into our private meeting, I noticed that the guy sitting directly in front of me, a stocky, forty-year-old surfer with long blond hair and a deep tan, was undergoing a noticeable change: the veins in his neck and forehead started to stick out. He began sweating freely. His face turned beet red. His eyes narrowed. Short of his experiencing a heart attack, I could sense things were not shaping up as I had hoped. Finally he couldn't take another moment. He stood up, got right in my face, and said in a tone of pure unadulterated maniacal menace: "Listen to this carefully. I'm only going to say this once. The sand of Avalon Beach is my flesh. The water is my blood. I will do *anything* to keep you from coming here. Anything!" Without another word he stormed out of the room. So much for civil discourse.

As I headed back to my hotel, I knew that it was over for *Baywatch* in Avalon. I couldn't bring our crew and actors into a place where their safety might be jeopardized. The only thing that remained was a graceful retreat from Avalon, after which I would pursue another beach location somewhere else in Australia. It is, after all, a very big country with about 10,000 miles of shoreline.

The legacy lives on. From left: Brandy Ledford, Simmone Mackinnon, Stacy Kamano, Brooke Burns.

Rather than cancel the community meeting the following night, I went anyway. I wanted to hear the Avalon concerns in hopes that I could learn something that could be applied when we sought out other locations. At the community meeting I did my best to answer the critics: No, we wouldn't prevent people from surfing. No, we wouldn't ruin the sand dunes. No, we wouldn't kick people off the beach or out of the rock pool.

I tried to explain that we hadn't done those things back in L.A. during nine years of production—why would we start now?

My answers went mostly unheard due to the near riot unfolding in front of me. The voices that rang most clearly were those of the three men I'd met the night before. They repeatedly shouted, screamed, wailed and generally carried on—and all their antics were captured on video and subsequently shown on Aussie network news. Once that footage hit the airways (and was shown again and again), the debate became front-page news throughout Australia. Should *Baywatch* be allowed to invade the quiet hamlet of Avalon? Even Prime

Minister John Howard waded in, criticizing his fellow Aussies for jeopardizing such a great economic opportunity.

The nature of the debate—glitzy *Baywatch* versus quiet beachside hamlet; employment opportunities versus a "no-change, locals-only, maintain-the-status-quo" mentality—caught the interest of the national press.

The premiere of the adjacent state of Queensland immediately stepped forward and offered Queensland as a home for *Baywatch*. It didn't hurt that unemployment was high in Australia and that their economy was stagnant—and that this was an election year. The Queensland politicos wanted their residents to get the jobs that were up for grabs. We had plans to employ over 200 Australians and spend $20 million—as well as put our new location on the map by broadcasting it to 140 countries and millions of people, which would help attract tourists.

I drew up a wish list of things I considered essential in order for *Baywatch* to move north to Queensland. While my wish list was being considered, I toured the coast of Queensland by car. The press followed me closely throughout the day from place to place; we were literally a parade of cars zooming down the highway. Each time I pulled over to check out a beach, reporters jumped out of their cars and shouted, "Is this the place where you'll put *Baywatch*?"

The phenomenal power of television was immediately demonstrated to me. By the time the footage of my beach tour hit the evening news, any semblance of privacy I might have enjoyed was shot to hell. Nine years of producing *Baywatch* in the U.S. hadn't put the slightest dent in my personal space. In Australia, it was gone in a single day. In restaurants, in the hotel lobby, literally everywhere I went, I heard the line: "You're the *Baywatch* guy, aren't you?"

Because of the worldwide popularity of our show, the story of the whole Avalon

Nothing takes place in secret anymore. It seems like the entire world was looking on as Hawaii and Australia tried to land the new Baywatch *show. The Hawaiian newspapers were particularly good at depicting the conpetition. This view, drawn by Dick Adair for the* Honolulu Advertiser, *is not, I assure you, how it actually happened.*

upheaval quickly became international news. I had friends in Turkey call me to say they'd read about it in the *Istanbul Times*. It was inevitable that the news would reach the governor's office in Hawaii.

From the beginning, one of the strongest contenders for a potential location for the new *Baywatch* was Hawaii. There is a long tradition of television series that were based in the Islands, starting with *Hawaii 5-0*, which ran twelve years. *Magnum P.I.* followed for eight years. Besides providing needed employment for Hawaiian production crews, these shows served as beautiful picture postcards of the Islands, enticing tourists to visit. Recently, Hawaii's television production business has fallen on hard times. The series *Wind on Water* lasted barely two episodes. *Fantasy Island* lasted a little longer. This series, by its nature, never even mentioned Hawaii as the location, which did little to promote the Islands.

Certainly a new series, one that would proudly show the best of Hawaii, would be welcome. But filming in Hawaii traditionally has been extremely costly. I didn't want to re-invent *Baywatch* only to discover that it cost more than the old incarnation. The purpose, hopefully, would be for the show to cost less but still give us the high production value we needed. Expensive Hawaii seemed inherently out of the question.

Assisting the governor in bringing new film production to the Islands was an energetic woman, April Masini, and her equally energetic husband, Al. One of the best-known producers in Hollywood, Al Masini created such shows as *Entertainment Tonight* and *Lifestyles of the Rich and Famous*. Several years earlier he had moved to Hawaii to retire. At the time, however, I didn't know either of them. After returning from Australia, I got a call from April Masini. I remember thinking, Who the heck is this?

April asked me what it would take to bring *Baywatch* to Hawaii. Because of our Queensland negotiation, I had the list right in front of me.

- office space and infrastructure
- a beach interior/exterior location and set like the one at Will Rogers lifeguard headquarters
- a warehouse sound stage for interiors
- a tank for underwater filming
- hotel accommodations
- first-class, round-trip plane tickets
- shipping of equipment, uniforms, set pieces, the two Scarab rescue boats, and the newer Luhrs boat

I read off the items to April, plus I added one more: I wanted these items for the life of the show, not just for one season, as had been the case in Australia. Thirty minutes later she called back and said she'd be able to get everything I'd requested.

Now the battle was joined: Hawaii versus Queensland, Australia. Each place had its advantages. Hawaii is a hell of a lot closer to the mainland—five hours flying time to Honolulu versus eighteen hours to Queensland. For a variety of reasons (all of them valid), our new parent company, Pearson, preferred that we be closer to the U.S. mainland. My colleagues in this whole ordeal, Frank Conway and Craig Kwasizur, worked closely with me to sort out the advantages each place presented.

In the big picture, we were all pleasantly surprised that the new *Baywatch* had become such a hot property—hotter than I ever would have imagined.

As we continued exploring the options, the final two episodes of *Baywatch* that had been shot in Australia finally aired. The ratings, unfortunately, were lousy. This did not bode well for moving the whole show Down Under.

The day after the airing of the Australia episodes, I was in a theater watching *October Sky* with Tai, one of our few moments together in recent weeks, when Frank Conway tapped me on the shoulder. After I came off the ceiling, Frank said, "The prime minister of Australia is on the phone. He wants to talk to you. Right now!" I had a long talk with the prime minister, who said in no uncertain terms how important it was to the "perception, economy, and spirit of Australia" that *Baywatch* come there.

The next day Frank Conway went to Hawaii in order to research the Masini's offer. I went back to Queensland yet again to further—and possibly conclude—negotiations. During this trip I decided we simply could not find a better place to locate the show than Queensland. Because of the recession in Australia, our U.S. dollars could get us 40 percent more buying power. The high costs in Hawaii, on the other hand, meant that one U.S. dollar would be discounted by 30 percent. On every front Australia seemed ideal. As I concluded one final meeting in Queensland, Frank Conway reached me by phone. Before I could say hello, he literally shouted, "Don't sign anything! It's unbelievable here. Trust me."

I explained to the Queenslanders that I couldn't commit to anything because Hawaii had made a significant offer. My business associate in this deal was insisting that I look before I signed anything. I owed it to him to do that. I left Queensland saying that I was going to Hawaii with an open mind.

Throughout these negotiations the Internet played a big role. All major newspapers are posted on the Internet. April Masini in Hawaii could read about our ongoing tribulations in Australia through the *Sydney Herald* Website rather than get the information days later or secondhand. This rapid exchange of information is the wave of the future, although it certainly made the time-honored strategy of bluffing nearly impossible.

I was met at the Honolulu airport by April and Al Masini, and we went straight to the governor's mansion. The governor, Ben Cayatano, made a promise that he would do whatever he could to get us there. This turned out to be a solid promise on his part.

Later we went to the Hawaii Film Studios, set in the shadow of Diamond Head, which we would be using should we decide to move to Hawaii. The scattered leaves crunched under the tires of our limousine as we made our way through the deserted compound. It looked as if no one had paid a visit in quite a few months. We parked and I walked into a small bungalow. Smack, right in the face, I walked into a huge spider web. After retreating outside, I looked around. Spider webs and iffy landscaping aside, I could see tremendous potential. In the same way that we had transformed a vacant warehouse on Beethoven Street into a great, functioning studio, I could see that with a couple of months of intense work these old bungalows and the sound stage could be transformed into a magnificent site for creating the new show.

The next day, after a day of touring the island of Oahu, I could see that Frank Conway had been unequivocally right. The whole setting was superb. Hawaii was giving us everything we wanted. It was much closer to the U.S. mainland. The weather was far better (we would have been filming in the dead of winter in Australia—a much-less-agreeable prospect than filming in the summer in Hawaii.) And by keeping the show in the U.S. we would be providing employment for American citizens.

The governor and his advisors, including Tony Vericella, president and CEO of the Hawaii Vistors and Convention Bureau, wanted only two items: first, a two-year guarantee; second, they wanted "Hawaii" in the title. I was happy to oblige. The new home of *Baywatch* would be Hawaii.

'Baywatch' says aloha

By TIM RYAN

HONOLULU — "Baywatch" will change names and locations for the next season — its 10th — beginning with its 200th episode, tentatively titled "Aloha Baywatch."

Announcement that the hourlong syndicated lifeguard drama will relocate to Hawaii came Friday at a news conference — appropriately held on Waikiki Beach — given by "Baywatch" exec producer Greg Bonann, Gov. Ben Cayetano, other government officials and union heads.

"Baywatch Hawaii" — the show's new name is part of a deal with the state — will film on Oahu in late June through early December, Bonann said.

"I cannot think of a better place for 'Baywatch' to be," the producer said. "Now we have to live up to the efforts and sacrifices everyone has made to get us to the Aloha State."

Final approval came last Thursday minutes before a deadline imposed by Pearson Television, owners of "Baywatch," who agreed to increase the show's Hawaii budget from the originally proposed $835,000 per episode to $870,000 ($19 million for the 22-seg season). When the show appeared destined for Australia, that budget was $16.2 million.

Turn to page 13

As of today, January 2000, we have filmed one full season, 22 episodes, in our new home. The experience has been better than anything I could have predicted. The creative challenge was never in doubt—not with such truly awesome settings to choose from and new, enthusiastic cast members. We are developing a story line that involves the creation of a *Top Gun*-style school for lifeguards based on the North Shore of Ohau. This will allow us to bring in a constant stream of new characters from around the world.

The financial side has worked out well. We've kept our costs under control without sacrificing production values. Fortunately our owner, Pearson, has worked with us all along to make the show a financial success.

The most satisfying has been the technical side, specifically working with Hawaii residents. Rather than treat Hawaii as though it were a "back lot" on the outskirts of L.A., we have tried to do as much as we can here. This includes writing (and rewriting), filming, and performing post-production in Hawaii.

When I came over from the mainland, I didn't bring all my production heads to run the show. As much as possible we hired people from the Islands. We could not find experienced editors so we hired guys to serve as assistant editors. I'm hoping that someday, much like with Tommy Erwin a decade ago, these assistant editors will become full editors.

Since making the move I've had the true honor of working with some of the best watermen in the world: Dennis Gouveia, Archie Kalepa, Ralph Goto, and Brian Keaulana, whose father is

One of our rising stars,
Jason Momoa.

the legendary Buffalo Keaulana. Just having guys like Brian, Ralph, Archie, and Dennis around seems to bless the show.

After only eight months in Hawaii, I'm more well known than I was after working nine years in Southern California. In restaurants, in the supermarket, I've been told dozens of times, "Thank you for bringing *Baywatch* to Hawaii." The positive spirit of the people keeps us charged up and trying our hardest to make the best show possible.

At our wrap party, I told the cast and crew, "We may never be challenged like this again in our professional lives. I know that this last year you have all risen to the challenge. Together we've created a whole new *Baywatch* family. My greatest wish at this point is for our family to continue working together for years to come."

Baywatch Hawai'i is now well underway—a year's worth of episodes in the can and hopefully more on the way. But I haven't forgotten our original version of *Baywatch*. We completed 199 episodes, the series spanning the whole, remarkable decade of the '90's. Driving along Pacific Coast Highway in the area below Pacific Palisades will forever bring back the best of memories. I spent a lot of time on that road, going from my house in Malibu to the Will Rogers set and to our Beethoven Street headquarters. I remember many years ago driving with my dad to take the lifeguard swim test. I remember driving to Will Rogers Beach on my way to film the *Boys of Summer* presentation, which helped sell the show to Brandon Tartikoff. I remember driving to the first day of filming for the *Baywatch* pilot and later being given a chance to direct first unit, seeing the production trucks lined up by the dozen and everyone standing around, waiting for me. I was lucky to have shared the adventure with my friends and family.

It was a remarkable time, a dream brought to life, an adventure I could never have imagined beforehand. Mahalo.

Charlie

As I was sitting on the deck of my home working over the final pages of this manuscript, I looked up to see five lifeguard rescue boats slowly motoring up the coast toward Point Dume. The lifeguard on one of the rescue boats waved to me. I waved back. The passing of the boats reminded me that it was time to put down these pages and get moving.

For the first three years of production we had about a dozen spectators watching us whenever we filmed at Will Rogers State Beach. By the end we were attracting over 2,000 people a day. Fans of the show were continually making their way from Toronto or Tokyo or Toledo (Ohio and Spain), just to watch us film.

Sometimes an interesting individual or two comes out of the crowd. This last season, when I was directing an episode, Tai brought a young woman and her 12-year-old son to meet me.

You could tell right away that this mother and child were somehow different. For starters, the mother, Susan Hayes, was remarkably beautiful. You would have thought that she was a fashion model—tall, lean, poised, but a little sad, too. Her son, Charlie, was curious, excited, and very interested at the sight of *Baywatch* under construction. But he also seemed a little tired.

Susan and Charlie's outing did not have the usual lighthearted demeanor one might expect.

(Opposite) Charlie in his dry suit after our excursion beyond the waves.

Far from it. Susan had brought Charlie to the set of *Baywatch* to satisfy one of his wishes, a dying wish. Charlie had terminal cancer.

While at the beach, Charlie's mother noticed that he seemed much healthier and happier. Thanks to a gentleman in Malibu who lent them the use of his house, their brief visit turned into a longer stay. Over the next few months, Charlie and Susan were frequent guests at the communal dinner at my home on Sunday nights. And often they visited the set of *Baywatch*. Naturally, Tai and I came to know Charlie and his mother quite well.

During one visit to the set, Charlie had one of his greatest delights: I let him direct a scene. When I gave him the high sign, he said through the megaphone, "Action." On cue, the actors acted. Finally I gave him another sign, and he said, "Cut." Then we conferred. Did it go okay? Yes, it did. Okay, let's move to the next shot. On certain days, being the boss of *Baywatch* is torture, with more hassles than this book has pages. But on other days, being the boss is the world's greatest job. If I want a 12-year-old kid to direct a scene, he directs.

At the time I met him, Charlie Hayes was not expected to survive more than a few weeks. But despite having a particularly virulent form of cancer, Charlie also had a resilient constitution and a healthy heart that wanted nothing more than to keep him alive. At times Charlie would grow frighteningly weak, then he would rally and for a while you'd hardly know he was ill.

Certain milestones served as magnificent motivation for strengthening his will to live. We dedicated an episode to him. He wanted to see his name on the screen. We had him act in an episode. He wanted to see his image on the screen. He directed a scene in an episode. He wanted to stick around long enough to see his work on the screen.

He wanted to go swimming. For most people, the desire to go swimming can be realized by

Charlie Hayes on the set directing the episode "Let the Games Begin."

simply putting on a pair of swim trunks and diving into the ocean or the nearest pool. Charlie, with an IV permanently fastened into the vein of his left arm, could not go swimming, at least not without special preparation.

We had a custom dry suit made for Charlie that would allow him to go into the water. Unfortunately, on the day of his inaugural swim, he was too weak and tired to put the dry suit on, much less go swimming. Instead he spent the day on the couch at my house, sleeping in the sun. Later that night, long after I'd carried him to his mom's car and he went home, Charlie called Tai on the phone. In his lowest, most conspiratorial voice, he said, "I've got my dry suit on right now. Don't tell my mom."

Charlie Hayes asleep on my sofa.

Charlie's earnestness and suffering touched us all very deeply, particularly myself. He was a remarkable individual. Because of Charlie I came to realize the huge impact that our show was having around the country and around the world. This young boy, whose home was in Utah, saw *Baywatch* and fell in love with the show and everything it represented. More than anything, it made him want see the Pacific Ocean in person, to see the *Baywatch* characters in person. For Charlie, our show opened up a whole world, which he found tremendously inspiring. For Charlie, we had an obligation to make sure that *Baywatch* stayed special.

Charlie did go swimming, and then we went paddling on a surf ski, far out into the ocean. He said he wanted to see what the world looked like from the watery side. As we were turning around to paddle in, he said, "Can I ask you a favor?" I said of course. "Yesterday my mom told me she really liked the swimsuit Tai was wearing. Could you get one like it for her?"

Finally the cancer overtook his phenomenal spirit.

park my car at a bluff overlooking the ocean a few miles up the coast. Almost immediately the Coast Guard jet helicopter flies in low and hovers just overhead, the pilot dipping the nose of the helicopter in a salute to Charlie and his mother Susan. Then it roars off, disappearing as quickly as it came. Next his friends, his nurse, his mother, his brother, Tai, and I say a few words about how much we will miss Charlie. He was a good friend.

After everyone has spoken, we look toward the ocean, at the five lifeguard rescue boats that have been idling quietly offshore. We watch as a lifeguard on the middle boat places a wreath in the water. Then, in formation, the boats head into the ocean. As far as I know, Charlie is the only non-lifeguard ever to have been given this traditional lifeguard farewell.

A few moments later, the rescue boat on the left, Charlie's favorite, turns hard to port and goes alone: missing man formation.

THE *BAYWATCH* EPISODES

SEASON 1

1 and 2 (Pilot) Panic at Malibu Pier
Written by: Michael Berk & Doug Schwartz and Greg Bonann; Directed by: Richard Compton; Montages: "Save Me" performed by Peter Cetera; "Look Out Any Window" performed by Bruce Hornsby; "The Show Goes On" performed by Bruce Hornsby. $2,000,000 over budget. A network type overage.

3 In Deep
Written by: Michael Berk and Doug Schwartz; Directed by: Peter Hunt; Montage: "Life Is a Carnival" performed by The Band. 2 days over schedule (that's 25%).

4 Heat Wave
Written by: Rolf Wallengren; Directed by: Gus Trikonis; Montages: "Room to Move" performed by Animotion; "Working on It" performed by Chris Rea. 1 day over schedule = $75,000.

5 Second Wave
Written by: Jill Donner; Directed by: Scott Brazil; Montage: "Don't Look Back" performed by Charlie Sexton. Fantastic aerial photography, 2nd Unit. On schedule!

6 Message in a Bottle
Written by: Terry Erwin; Directed by: Kim Manners; Montages: "Something So Strong" performed by Jim Capaldi; "Touch" performed by Noiseworks; "Roam" by B-52's. Stu's son Terry's 1st episode as a writer.

7 Drowning Pool
Written by: William A. Schwartz; Directed by: Di Leo; Montage: An original music score by Cory/John. Had to fire Di Leo (the director), slow, slow, slow.

8 The Sky Is Falling
Written by: William Rabkin & Lee Goldberg; Directed by: Kim Manners; Montages: "As Days Go By" performed by Daryl Braithwaite; "Money—That's What I Want." Not a very good episode, too violent

9 Cretin of the Shallows
Written by: Rolf Wallengren & William A. Schwartz; Directed by: Vern Gillum; Montages: "Power of Suggestion" performed by Steve Stevens; "The Look" performed by Roxette. Typified all that was bad about the network version of *Baywatch*. Bad guys, violence, etc.

10 Rookie School
Written by: William Rabkin & Lee Goldberg; Directed by: Bruce Seth Green; Montage: "Stop the World" performed by Big Big Sun. Montage and girl "friendly."

11 Cruise Ship
Written by: William A. Schwartz & Jill Donner; Directed by: Tommy Lee Wallace; Off genre and over budget. All night shooting.

12 Shelter Me
Written by: Terry Erwin; Directed by: Scott Brazil; Montage: "True Love" performed by Glen Frey. Erika was really good in this, Brazil was slow.

13 The Reunion
Written by: Reed Moran; Directed by: Rob Bowman; Montages: "Showdown at Big Sky" performed by Robbie Robertson; "Healing Waters" performed by Starship; "I Get Up" performed by Julian Lennon. Bowman was a great director.

14 Armored Car
Written by: Lee Goldberg & William Rabkin; Directed by: Michael Rhodes; Montage: "Lay Your Hands On Me" performed by Bon Jovi. Great concept, fun 2nd unit.

15 Home Court
Written by: Terry Erwin and William A. Schwartz; Directed by: Paul Schneider; Montage: "No One Else" performed by East of Eden. Introduction of John Allen Nelson. You couldn't not like him.

16 We Need a Vacation
Written by: William Rabkin & Lee Goldberg; Directed by: Gus Trikonis; Montage; "Vacation" performed by Tom Cochran. Guys go to Mexico surfing—wow!

17 Muddy Waters
Written by: Terry Erwin and William A. Schwartz; Directed by: Paul Schneider; Montage: "Whole Lotta Shakin' Goin' On" performed by Georgia Sattelites. Baywatch solves crime at water park—what imagination!

18 Snake Eyes
Written by: Kate Boutilier; Directed by: Gus Trikonis; Montage: "One Good Woman" performed by Peter Cetera. Baywatch goes gambling—a little off genre again.

19 Eclipse
Written by: Claire Whitaker; Directed by: Paul Schneider; Montage: "Breaking Point" performed by The Moody Blues. Great montage! Lousy story.

20 Shark Derby
Written by: Kate Boutilier & Terry Erwin; Directed by: Greg Bonann; Montage: "Goodbye My Friend" performed by Linda Ronstadt. Shawn Weatherly gets killed by shark, she leaves show. My first directing gig.

21 The Big Race
Written by: Rolf Wallengren; Directed by: Kevin Inch; Montages: "When the Going Gets Rough" performed by Billy Ocean; "Dipping Low in the Lap of Luxury" performed by ZZ Top; "Bad Blood" by 10 Years After; An original score by Cory/John. Still going over budget.

22 Old Friends
Written by: William A. Schwartz; Directed by: Doug Schwartz; Montage: "Miss You Now" performed by Trevor Rabin. Doug's first directing gig.

23 The End?
Written by: William Rabkin & Lee Goldberg; Directed by: Badiyi; The writers of this episode really thought it would be our last. . .instead it was their last.

SEASON 2

24/25 Nightmare Bay Pt. 1 & 2
Written by: Michael Berk & Doug Schwartz; Directed by: Greg Bonann; Montages: An original score by Cory/John; "Get Up" performed by Mike and the Mechanics; "Rock Hard" performed by Jimmy Jamison; "Keep Me Running" performed by Noiseworks; "Current of Love" performed by David Hasselhoff. We're back and under budget. Our 1st show on our own.

26 Money Honey
Written by: Alan Swyer; Directed by: Monty Markham; Montages: "Boom Band Boom" performed by Steve Schiff; "Summertime Girls" performed by Y&T. Monty's 1st directing. . . under budget.

27 Buchannon Boys
Written by: David Braff & Reed Moran; Directed by: Gus Trikonis; Montages: "All the Best Things" performed by The Fixx; "Cloud 8" performed by Frazer Chorus. We introduce a brother for Mitch.

28 Reunion
Written by: Michael Berk & Jill Donner; Directed by: Gus Trikonis; Montage: An original score by Cory/John. Gus Trikonis was a really good director.

29 The One That Got Away
Written by: Ronnie Kern; Directed by: Gus Trikonis; Montages: "Don't Do That" performed by Marshall Crenshaw; "When Love Comes Down" performed by Jimmy Jamison. ITV (England) rejected this one. A "knife" and a woman in jeopardy.

30 Thin or Die
Written by: Doug Schwartz & Deborah Schwartz; Directed by: Doug Schwartz; Montages: "So Quiet and So Still" performed by Natalie Archangel; "Indian Rap" performed by Scott Roewe. Erika was great! But something was wrong.

31 Point of Attack
Written by: Alan Swyer; Directed by: Alan Myerson; Montages: "Crazy" performed by Seal; "All Love" performed by Ziggy Marley. Our 1st gang show, huge ratings.

32 If Looks Could Kill
Written by: Michael Berk; Directed by: Doug Schwartz; Montages: "Lilly Was Here" performed by Candy Dulfer; "To Have and to Hold" performed by David Halliday. Shannon Tweed guests as a murderess.

33 Sandcastles
Written by: Garner Simmons; Directed by: Monte Markham; Montages: "Future Love Paradise" performed by Seal; "I Just Wanna Be with You" performed by Tranvision Vamp. Guest star Nicki Cox—her first gig.

34 The Chamber
Written by: Alan Swyer & Gregg Segal; Directed by: Greg Bonann; Montages: "Point of Origin" performed by Yanni; "After the Sunrise" performed by Yanni. Our 1st bottle show: a show shot "in a bottle" that is—on one set. $180,000 under budget.

35 Sea of Flames
Written by: Michael Berk and Doug Schwartz; Directed by: Greg Bonann; Montages: "Tear It Up" performed by 38 Special; "Can't Slow Down" performed by Joe Satriani. Doug got sick and I took over directing. It turned out O.K. but was difficult.

36 Game of Chance
Written by: David Braff; Directed by: Georg Fenady; Montages: "Ooh La La" performed by David Halliday; "Horses" performed by Daryl Braithwaite. Erika's not the same.

37 Big Monday
Written by: Gary Capo & Julian Whatley and Michael Beck; Directed by: Greg Bonann; Montages: "Life Holds On" performed by Beth Neilson Chapman; "Heat of the Jungle" performed by Chris Isaak. Written by our 2nd Unit D.P. and his 1st Assistant—good show!

38 War of Nerves
Written by: Deborah Schwartz & Doug Schwartz; Directed by: Doug Schwartz; Montages: "Real Thing" performed by Brent Bougois; "Saltwater" performed by Jullian Lennon. Cary Tagowa guests as a martial arts gangster—way over $.

39 The Big Spill
Written by: David Braff; Directed by: Cliff Bole; Montages: "Another Nice Day in L.A." performed by Eddie Money; The Bug" performed by Dire Straits; "When the World Was Young" performed by John Cafferty; "Different Destinations" performed by David Halliday. Environmental theme—low ratings.

40 Now Sit Right Back
Written by: Lloyd Schwartz; Directed by: Doug Schwartz; Montage: Theme song to *Gilligan's Island*. Erika wants off the show. Says she's had enough!

41 Shark's Cove
Written by: Deborah Schwartz & Doug Schwartz; Directed by: Monty Markham; Montages: "After Venus" performed by Enya; "House Full of Reasons" performed by Jude Cole. Monty Markham another great job. On budget on schedule.

42 Lost Treasure of Tower 12
Written by: Glenn Bruce & David Braff; Directed by: Cliff Bole; Montages: "Women in Chains" performed by Tears for Fears; Cole Porter's "Night and Day"; "Sound of Your Voice" performed by 38 Special. Erika's wonderful in the episode, but very unhappy.

43 Summer of '85
Written by: Michael Berk; Directed by: Michael Berk; Montage: "About You" performed by David Halliday. Billy gets into a fight with Michael Berk—everyone is shocked. We knew he's gone.

44/45 The Trophy Pt. 1 & 2
Written by: David Braff; Directed by: Doug Schwartz; Montages: An original score by Cory/John; "Fascination" performed by The West End Girls; "Dream in Color" performed by Starship; "Angry Young Man" performed by Jimmy Jamison. Our 1st unplanned 2-part episode—ultimately under budget.

46/47 River of No Return Pt. 1 &2
Written by: Michael Berk and Doug Schwartz; Directed by: Doug Schwartz; Montages: "Poison Girl" performed by Chris Whitley; "All My Life" performed by Linda Ronstadt. Pamela Anderson introduced playing the sax!

48 Rookie of the Year
Written by: Deborah Schwartz and Greg Bonann; Directed by: Gus Trikonis; Montages: "Color Me You" performed by Colorhaus; "Guardian of the Breath" performed by Howard Jones. David Charvet and Alexandra Paul introduced.

49 Tequila Bay
Written by: David Braff; Directed by: Lyndon Chubbuck; Montages: "Diamente" performed by Zucchero; "As Time Goes By" performed by Harry Nillson. Kelly Slater introduced.

50 Pier Pressure
Written by: Deborah Schwartz & Doug Schwartz; Directed by: Gus Trikonis; Montages: "Drag" performed by Steve Wynn; "One Summer" performed by Daryl Braithwaite; "Nobody Does Me" performed by Susan Anton. I met Tai doing 2nd Unit—WOW!!

51 Dead of Summer
Written by: Terry Erwin; Directed by: Cliff Bole; Montages: "Class War" performed by Blackbird; "Reach Out" performed by The Zoo; "Don't Play with My Heart," "Lonely without Your Love," "Don't Stop the Beat" performed by TAG. Stu Erwin's son returns to write one for us.

52 A Matter of Life and Death
Written by: Gary Capo & Julian Whatley and Michael Berk; Directed by: Sidney Hayers; Montages: "Carribean Blue" performed by Enya; "Life Is a Highway" performed by Tom Cochran. Hayers—a class act directing.

53 The Princess of Tides
Written by: Michael Berk & Peter Kiwitt; Directed by: Doug Schwartz; Montages: "In the Hands of Time" performed by Hardine; "Killer" performed by Seal. We ripped off an old classic story and it worked!

54 Point Doom
Written by: Dan Peterson & David Trim; Directed by: Greg Bonann; Montages: "Who Do You Think You Are?" by Sass Jordan; "I'm Too Sexy" performed by Right Said Fred; "Save Me Tonight" performed by Giant. Jennifer Lynn Campbell introduced. What a montage!

55 Lifeguards Can't Jump
Written by: Lloyd Schwartz; Directed by: Greg Bonann; Montages: "Running Wild" performed by Soup Dragons; "Taste of Love" performed by Jimmy Jamison; "Good Times" performed by Arc Angels. Greg Alan Williams looses his temper—wow!

56 Masquerade
Written by: I. C. Rapoport; Directed by: Heather Hill; Montage: "Evening" performed by Pat Benetar. Alexandra Paul and David Hasselhoff play dress up.

57 Showdown at Malibu Pier
Written by: Michael Berk and Doug Schwartz; Directed by: Doug Schwartz; Montages: "Young Love" performed by The Outfield; "I Just Wanna Make Love to You" performed by The Rythmn Syndicate; "Freedom" performed by Noiseworks. Great action adventure.

58/59 Vacation Pt. 1 & 2
Written by: David Braff; Directed by: Gus Trikonis; Montages: "A Kissed Out Float Boat" performed by The Cocteau Twins; "All I Need Is You" performed by Blue Train; "Heaven's Gate" performed by Toni Childs. On board a cruise ship with the whole company.

60 Island of Romance
Written by: Michael Berk and Doug Schwartz; Directed by: Greg Bonann; Montages: "Sighs Smell of Farewell" performed by The Cocteau Twins; "I Just Wanna Be With You" performed by Chris Rea. 3 girls get hot, hot, hot.

61 Stakeout at Surfrider
Written by: David Braff; Directed by: Parker Stevenson; Montages: "Working Man" performed by Glen Frey; "Damn I Wish I Was Your Lover" performed by Sophie B. Hawkins. Parker's 1st episode ever! Fantastic!!

62 Stranger among Us
Written by: John Whelpley; Directed by: Alan Myerson; Montages: "Around the World" performed by The Weathermen; "Bare" performed by Geoffrey Williams. We try everything—this time an alien.

63 Kicks
Written by: Peter Kiwitt & Trish Garland and Michele Rogers; Directed by: Michael Berk; Montages: "Here Comes Trouble" performed by Bad Company; "Love in the 21st Century" performed by Glen Frey. Kickboxing is not our show—but we tried!

64 Fatal Exchange
Written by: David Braff; Directed by: Paul Cajero; Montages: "Take Me" performed by Blackbird; "Senza Una Donna" performed by Zucchero and P. Yound. Paul Cajero, our Line Producer, directs.

65 The Tower
Written by: Doug Schwartz and Michael Berk; Directed by: Greg Bonann; Montages: "Chase the Clouds" performed by The Rembrandts; "Sentinel" performed by Tubular Bells. My 2nd bottle show—$120,000 under.

66/67 Shattered Pt.1 & 2
Written by: Deborah Schwartz; Directed by: Doug Schwartz; Montages: "Right Till the End" performed by Terry Reid; "5th of July" performed by Terry Reid. Our 2nd unplanned 2-part episode—Doug made a silk purse out of a sow's ear.

S E A S O N   4

68/69 Race against Time Pt. 1 & 2
Written by: Michael Berk and Doug Schwartz; Directed by: Greg Bonann; Montages: "Wheels in Motion" performed by Jimmy Barnes; "Searchin' My Soul" performed by Vonda Shepard; "I Would Die for You" performed by Jann Arden; "Hungry Town" performed by Big Pig. Biggest episode yet. Lotsa $, lotsa work, great episode.

70 Ironman Buchannon
Written by: David Braff; Directed by: Doug Schwartz; Montages: "Dream On" performed by Beloved; "You Want It All" performed by The Weathermen. Mitch Buchannon turns 40 and wins race.

71 Lover's Cove
Written by: Steven Barnes; Directed by: Gus Trikonis; Montages: "Hunny Bunny" performed by Book of Love; "Once in a Lifetime" performed by Sarah Brightman; "River of Time" performed by Laura Christy. A very tough episode about a terminal child whom Hobie falls in love with.

72 Red Knights
Written by: Deborah Schwartz; Directed by: Cliff Bole; Montages: "Ordinary World" performed by Duran Duran; "Anything You Ask" performed by Susan Anton. Richard Jaeckel's last episode and we all knew it. He was wonderful and I cried watching him.

73 Second Time Around
Written by: Garner Simmons; Directed by: Lyndon Chubbuck; Montages: "Sail Across the Water" performed by Jane Sibury; "Rock On" performed by David Essex; "Tighter Tighter" performed by David Hasselhoff. Alexandra Paul can carry a show all by herself.

74 Tower of Power
Written by: David Braff; Directed by: Gus Trikonis; Montages: "Elemental" performed by Tears for Fears; "Just Another Day" performed by Jon Secada. Our 2nd gang episode. Ratings thru the roof.

75 Blindside
Written by: Deborah Schwartz; Directed by: Doug Schwartz; Montages: "Spirit" performed by Beloved; "Pelican Man" performed by Jimmy Hart. Pamela Anderson and John Allen Nelson are good in a episode dealing with the disease—retinitis pigmentosa.

76 Sky Rider
Written by: Sherri Ziff & Michael Berk; Directed by: Lyndon Chubbuck; Montages: "Treaty" performed by Yothu Yindi; "Book of Days" performed by Enya. Pam at her best.

77/78 Coronado del Soul Pt.1 & 2
Written by: David Braff; Directed by: Gus Trikonis; Montages: An original score by Cory/John; "Running into the Sun" performed by Noel; "State of Grace" performed by Tia Carrere. The company goes to the Hotel del Coranado in San Diego.

79 The Child Inside
Written by: Deborah Schwartz; Directed by: Doug Schwartz; Montages: "The Best Is Yet to Come" performed by David Hasselhoff; "The Child Inside" performed by Robin and Judithe Randall. Mary Lou Retton guests—high rating.

80 Trading Places
Written by: David Braff; Directed by: Paul Cajero; Montage: "Stand Up" performed by Jimmy Barnes. U.S. Coast Guard stars with Alexandra.

81 Mirror, Mirror
Written by: Deborah Schwartz; Directed by: Doug Schwartz; Montage: An original score by Cory/John. Off genre—crazy twins go berserk.

82 Rescue Bay
Written by: Steven Barnes; Directed by: Greg Bonann; Montages: "Lie to Me" performed by Paul Norton; "I Want You" performed by Nikoli Steen; "Art of Living" performed by The Boomers. Jeff Altman guest stars. Take off on ourselves. Producer creates beach lifeguard series for TV.

83 Submersion
Written by: Michael Berk; Directed by: Greg Bonann; Montage: "Ordinary Day" performed by Jim Jacobson. Best show Michael ever wrote, best acting Hassel ever did.

84 Guys & Dolls
Written by: David Braff; Directed by: Cliff Bole; Montages: "Beautiful" performed by Babble; "Dream a Perfect Dream" performed by Tia Carrere. One of our most forgettable shows.

85 The Life You Save
Written by: Michael Berk; Directed by: Michael Berk; Montages: "Sunshine Like You" performed by The Waterlillies; "Climb On" performed by Shawn Colvin. Fantastic montage opens the show about kids and our future.

86 The Falcon Manifesto
Written by: Michael Berk; Directed by: Chuck Baverman; Montage: "Looking For Something" performed by Vonda Shepard. Mystery and action. Gorgeous girl guests.

87 Western Exposure
Written by: Deborah Schwartz; Directed by: Doug Schwartz; Montages: "Talking to God" performed by Ricky Van Shelton; "My Baby Loves Me" performed by Martina McBride; "Life #9" performed by Martina McBride; "Where Was I" performed by Ricky Van Shelton. 4 montages. A country western delight.

88 Tentacles Pt. 1
Written by: Sherri Ziff and Michael Berk; Directed by: Lyndon Chubbuck; Montage: "Fly" performed by His Boy Elroy. Another 2-part mistake—we were so far over budget We had to stretch it to 2 parts.

89 Tentacles Pt. 2
Written by: Michael Berk; Directed by: Greg Bonann; Montages: "Water x 3" performed by Sun 60; "Enchanted" performed by Book of Love. It turned out well thanks to the scariest giant squid ever.

S E A S O N   5

90/91 Fault Line Pt. 1 & 2
Written by: Michael Berk; Directed by: Greg Bonann; Montages: "Off the Hook" performed by Peter Frampton; "You Can Run" performed by Jeremy Jackson; "I'm Gonna Miss You" performed by Jeremy Jackson; "Meanwhile" performed by 3rd Matinee. Huge show—Earthquake and big $.

92 Aftershock
Written by: David Braff; Directed by: Gus Trikonis; Montages: "Summer of Love" performed by David Hasselhoff; "Return to Me" performed by October Project. After the big show, we needed a small show.

93 Baja Run
Written by: Deborah Schwartz; Directed by: Doug Schwartz; Montages: "LaBamba" performed by Los Lobos; "Silver" performed by The Williams Brothers. Dune buggies send us flying over budget.

94 Air Buchannon
Written by: David Braff; Directed by: Gus Trikonis; Montages: "The Limit" performed by Jim Jacobson; "Everyone's a Star" performed by Francis Dunnery; "Lessons of Love" performed by Lea Solanga. Silly but fun.

95 Short Sighted
Written by: Deborah Schwartz; Directed by: Doug Schwartz; Montages: "Ri Na Cruinne" performed by Clanned; "Best of Whatever You Are" performed by Robin and Judithe Randall. Doug and retinitis pigmentosa sequel.

96 Someone to Baywatch over Me
Written by: Kimmer Ringwald; Directed by: Reza Badiyi; Montages: "Cantaloop" performed by US3; "If You Go" performed by Jon Secada. True story unfulfilled.

97 I Spike
Written by: Michael Berk; Directed by: Greg Bonann; Montages: "Knock Me Down" performed by Jimmy Barnes; "I'll Drown In My Tears" performed by Greg Alan-Willams. Kent Steffes and Karch Kiraly guest—#1 volleyball team in the world at the time.

98 KGAS and the Groove
Written by: Reuben Leder; Directed by: Charles Winkler; Montages: "Summer of Love" performed by The Beach Boys; "You Can Get It If You Really Want It" performed by Desmond Dekker; "Daydream" performed by Sarah Vaughn. Pam did some incredible underwater work.

99 Rubber Ducky
Written by: David Braff; Directed by: Greg Bonann; Montages: "Mystery Game" performed by Clanned; "Celtic Warrior" performed by Stephen Housden. Introduce Rebecca Carlton—gorgeous Aussie.

100 Deep Trouble
Written by: John Allen Nelson & Max Strom; Directed by: Gus Trikonis; Montages: "Falling Forward" performed by Julia Fordham; "I Love You. . . I'll Kill You" performed by Enigma. Our 100th episode!

101 Father's Day
Written by: Tai Collins; Directed by: Greg Bonann; Montage: "A Gentle Place" performed by Clanned. Tai's 1st episode as a writer.

102 Red Wind
Written by: Eric Blakeney; Directed by: Greg Bonann; Montages: "What Silence Knows" performed by Shara Nelson; "Don't Force It" performed by Arrow; "Adouma" performed by Angelique Kidjo. Sexy show—WOW!

103 Wet and Wild
Written by: Kimmer Ringwald; Directed by: Paul Lazarus; Montages: "Our World, Our Times" performed by Alannah Myles; "Sun's Gonna Rise" performed by Sass Jordan. A new director—an interesting show.

104 Promised Land
Written by: David Braff; Directed by: Paul Cajero; Montages: "Inside Job" performed by Michael Lanning; "Boom Papa Boom" performed by Jimmy Vaughan. Torn from the headlines—boat people.

105 Seize the Day
Written by: Deborah Schwartz; Directed by: Doug Schwartz; Montages: "Days of Our Love" performed by David Hasselhoff; "If I Could Touch You One More Time" performed by Robin and Judithe Randall. Rebecca's character Tracy dies of cancer.

106 A Little Help
Written by: Michele Rogers Berk & Susan Hamilton Brin; Directed by: Michael Berk; A bottle show that wasn't.

107 The Runaways
Written by: David Braff; Directed by: Lou Stout; Montages: "Until the Last Teardrop" performed by David Hasselhoff and Jayne Collins; "No Turning Back" performed by Jayne Collins; "Good Golly Miss Molly" performed by Little Richard. Stout did a great job on his 1st show.

108 Fire with Fire
Written by: David Braff; Directed by: Richard Preece; Montages: "The Fire" performed by Jim Jacobson; "Here We Go" performed by Stakka Bo. Braff wrote this under fire in 4 days!

109 Homecoming
Written by: Steven Barnes; Directed by: Gus Trikonis; Montages: "Jebbas" performed by David Foster; "Generator" performed by Royal Jelly. Barnes was our most creative freelancer. This was another interesting story and show.

110/111 Silent Night Pt. 1 & 2
Written by: Deborah Schwartz; Directed by: Doug Schwartz; Montages: "Let It Snow" performed by Leon Redbone; "Santa Baby," "Have Yourself a Merry Little Christmas," and "Winter Wonderland" all performed as instrumentals; "Black Coffee" performed by Angela Teek. Snow on the beach? 2 parts, what a mess, great fun.

112/113
Trapped beneath the Sea Pt. 1 & 2
Written by: Michael Berk; Directed by: Greg Bonann; Montages: "Casablanca" performed by The Ambush; "Cursum Perficio" performed by Enya. Huge, huge, show!! Michael and I collaborate well. 3rd year in a row we start out big.

114 Face of Fear
Written by: Deborah Schwartz; Directed by: Doug Schwartz; Montages: An original score by Cory/John; "You Painted Smile" performed by Bryan Adams. After a big show—"you know what."

115 Leap of Faith
Written by: Deborah Schwartz; Directed by: Doug Schwartz; Montages: "Garden of Eden" performed by Paula Cole; "I'm Always Here" performed by Jimmi Jackson. Teen suicide show. ITV rejected it.

116 Surf's Up
Written by: David Braff; Directed by: Gus Trikonis; Montages: "Surfer Girl," "California Girls," "Fun, Fun, Fun," "Don't Worry Baby," "Summer of Love" all performed by The Beach Boys. Yasmine Bleeth carries the show.

117 Beauty and the Beast
Written by: David Braff; Directed by: David Hagar; Montages: "Supermodel Sandwich" performed by Terence Trent D'Arby; "Adiemus" performed by Adiemus. David Hagar's directorial debut—an alligator and huge ratings.

118 There Is a Season
Written by: Deborah Schwartz; Directed by: Doug Schwartz; Montages: "Stranger In Paradise" performed by Kourosh; "Only a Matter of Time" performed by Robin and Judithe Randall. Doug and Debbie collaborate again. A little off genre.

119 Hot Stuff
Written by: David Braff; Directed by: Georg Fenady; Montages: "Crazy Cool" performed by Paula Abdul; an original score by Cory/John. Gena Lee Nolin gets hot!!

120 Hit and Run
Written by: Grant Rosenberg; Directed by: Gus Trikonis; Montage: "Could I Be Your Girl" performed by Jann Arden. Not very original but a good show.

121 Lost and Found
Written by: Evan Somers; Directed by: Reza Badiyi; Montages: "Day in the Sun" performed by Peter Frampton; "(Let's) Get Together" performed by The Youngbloods; "Can't Wait for You" performed by Kindred Spirit. A very forgettable show. They can't all be great.

122 Sail Away
Written by: David Braff; Directed by: Paul Cajero; Hasselhoff carries the show and the day.

123 Go for the Gold
Written by: David Braff; Directed by: Greg Bonann; Montages: "Search for the Hero" performed by M People; "Way Down Deep" performed by Jennifer Warnes. The 2nd unit goes Olympics again—what fun.

124 The Incident
Written by: Kimmer Ringwald; Directed by: Greg Bonann; Montages: "Throwing Fire at the Sun" performed by Heather Nova; "Pleasure Grounds" performed by Mae Moore. Great story, great action. Yaz looses victim.

125 Bash at the Beach
Written by: Deborah Schwartz; Directed by: Doug Schwartz; Montage: "American Made" performed by Hulk Hogan and Hulk's Boot Band. Hulk Hogan guest stars. Stephanie gets melanoma

126 Last Wave
Written by: David Braff & Tai Collins; Directed by: Reza Badiyi; Montages: "Tintinnabulum" performed by Adiemus; "Deep as You Go" performed by October Project; "Blue Hills" performed by Daryl Braithwaite; "Memorial Beach" performed by A-Ha. Mark Fo's real-life tragedy.

127 Sweet Dreams
Written by: Tai Collins; Directed by: Greg Bonann; "Everything You Do" performed by Keely Hawkes; "Stonage" performed by Stone Edge. A baby comes to *Baywatch*. Logan has a history.

128 Desperate Encounters
Written by: Deborah Schwartz; Directed by: Doug Schwartz; Montages: "Pretty Woman," "One Last Chance," and "Backroads" all performed by Ricky Van Shelton. Too dark and off genre.

129 Baywatch Angels
Written by: Michele Rogers Berk & Susan Hamilton Brin; Directed by: Michael Berk; Montage: "Funky Junky" performed by Peter Andre. Great idea, didn't work. Charlie's Angels go *Baywatch*.

130 Where the Heat Is
Written by: Michael Berk; Directed by: Lou Stout; Montage: An original score by Cory/John. Stout pitches in with a great show.

131 Freefall
Written by: Michael Berk; Directed by: Michael Berk; "Over My Shoulder" performed by Mike and the Mechanics; "Welcome to the Real World" performed by Frankie Knuckles; "I Believe" performed by David Hasselhoff; "Lovin' Me Insane" performed by The Rembrandts.

Bottle show. Michael Berk wrote and directed.

132/133 Forbidden Paradise Pt. 1 & 2
Written by: Deborah Schwartz; Directed by: Doug Schwartz; Montages: "Couple of Days Off" performed by Huey Lewis and the News; "Cruisin on Hawaiian Time" performed by Dave Jenkins and Kabpono; "Funky Jam" performed by Primal Scream; "Bone Down" performed by T-Ride. Hawaii. The waterfall with Pam and Charvet . . . hot, hot, hot!

134 Liquid Assets
Written by: Michael Berk; Directed by: Georg Fenady; Montages: "Venice Grooves" performed by Jim Jacobson; "Runaway" performed by The Cors. We did parts of this show last season to save $.

135 Bachelor of the Month
Written by: David Braff; Directed by: Reza Badiyi; Montages: "Heaven Help My Heart" performed by Tina Arena; "Bring Out the Elvis" performed by Louise Hoffsten; "Grooving" performed by The Hunting Party. Hasselhoff stranded on a deserted beach with the date from hell.

136 Shark Fever
Written by: David Braff; Directed by: Greg Bonann; Montages: "Chains" performed by Tina Arena; "Nice Doin' Business" performed by Louise Hoffsten. Jaason Simmons last show. He becomes a director in story and leaves for Hollywood.

137 Chance of a Lifetime
Written by: Deborah Schwartz; Directed by: Doug Schwartz; Montage: "Bless a Brand New Angel" performed by Judithe Randall. We kill Alexandra's character off.

138 Buried
Written by: David Braff; Directed by: David Hagar; Montages: "She's a River" performed by Simple Minds; "Ready to Go" performed by Republica. Hagar directs a great episode underground.

139 Talk Show
Written by: Kimmer Ringwald; Directed by: Greg Bonann; Montages: "Dog" performed by Milo Z; "The Only Thing That Looks Good on You Is Me" performed by Bryan Adams. Guest star—Jay Leno. But a dog steals the show.

140 Hot Water
Written by: Michelle Rogers Berk & Susan Hamilton Brin; Directed by: Lou Stout; Another "environmental" fiasco.

141 Windswept
Written by: David Braff; Directed by: Georg Fenady; Montage: "The Life" performed by Mark Tschanz. Clever of Braff, Georg brought it under.

142 The Contest
Written by: Michael Berk; Directed by: Reza Badiyi; Montages: "Sun" performed by Babble; "I Just Wanna Be Your Underwear" performed by Bryan Adams; "PCH" performed by ZZ Top. A bikini showcase.

143 Scorcher
Written by: Kimmer Ringwald; Directed by: Greg Bonann; Montages: "In the Summertime" performed by Shaggy; "Soul" performed by Sovory. Charlie came into our lives and we are changed forever.

144 Let The Games Begin
Written by: Tai Collins; Directed by: Greg Bonann; Montages: "The Celts" performed by Enya; "You're the Voice" performed by David Foster; "Happy" performed by Mark Tschantz. 25 Australian Ironmen guest stars from Oz.

145 Rendezvous
Written by: Kimmer Ringwald; Directed by: Gus Trikonis; Montages: "Children" performed by Robert Miles; "Cool Water" performed by Joy Askew. Good action and underwater work.

146 Trial by Fire
Written by: David Braff; Directed by: Lou Stout; Montage: "Miricle" performed by Heidi Berry. Montage was great; music fantastic.

147 Baywatch at Seaworld
Written by: Deborah Schwartz; Directed by: Doug Schwartz; Montages: "18 'til I Die" performed by Bryan Adams; "The Giving Sea" performed by Crusoe. We go to San Diego again.

148 Heal the Bay
Written by: Kimmer Ringwald; Directed by: Gus Trikonis; Montages: "That Girl" performed by Maxi Priest; "Beyond the Invisible" performed by Enigma. Our last environmental show—boring.

149 Nevermore
Written by: Deborah Schwartz; Directed by: Doug Schwartz; Montage: "Mine" performed by The Hoodoo Gurus. Cute and over budget.

150 Beach Blast
Written by: Deborah Schwartz; Directed by: Doug Schwartz; Montages: "Cat on the Loose" performed by Catonda Loose; "House Is Rockin'" performed by The Brian Setzer Orchestra. 150 episodes and counting!

151 Golden Girls
Written by: David Braff; Directed by: Gus Trikonis; Montages: "Keep Up" performed by Christine Anu; "I Wanna Know" performed by Michael English. A very sexy show.

152 Guess Who's Coming to Dinner
Written by: Deborah Schwartz; Directed by: Doug Schwartz; Rather cliché but a fun show.

153 Lifeguardian
Written by: Tai Collins; Directed by: Greg Bonann; Montages: "Greatest Gift" performed by Tina Arena; "Watching the World" performed by Maxi Priest. An angel introduces us to Camp Baywatch.

154 Matter of the Heart
Written by: Kimmer Ringwald; Directed by: Michael Berk; Montages: "High Time" performed by Cory Lerios; "Da Roof" performed by War. Cory and John composed a fantastic show.

155 Search and Rescue
Written by: Michael Berk; Directed by: Greg Bonann; Montages: "The Band Played On" performed by Simple Minds; "Survival" performed by Martin Okasili. Pilot for a possible new series—All American decided not to do it. . . what a mistake #2.

S E A S O N   8

156 Rookie Summer
Written by: David Braff; Directed by: Greg Bonann; Montage: "Leave Your Hat On" performed by Alex Fox. I directed the 1st five shows to air—too much.

157 The Choice
Written by: Gillian Horvath; Directed by: Greg Bonann; Montages: "Satisfied" performed by Bus Stop; "Proud Man" performed by Jon Stevens. Angelica's introduction—we couldn't make her look good.

158 Memorial Day
Written by: Kimmer Ringwald; Directed by: Greg Bonann; Montages: "Freedom" performed by Michael English; "Cellophane Girl" performed by Louis Says; "Believer" performed by Chantal Kreviazuk. A bottle show with Dick Martin as guest star.

159 Lifeguard Confidential
Written by: Michael Berk; Directed by: David Hagar; Montages: "Right On" performed by Pianoboy; "Something between You and I" performed by Say-So. Hagar's best episode ever.

160 Charlie
Written by: Tai Collins; Directed by: Greg Bonann; Montages: "Peace and Love" performed by The Blessed Union of Souls; "Sarangi" performed by Hooverphonic; "Make a Difference" performed by Michael Cuccione. Tai's script for little Charlie Hayes. We cried through the whole thing.

161 To the Max
Written by: Deborah Schwartz; Directed by: Doug Schwartz; Montage: "To the Max" performed by Robin and Judithe Randall. Very off genre; very boring.

162 Out of the Blue
Written by: David Braff; Directed by: Parker Stevenson; Montages: "Searching" performed by Cyndi Lauper; "Ouch" performed by Camus. Tracy Bingham can't act, even Park agreed.

163 Eel Nino
Written by: Gillian Horvath; Directed by: Doug Schwartz; Great show about giant eel—big numbers.

164 Homecoming
Written by: Kimmer Ringwald; Directed by: Paul Cajero; Montages: "Gitch Manido" and "Ly Oley Ale Loya" performed by Sacred Spirits. Malibu history - re: native Indians—great show!

165 Full Throttle
Written by: Kimmer Ringwald; Directed by: Lou Stout; Montages: "Summertime" performed by The Sundays; "Friends" performed by Wannadies. An editing victory for Latham—saved in post again.

166 Hijacked
Written by: Gillian Horvath; Directed by: Robbie Weaver; Montages: "Getting Scared" performed by Imogen Heap; "Footsteps" performed by Annika. Robbie Weaver was fantastic directing. This guy is good.

167 Night of the Dolphin
Written by: Kimmer Ringwald; Directed by: Tracy Britton; Montage: "Meil" performed by Imogen Heap. High energy, low yield.

168 Next Generation
Written by: David Braff; Directed by: Greg Bonann; Montages: "Desire" performed by Toad the Wet Sprocket; "Good Vibrations" performed by The Beach Boys. Too many cast members—Carmen Electra introduced.

169 Bon Voyage
Written by: David Braff; Directed by: Doug Schwartz; Montage: "Padded Bra" performed by Louise Hoffsten. Part 3 of the Alaska fiasco.

170/171 White Thunder Pt. 1 & 2

Written by: David Braff; Directed by: Doug Schwartz; Montages: "Wide Wide Blue" performed by Pianoboy; An original score by Cory/John; "I Wanna Wake Up" performed by Annika; "These Lovin' Eyes" performed by David Hasselhoff. Nightmare on board a cruise ship—$300,000 over budget and our 1st ever 3-part fiasco!!

172 Surf City

Written by: David Braff; Directed by: Greg Bonann; Montages: "Show Me Heaven" performed by Tina Arena; "Tears and Laughter" performed by The Odds; "Shine" performed by Louis Says. Bottle show to make up for Alaska fiasco.

173 Countdown

Written by: Tai Collins; Directed by: Rick Jacobson; Montages: "MmmBop" performed by Hanson; "The Reddest Rose" performed by Annika. Another bottle show to make up for Alaska.

174 Quarantine

Written by: Kim Weiskoff; Directed by: Doug Schwartz; Montages: "Party Time" performed by Gloria Estefan; "She Can Rock It" performed by Power Station; "Postcards" performed by Texas; "Walk the Walk" performed by Sylvia Powell. Bottle show. . .still paying off Alaska.

175 No Way Out

Written by: Tai Collins; Directed by: Greg Bonann; Montages: "Burn" performed by Tina Arena; An original score by Cory/John. Bottle show with Parker starring—$200,000 under.

176 Missing

Written by: David Braff; Directed by: Parker Stevenson; Montage: An original score by Cory/John. Braff's best script ever—right from the M.I.R.

177 Diabolique

Written by: Kimmer Ringwald; Directed by: Parker Stevenson; Montages: "Falling" performed by Olive; Johann Strauss's waltz "On the Blue Danube." The last bottle show to make up for Alaska.

S E A S O N   9

178/179 Crash Pt. 1 & 2

Written by: David Braff; Directed by: Greg Bonann; Montages: "Where You Are" performed by Jim Jacobson; "Wasn't It Good" performed by Tina Arena. Biggest show I ever attempted. (Oz still on horizon.)

180 Hot Summer Night

Written by: Kimmer Ringwald; Directed by: Rick Jacobson; Montage: "Sweet Religion: performed by Imogen Heap. Jeremy Jackson's best show ever.

181 The Big Blue

Written by: Tai Collins; Directed by: Greg Bonann; Montages: "Just Like You" performed by Babble; "How Far" performed by Vennesa Daou. The Golden Knights Army parachute team and Mehgan Heaney Grier guest star.

182 Sharks, Lies & Videotape

Written by: Maggie Marshall; Directed by: Parker Stevenson; Montages: "Real Woman" performed by Gloria Estefan; "Spice Up Your Life" performed by The Spice Girls. Mitzi and David had a great time.

183 Double Jeopardy

Written by: Chad Hayes & Carey Hayes; Directed by: Parker Stevenson; Montage: "Letter of Fate" performed by Goldie. Parker proved himself in the water.

184 Water Dance

Written by: John Whelpley; Directed by: Doug Schwartz; Montage: "Aquamarine" performed by Linda Lampenius. An absolute fiasco with guest star violinist.

185 Drop Zone

Written by: Kimmer Ringwald; Directed by: David Hagar; Montage: "Angry Angel" performed by Imogen Heap. Great show, great script, real lifeguarding.

186 Dolphin Quest

Written by: Tai Collins; Directed by: Greg Bonann; Montages: "Our World" performed by Maire Brennan; "You Can Fly" performed by Wade Hubbard. Hawaii with the dolphins, Mitzi's 1st show.

187 The Natural

Written by: Ziff Lester; Directed by: Rick Jacobson; Montage: "Girl on Fire" performed by INXS. Brooke Burns is introduced—wow!

188 Swept Away

Written by: David Braff; Directed by: Lou Stout; "Halfway" performed by Gloritone. Big budget, Lou and Frank did a great job.

189 Boys Will Be Boys

Written by: Kimmer Ringwald; Directed by: Georg Fenady; Montages: "Free My Soul" performed by Jon Stevens; "Walk Right On" performed by Stefan Anderson. Kimmer writes comedy beautifully.

190 The Edge

Written by: Steven Barnes; Directed by: Robbie Weaver; Montages: "Push It" performed by Garbage; "Airplane" performed by Imogen Heap. Chokie swims like an Olympian—his best show ever.

191 The Swimmer

Written by: Kimmer Ringwald; Directed by: Greg Bonann; Montages: "This the Trip" performed by Sister 7; "Is This Real" performed by Lisa Hall; "I'm the Man" performed by The Philosopher Kings. A bottle show ripped off from the Burt Lancaster movie.

192 Friends Forever

Written by: Deborah Schwartz; Directed by: Doug Schwartz; Montages: "We Can Do Anything" performed by Jeanette Clinger; "I'm Always Here" performed by Lerios/D'Andrea; "Forever Friends" performed by Robin and Judithe Randall. Doug wanted to do an ape show!!

193 Come Fly with Me

Written by: David Braff; Directed by: David Hasselhoff; Montage: "I'll Be the One" performed by Wade Hubbard. Hasselhoff's 1st directing gig—all hands supported magnificently.

194 Grand Prix

Written by: David Braff; Directed by: Georg Fenady; Montages: "Hey Now Now" performed by Swirl 360; "Hooray for Hollywood" performed by Jim Jacobson; "New Clear Days" performed by Crusoe. *Baywatch* goes NASCAR.

195 Wave Rage

Written by: Kimmèr Ringwald; Directed by: Parker Stevenson; Montages: "Holy Waters" performed by Angelique; "Ave Maria" performed by Ke'. Parker under pressure—no prep time—great show.

196 Galaxy Girls

Written by: Kimmer Ringwald; Directed by: Doug Schwartz; Montages: "Chinese Burn" performed by Curve; "Lose Your Mind" performed by Motorbaby. A great show with athletic women.

197 Castles in the Sand

Written by: David Braff; Directed by: Parker Stevenson; Montage: "Inconceivable" performed by Leah Andreone. Braff's last script. . . a great run.

198/199 Baywatch Down Under Pt. 1 & 2

Written by: Maurice Hurley; Directed by: Greg Bonann; Montages: ""Mouth to Mouth" performed by Vennesa Daou; "My Island Home" performed by Christina Anu; "The Show Goes On" performed by Bruce Hornsby. The biggest challenge I ever attempted—Frank and Craig were the heroes.

Baywatch is broadcast over regular television stations and satellite television networks in the following countries:

Albania .Greek	Guinea . . . . .French	Peru . . . . .Spanish
Andorra . . . . .Catalan	Guyana . . . . .English	Philippines . . . . .English
Angola . . . . .Portugese	Haiti . . . . .French	Poland . . . . .Polish
Antigua . . . . .Portugese	Honduras . . . . .Spanish	Portugal . . . . .Portugese
Argentina . . . . .Spanish	Hungary . . . . .Hungarian	Qatar .Arabic
Australia . . . . .English	Iceland . . . . .Icelandic	Romania . . . . .Romanian
Austria . . . . .German	India . . . . .Hindi	Russia . . . . .Russian
Azerbaijan . . . . .Russian	Indonesia . . . . .Malay	Saint Kitts . . . . .English
Bahamas . . . . .English	Iran . . . . .Farsi	Saint Lucia . . . . .English
Bahrain . . . . .Arabic	Iraq .Arabic	Saint Vincent . . . . .English
Bangladesh . . . . .English	Ireland . . . . .English	San Marino . . . . .Italian
Barbados . . . . .English	Isreal . . . . .Hebrew/Arabic	Sao Tome . . . . .Portugese
Belarus . . . . .Russian	Italy . . . . .Italian	Saudi Arabia . . . . .Arabic
Belgium . . . . .Flemish	Jamaica . . . . .English	Senegal . . . . .French
Belize . . . . .English	Japan . . . . .Japanese	Seychelles . . . . .English
Benin . . . . .French	Jordan . . . . .Arabic	Singapore . . . . .Chinese
Bhutan . . . . .Tibetan	Kazakstan . . . . .Russian	Slovakia . . . . .Slovak
Bolivia . . . . .Spanish	Kenya . . . . .Swahili/English	Slovenia . . . . .Slovenian
Brazil . . . . .Portugese	South Korea . . . . .Korean	Solomon Islands . . . . .English
Brunei . . . . .English	Kuwait . . . . .Arabic	South Africa . . . .English, plus ten others
Bulgaria . . . . .Bulgarian	Kyrgyzstan . . . . .Russian	Spain . . . . .Spanish
Burundi . . . . .French	Latvia . . . . .Russian	Sri Lanka . . . . .Sinhala
Cambodia . . . . .French	Lebanon . . . . .Arabic	Sudan . . . . .Arabic
Cameroon . . . . .English	Liechtenstein . . . . .German	Suriname . . . . .Dutch
Canada . . . . .English/French	Lithuania . . . . .Russian	Swaziland . . . . .English
Chile . . . . .Spanish	Luxembourg . . . . .French	Sweden . . . . .Swedish
China . . . . .Mandarin	Malaysia . . . . .Malay	Switzerland . . . . .Germany
Columbia . . . . .Spanish	Maldives . . . . .Divehi	Taiwan . . . . .Mandarin
Costa Rica . . . . .Spanish	Mali . . . . .French	Tajikistan . . . . .Russian
Cyprus . . . . .Greek	Malta . . . . .Maltese/English	Thailand . . . . .Thai
Czech Republic . . . . .Slovak	Marshall Islands . . . . .English	Togo . . . . .French
Denmark . . . . .Danish	Maurutania . . . . .Arabic	Tonga . . . . .English
Djibouti . . . . .French/Arabic	Mauritis . . . . .English	Trinidad/Tobago . . . . .English
Dominica . . . . .English	Mexico . . . . .Spanish	Tunisia . . . . .Arabic
Dominican Republic . . . . .Spanish	Micronesia . . . . .English	Turkey . . . . .Turkish
Ecuador . . . . .Spanish	Moldova . . . . .Russian	Tuvalu . . . . .English
Egypt .Arabic	Monaco . . . . .French	Ukraine . . . . .Russian
El Salvador . . . . .Spanish	Morocco . . . . .Arabic	United Arabic
England . . . . .English	Myanmar . . . . .Burmese	Emerates . . . . .Arabic
Estonia . . . . .Estonian	Namibia . . . . .German	United States . . . . .English
Fiji . . . . .English	Netherlands . . . . .Dutch	Uruguay . . . . .Spanish
Findland . . . . .Finnish/Swedish	New Zealand . . . . .English	Uzbekistan . . . . .Russian
France . . . . .French	Nicaragua . . . . .Spanish	Vanuatu . . . . .French
Gabon . . . . .French	Norway . . . . .Norwegian	Venezuela . . . . .Spanish
Gambia . . . . .English	Oman . . . . .Arabic	Western Samoa . . . . .English
Georgian Republic . . . . .Russian	Pakistan . . . . .Urdu	Yemen . . . . .Arabic
Germany . . . . .German	Palau . . . . .English	Yugoslavia . . . . .Serbo-
Greece . . . . .Greek	Panama . . . . .Spanish	Croatian
Grenada . . . . .English	Papua New Guinea . . . . .English	Zaire . . . . .French
Guatemala . . . . .Spanish	Paraguay . . . . .Spanish	Zambia . . . . .English

Each week, *Baywatch* is translated into the following languages:
Arabic, Bulgarian, Burmese, Catalan, Chinese, Danish, Divehi, Dutch, Estonian, English, Farsi, Finnish, Flemish, French, German, Greek, Hebrew, Hindi, Hungarian, Icelandic, Japanese, Korean, Italian, Malay, Maltese, Mandarin, Norwegian, Polish, Portugese, Romanian, Russian, Serbo-Croatian, Sinhala, Slovak, Slovenian, Spanish, Swahili, Swedish, Thai, Tibetan, Turkish, Urdu and more. It isn't called *Baywatch* in all these places. It's called: *Alert a Malibu* in France, *Los Vigilantes de la Playa* (Sand Vigilantes) in Spain, *Mares Vivas* (Sea Lives) in Potugal, *SOS Malibu* in Brazil, *Guardines de la Baja* (Guardians of the Baja) in most of Latin America; *Soul of the Sea* in China. Each year, the cast of *Baywatch* goes through: 306 pounds of body makeup; one 50-gallon drum of sunscreen; 1500 cases of bottled water; 900 sets of ear and nose plugs; 575 swimsuits; 50 cases of protein bars; 39 goggles, and 129 surfboards.

*B*aywatch—it has been a long, exciting journey. Hundreds of people have contributed to the success of the show. Through the course of this book, I have acknowledged most of them. A few important people, however, need to be recognized here.

I would like to thank the still photographers who worked on *Baywatch* over the years, especially Kim Carlsberg. Kim took many of the excellent photographs contained within these pages, including the lifeguard tower photographs heading each chapter. Her eye for capturing the essence of a moment has never been equaled. I would also like to thank Roman Salicki, who shot the cover photograph and Mario Perez, for his work in Hawaii.

I would like to thank the Lifeguard Division of the Los Angeles County Fire Department. Without the lifeguards, their stories, their camaraderie, their commitment, their inspiration, *Baywatch* would not exist.

I would like to thank the U.S. Coast Guard. They generously supported *Baywatch* over the years in a myriad of ways. I hope a few able recruits found their way into the Coast Guard as a result of watching *Baywatch*.

I would like to thank my friends at New Millennium Press, especially Michael Viner, Deborah Raffin, Paul McLaughlin, editor Shelly Kale, production coordinator Anita Keys, and book designer Kurt Wahlner.

Finally, I would to thank my right-hand man, Peter Hoffman. Peter—you *are* the man!

—G.B.

The author's share of proceeds from the sale of *Baywatch: Rescued from Prime Time* shall be donated to The Camp Baywatch Foundation. For more information about the camp, please write to:

The Camp Baywatch Foundation
15237 Sunset Boulevard, Suite 94
Pacific Palisades, California 90272